CONTEMPLATIVE LEADERSHIP FOR ENTREPRENEURIAL ORGANIZATIONS

CONTEMPLATIVE LEADERSHIP FOR ENTREPRENEURIAL ORGANIZATIONS

PARADIGMS, METAPHORS, AND WICKED PROBLEMS

NANCY J. EGGERT

Q

QUORUM BOOKS
Westport, Connecticut • London

HD
57.7
.E37
1998

Eggert, Nancy J.,
1948-
Contemplative
leadership for
entrepreneurial
organizations

Library of Congress Cataloging-in-Publication Data

Eggert, Nancy J., 1948-
 Contemplative leadership for entrepreneurial organizations :
paradigms, metaphors, and wicked problems / Nancy J. Eggert.
  p.   cm.
 Includes bibliographical references and index.
 ISBN 1-56720-190-3 (alk. paper)
 1. Leadership. 2. Organization. 3. Paradigms (Social sciences)
I. Title.
 HD57.7.E37   1998
 658.4'092—dc21   98-5288

British Library Cataloguing in Publication Data is available.

Library of Congress Catalog Card Number: 98-5288
ISBN: 1-56720-190-3

First published in 1998

Quorum Books, 88 Post Road West, Westport, CT 06881
An imprint of Greenwood Publishing Group, Inc.

Printed in the United States of America

The paper used in this book complies with the
Permanent Paper Standard issued by the National
Information Standards Organization (Z39.48-1984).

10 9 8 7 6 5 4 3 2 1

Copyright
Acknowledgments

In Memory of Dr. Bengt Hoffman

Contents

Preface

Not long ago I attended my niece's college graduation and heard the commencement speaker plead the cause of urban public schools. His pleas brought back memories of my own college graduation more than a quarter of a century earlier when, with the idealism of the 1960s, I decided to venture into the world of urban education with the express hope of reforming the inner-city schools. My first career was short, just a couple years of working with fellow graduate students and more-experienced educators in ambitious, creative—and dramatically unsuccessful—reform efforts in the local school system. I am disheartened, but not surprised, that 25 years later the plight of the urban public schools persists.

It helps to be able to name the experience: *wicked problems* (see Harmon & Mayer, 1986, pp. 8–9; Rittel & Webber). Those recurring, insidious tangles of contradictions keep popping out of the grave no matter what you do. They are not easy to pin down, have an amazing ability to change their appearance, and will kill you if you ignore them. Poverty, welfare, drug abuse, broken families—all were lurking around the urban education conundrum. I first encountered wicked problems in the urban schools, but sometimes these malignant creatures are not as obvious as broken windows and a littered schoolyard. They sometimes appear as impossible conflicts between opposing forces: family pressures and work demands, meeting customer needs while maintaining a consistent and focused product, or assimilation of technological change while maintaining core values and culture. No organization can escape. *Wicked problems* are never solved, only addressed with a variety of approaches—approaches that need to shift as the problem mutates.

But where do we find the new approaches to the wicked problems that bedevil our organizations? I am suggesting that another perspective, another worldview, another paradigm would yield additional ways of thinking, perceiving, valuing, inquiring, and acting that could be brought to bear on these tricky and slippery complexes of problems. We all know what happened when we stopped thinking about the earth as the center of the universe. As the culture's perspective radically shifted, new doors were opened for exploration and discovery. This book is an invitation to explore the world of alternative perspectives, alternative paradigms.

Here, we explore what may seem to be a distinctly foreign land—the worldview, the paradigm of the contemplatives. Using medieval German mystic Meister Eckhart as a guide, the journey takes us into the contemplative experience itself and the fundamental assumptions of the contemplative paradigm. Recruiting Meister Eckhart as a guide poses a practical problem with language, image, and metaphor. Eckhart's medieval language and concepts are different from what we ordinarily use on the job. Eckhart often uses what we term *religious* language, which was, for his fellow medieval colleagues, simply *language*. In essence, Eckhart is using language that is both foreign—because we do not ordinarily use it in management literature—and familiar—because it is used in other contexts in our contemporary culture. It is language—that is, *God talk*—that for contemporary Western culture is encrusted with centuries of meaning and often laden with emotion. It might be easier to investigate the paradigm of the South American Yanomamo tribe or the 19th-century Australian aboriginals, using their distinct mythology and metaphor than it is to explore Eckhart's worldview using the language and imagery of this time—language and imagery that overlaps the language and imagery of our own culture. The reader is invited to approach Meister Eckhart and his colleagues with the same openness, respect, and curiosity that would be accorded a totally *other* culture such as the Yanomamo tribe or the Australian aboriginals. But despite beginning the journey in the 14th century, the contemplative pilgrimage takes on a familiar look as it leads us into the contemporary physical sciences and management literature, and finally, into a sketch of the leadership style that might arise from the contemplative paradigm.

This book offers no solutions, no quick fix for your wicked problems, only an invitation to begin your own journey into alternative ways of thinking, perceiving, inquiring, valuing, and acting.

Many thanks to my family and friends for their patience, support, and encouragement; their withstanding years of neglect while this project was stewing; and their willingness to listen to endless progress reports. Special thanks is due my brother, Dr. John Eggert, a leader of an entrepreneurial organization, for being my lifelong intellectual sparring partner and exemplar of creativity and hard work. I also acknowledge my debt of gratitude to the many colleagues at the Institute of Cultural Affairs and the Shalem Institute for Spiritual Formation, organizations that have, over the decades, generated the bulk of the foundational work that I have shamelessly borrowed here. Thanks to Ms. Kathy Lesesne for her word-processing magic and to my editor, Eric Valentine, for walking me through the process. There are many who have shaped this project. I offer special thanks to Dr. Ron Stupak, Dr. Judy Lombard, Dr. John Kirlin, Dr. Wayne Matthews, Paul Waldo, and Dr. Chris Bellavita, for their help in developing the concepts, critiquing earlier manuscripts, and offering encouragement.

I am especially grateful to the late Dr. Bengt Hoffman and his wife Pearl, not only for their assistance with this book but for their courage and unselfish service around the globe, and for offering me comfort, inspiration, and a contemplative environment.

Wicked Problems, Paradigms, and Metaphors

New Possibilities for Thought and Action

We are confronted today with many wicked problems, those problems with no solutions, only temporary and imperfect resolutions (Harmon & Mayer, 1986, pp. 8–9). Wicked problems are not easily defined and resist traditional solutions. Despite the efforts of the best minds, despite billions of dollars, we are still bedeviled by intractable, complex issues such as poverty; clashing of work and family life; and racial, ethnic, and other diversity conflicts. Those who address themselves to these issues have generated a multiplicity of creative ideas and approaches—from urban enterprise zones, affirmative action, and family leave policies to alternative dispute-resolution techniques, flextime, and on-site daycare—each approach enjoying a varying degree of success.

PARADIGM AS THE MOTHER OF THOUGHT AND ACTION

Each of these attempts to deal with one of today's wicked problems grew out of a particular way of looking at the situation, a particular worldview, a particular set of assumptions about how the world works—a particular paradigm. A paradigm, according to Willis Harman, consists of "the basic ways of perceiving, thinking, valuing and doing associated with a particular view of reality" (Harman, 1988, p.

10). A paradigm is usually taken for granted and treated as common sense, that is, our familiar grasp of life, our ordinary way of making sense of things, that we all have in common. Our operating paradigm is as important and as invisible as the air we breathe. This set of fundamental assumptions and patterns gives rise to methods, roles, procedures, language, and structures that form the backbone of our culture.

Paradigms are the most basic level of the maps that we use to maneuver in everyday life. Paradigms are the foundation for the theories, metaphors, and images that form the architecture of intellectual constructs we regularly employ. A paradigm is made up of the underlying rules of the game applicable to metaphors and theories. In a natural science context, for example, a physicist, operating out of the rationalist-functionalist paradigm, the dominant paradigm for our Western 20th-century society, in the process of building a theory about the motion of the planets, will almost certainly ground his or her theories on, or even take for granted, basic assumptions of this dominant paradigm about such matters as repeatability, causality, and observability of certain phenomena. The physicist will probably also build on other, well-established theories regarding gravitational force and its relation to mass, distance, and the like. Each of these established theories is, in turn, grounded in the dominant paradigm that has been with us since the Enlightenment.

Although it may be difficult to draw clear distinctions between theories and metaphors or metaphors and other maps of reality, paradigm here is defined as the most basic, fundamental assumptions that form our primary view of reality.

DISCOUNTED POSSIBILITIES

A particular paradigm, a particular manner of approaching life or understanding a situation, opens up particular possibilities for perceiving, thinking, organizing, and acting, but also closes off other possibilities. For example, the physicist operating out of the dominant paradigm would discount, among other things, any possibility of supernatural or divine forces affecting the movement of the planets. (The same could not be said for inquirers in some other civilizations, operating out of their unique dominant paradigm.) This discounting of certain factors or concepts is part of the basic rules of the game, one of our taken-for-granted operating assumptions.

Thomas Kuhn, in his seminal book on paradigms, *The Structure of Scientific Revolutions*, notes how certain experiences, data, and ideas, at least in a natural science context, are dismissed as anomalous and unworthy of attention because they do not fit into the dominant paradigm. In fact, according to Kuhn, as more anomalous data are collected, they become more difficult to ignore, and the dominant theories lose their prior ability to help people understand their world and to solve problems. When that failure occurs, when the data no longer fit within the current paradigm, the way is prepared for a new paradigm to come into favor, that is, for a paradigm shift.

One example cited by Kuhn (1970, pp. 68f) as a paradigm shift is Copernicus's dethroning of the planet earth as the center of the universe. Ptolemy's earlier, earth-centered system of astronomy was fairly successful in determining the position of planets. But his predictions about planetary positions never quite matched the actual observations of astronomers. The scientific community of Copernicus's day slowly came to realize that there was a breakdown in the normal technical puzzle-solving activity (Kuhn, 1970, p. 69) based on Ptolemy's system. Copernicus's new way of looking at the universe, sans the obvious assumption that the earth was the center of the universe, offered new possibilities for dealing with this break-down. Copernicus's new paradigm offered an alternative way of thinking, perceiving, inquiring, and acting (and even valuing) that led to new approaches to old problems.

IDENTIFYING BASIC OPERATING ASSUMPTIONS

Each sphere of professional or academic activity—whether organizational development, public policy, or business—also has a set of commonly accepted ways of thinking, assumptions about human beings, about public life, about the economy, about the nature of the world in which we live, which are shared to some extent (but perhaps not entirely) by society at large. As with any paradigm, these assumptions both direct and constrain our thinking and action. The range of options for dealing with problem situations in any field is affected by our most basic understandings of life, that is, by our operating paradigm.

Although we rarely examine our operating paradigm, it is not unusual to critique the metaphors or theories that are grounded in the dominant paradigm. This critical examination of theories and metaphors is often thought provoking and fruitful. Focusing on organizational life—although one might substitute "the economy" or "government" or some other area of interest—Gareth Morgan (1986) states the basic premise of his book, *Images of Organization*:

[O]ur theories and explanations of organizational life are based on metaphors that lead us to see and understand organizations in distinctive yet partial ways. . . . For the use of metaphor implies *a way of thinking* and *a way of seeing* that pervade how we understand our world generally. (p. 12)

Morgan then explores eight different metaphors for organization, each metaphor having distinct strengths and limitations, each reflecting a distinct way of thinking and perceiving. One's choice of metaphor is neither incidental nor insignificant.

But, according to Morgan (1986), our choice of metaphor affects not only our possibilities for thinking and perceiving but also the range of available actions:

> By using different metaphors to understand the complex and paradoxical character of organizational life, we are able to manage and design organizations in ways that we may not have thought possible before. (p. 13)

> Images and metaphors are not only interpretive constructs or ways of seeing; they also provide frameworks for action. Their use creates insights that often allow us to act in ways that we may not have thought possible before. (p. 343)

In a similar manner, using theories rather than metaphors, Harmon and Mayer (1986), in *Organization Theory for Public Administration,* examine six public administration perspectives on organization theory, each of which "illuminate different aspects of the public administration framework" (p. 119). The authors observe, "Each [theoretical] perspective addresses only certain aspects of the public administrator's world, while ignoring, deemphasizing or even skewing other parts of it" (p. 119). The authors "attempt to show how theory may be of use in making sense of the past and present in order to suggest future possibilities for action" (p. 1). For them, "Thinking about organizational activity is always grounded in assumptions about human nature, in the purposes of examining such activity, and in the suppositions about the relationship between theory and practice" (p. 2). One might also venture to say that if the assumptions are altered, thinking and action will also change.

ALTERNATIVE PARADIGMS, NEW POSSIBILITIES

If alternative metaphors and alternative theories open up new possibilities for thinking and acting, in the field of organizational development or in life in general, perhaps what we need, in order to deal with today's wicked problems, is another way of looking at our situation, a new map of reality, an alternative paradigm. Physicist and social theorist Fritjof Capra (1982) boldly identifies the real problem that underlies our crisis of ideas regarding persistent problems as "the fact that most academics [and others, I am sure] subscribe to narrow perceptions of reality which are inadequate for dealing with the major problems of our time" (p. 25). In addition, others, in a wide variety of fields, have nominated new or emerging paradigms to replace the old (Harman, 1988; Capra, 1982; Harman & Rheingold, 1984; Schaef & Fassel, 1988; Thayer, 1981; Beam & Simpson, 1984; Eisler, 1987; Fox, 1983; Theobald, 1987; Lenz & Myerhoff, 1985; Ferguson, 1980). Most of these works include a critique of our own, currently reigning, rationalist-functionalist paradigm. The real conundrum, of course, is determining which alternate view or views of reality would open the door to effective thinking and action. Unfortunately, this book does not identify—or even attempt to identify—*the* alternative paradigm that would lead to solutions for our wicked problems. Instead, in the pages that follow, we explore together an alternative worldview, that is, the *contemplative* paradigm, that is in contrast to the dominant paradigm. We examine the patterns of thinking, perception, inquiry, valuing, and action that arise from the assumptions of the alternative, contemplative paradigm and consider the possibility of opening our imaginations not only to alternative theories and metaphors but also to alternative paradigms. Particular attention will be given to the style of leadership that might arise from this alternative paradigm, that is, *contemplative* leadership.

AN ALTERNATIVE: THE CONTEMPLATIVE PARADIGM

It might have been possible to choose at random an alternative paradigm to explore, for example, the values, assumptions, and worldview of the 19th-century Australian aboriginals, and then to consider the thinking and action that might emanate from such a paradigm. Or one could invent an entirely new worldview from scratch to see if that would open up new possibilities for thinking and action that might address our wicked problems. But that is not what happened.

I did not intentionally choose an alternative paradigm. Neither did I invent an entirely new one. Rather, an alternative paradigm presented itself to me. I did not recognize it at first. Beginning in the early 1970s, I experienced some nontraditional planning processes used by businesses, community groups, and nonprofit organizations. Times of silence, music, intuition exercises, rituals, various arts and crafts activities, and reflective techniques were part of the methodological tool kit for the planning sessions. These approaches were interesting, helpful, and fun, and I incorporated them into my work without giving much thought to their origins or their underlying rationale.

However, when I later began to encounter a contemplative approach to life—whether from a Tai Chi workshop at the YMCA or a study of the medieval mystics in a formal classroom setting—it eventually occurred to me that those nontraditional planning processes had a distinctly contemplative flavor. I wondered whether there might be something that could be described as a contemplative paradigm—and whether some of the planning methods were grounded in that worldview. I have since answered these two questions for myself in the affirmative and have embraced the challenge of articulating the contemplative paradigm in a manner that would be accessible to our contemporary organizational culture.

The sources for the contemplative paradigm outlined in the later chapters include some original early contemplative writings, such as St. Teresa of Avila, St. John of the Cross, and St. Ignatius Loyola, as well as contemporary authors Tilden Edwards, Gerald May, Thomas Keating, and others. I have also relied on the analysis of scholars who have devoted their lives to the study of contemplative writings. Matthew Fox, a contemporary theologian who has analyzed the work of a diverse collection of contemplative writers over the centuries, provides the fourfold path framework for the contemplative paradigm, relying to a great extent on 13th-century German mystic Meister Eckhart. It is not surprising that neither Fox nor Eckhart focused his thoughts or writings on the issues of 21st-century organizations. Accordingly, it is necessary to recast the work of Fox, Eckhart, and others in contemporary concepts so that this alternative approach to life, the contemplative paradigm, is accessible to those who are confronted with today's wicked problems. Finally, the concept of contemplative leadership provides a focus for exploration of the contemplative paradigm by considering the style of leadership that would emerge from the assumptions of the contemplative paradigm.

THE JOURNEY TOWARD AN ALTERNATIVE PARADIGM

The reader is invited to embark on a journey, to jump from one series of stepping-stones to another in traveling from wicked problems to the contemplative paradigm and, finally, to contemplative leadership. The first segment of the journey is a consideration of how our basic intellectual constructs direct and constrain our possibilities for thinking, perceiving, inquiring, valuing, and acting. The first three stepping-stones in this series are Kuhn's explanation of the role of paradigms, Lakoff and Johnson's view of the function of metaphor, and Boulding's description of maps and images, not only in our thinking and acting, but also in our perceiving, valuing, and inquiry. This segment of the journey will pause for a reflection on the role of these intellectual constructs, that is, for a consideration of a theory of paradigms.

Our pilgrimage will then take three steps on a parallel path to consider the role of paradigms, images, and theories in organizations, using, respectively, Burrell and Morgan's (1979) *Sociological Paradigms and Organisational Analysis*, Morgan's (1986) *Images of Organization*, and Harmon and Mayer's (1986) *Organization Theory for Public Administration*.

The exploration then takes a sharp turn into the second segment of the journey, the articulation of the contemplative paradigm by first getting a solid footing on the nature of the current dominant paradigm, and then exploring the nature of the contemplative experience itself. The journey shifts to the fourfold path of Meister Eckhart for a detailed map of the contemplative paradigm with the final step of restating the fourfold path in contemporary terms.

The third and final segment of the journey shifts the focus to contemporary organizational life with a step into the style of contemplative leadership.

PART I

How Paradigms, Metaphors, and Images Affect Thinking, Perception, Inquiry, Valuing, and Action

Before considering an alternative paradigm, it is necessary to explore the role of paradigms, metaphors, images, and other intellectual constructs that are used as maps of reality. Part I draws upon contributions in several diverse fields—the history of science, linguistics, philosophy, and sociology—to develop a general theory of how paradigms affect thinking, perceiving, valuing, inquiry, and action.

Chapter 2 examines the role of paradigms, the most fundamental of the intellectual constructs employed in interactions with the world about us, using Thomas Kuhn's seminal work, *The Structure of Scientific Revolutions*. Kuhn surveys the history of science, focusing on the dynamics of those intellectual crises that signal a radical shift in the direction of a field of science. But the significance of Kuhn's work is not limited to the history of science. Kuhn carefully presents evidence that the way we think, perceive, value, inquire, and act is shaped by our most basic assumptions about life—that is, by our operating paradigm. The range of possibilities for our thinking, inquiry, valuing, action—and even perception—is directed and constrained by our fundamental worldview.

Chapter 3 considers the work of George Lakoff and Mark Johnson, *Metaphors We Live By*. Lakoff and Johnson zero in on the role of metaphor in daily interactions and explain how metaphors profoundly shape how we perceive, think, experience, value, and act.

Chapter 4 explores Kenneth Boulding's *Images*. Boulding investigates the concept of interior maps or images that we regularly—and often unconsciously—employ to situate ourselves in our world and describes how these images form our internal knowledge structure, govern our behavior, and shape our values.

Chapter 5 uses these three intellectual building blocks to construct a brief theory of paradigms, and clarifies the relationship among fundamental concepts such as *paradigm*, *metaphor*, and *theory*.

Part II, Chapters 6–8, shifts attention specifically to organizational theory and further explore the role of paradigm, image, and theory in organizational life. Three primary works—Burrell and Morgan's (1979) *Sociological Paradigms and Organisational Analysis*, Gareth Morgan's (1986) *Images of Organization*, and Harmon and Mayer's (1986) *Organization Theory for Public Administration*—consider, respectively, the role of paradigm, image, and theory, in shaping thinking, perceiving, valuing, inquiry, and action with respect to organizations.

Thomas Kuhn and
the Role of Paradigms

Thomas Kuhn's *The Structure of Scientific Revolutions*, first published in 1962, is the cornerstone for a study of paradigms. Although Kuhn considers the concept of paradigm from a slightly different perspective than do later authors such as Willis Harman, Kuhn's historical analysis lays the foundation for those who come after him. *The Structure of Scientific Revolutions* is grounded in a natural science context; nevertheless, it describes and illustrates the concept of paradigm and dramatizes the role of paradigms in the fundamental shifts in thinking, perceiving, inquiring, and acting that occur in scientific disciplines and even in society at large.

Using an historical approach, Kuhn examines the process by which fundamental understandings and approaches in the field of natural science are overturned and overtaken by rival understandings and approaches, that is, how scientific revolutions take place. The changes described by Kuhn (1970) are fundamental:

> Examining the record of past research from the vantage of the contemporary historiography, the historian of science may be tempted to exclaim that when paradigms change, the world itself changes with them. Led by a new paradigm, scientists adopt new instruments and look in new places. Even more important, during revolutions scientists see new and different

things when looking with familiar instruments in places they have looked before. It is rather as if the professional community had been suddenly transported to another planet where familiar objects are seen in a different light and are joined by unfamiliar ones as well. Of course, nothing of quite that sort does occur: There is no geographical transplantation; outside the laboratory everyday affairs continue as before. Nevertheless, paradigm changes do cause scientists to see the world of their research-engagement differently. In so far as their only recourse to that world is through what they see and do, we may want to say that after a revolution scientists are responding to a different world. (p. 111)

The world changes for the scientist—or at least the perception of it—when the paradigm changes. Before examining these revolutionary shifts in perception in more detail, it may be helpful to review Kuhn's concept of the *manner* in which a field of science changes.

HOW A FIELD OF SCIENCE CHANGES

Normal Science and the Established Paradigm

Let's return for a moment to our high school science fair days. We spend the first few months of the year acquiring some rudimentary knowledge of our field—biology, chemistry, or perhaps physics. We are introduced to basic theories about the world around us. There may be a few laws that we memorize. We learn techniques in the laboratory— some as basic as washing glassware or using a Bunsen burner or making various measurements. Perhaps we replicate a famous experiment or two. Then the science fair looms large, and we are given the opportunity to do original research. With some very rare exceptions, our science projects are variations on a theme that has been sung over and over again in that field. For example, some budding scientists may reflect on the world around them, formulate questions, and then use the basic theories, understandings, and techniques of their field to attempt a credible answer to that question. There are other science projects that feature novel variations in technique or applications of familiar theories to situations no one else had considered before. Although performed at a more basic level, the inquiry and research undertaken for a high school science fair is not unlike that undertaken by the vast majority of professional scientists. It can be termed normal science.

Kuhn (1970) uses the term *normal science* to refer to "research firmly based upon one or more past scientific achievements, achievements that some particular scientific community acknowledges for a time as sup- plying the foundation for its further practice" (p. 10). It is a body of ac- cepted theory that can be expounded, whose successful applications can be illustrated and compared with exemplary observations and experiments, that is, the body of work that might be found in a standard textbook (p. 10). Kuhn cites works by Aristotle, Ptolemy, Newton, and Lavoisier, as well as those standard-issue tomes that might be encountered in college chemistry or physics courses, as examples of normal science. These textbooks define the legitimate problems in a particular field and the methods of research for investigating those problems for the next generation of scientists. These cited works of scientific giants or their intellectual progeny have become standard texts not only because (a) their achievement was sufficiently unprecedented to attract an enduring group of adherents away from competing modes of scientific activity, but also because (b) the work was sufficiently open-ended to leave enough problems for the new group of adherents to resolve (p. 10).

An example of normal science might be Newtonian optics. Prior to Newton, there was no generally accepted understanding of the nature of light. There was a variety of schools. Some understood light to be particles emanating from material bodies; for others it was a change in the medium between the object and the eyes. Some said light was due to an interaction between the medium and something emanating from the eye. Each school relied on a particular set of observations that were in accord with a proposed theory. There was no standard set of methods or phenomena that each scientist was required to use and explain (Kuhn, 1970, p. 12). After Newton's *Opticks*, which taught that light was material *corpuscles*, this paradigm was embraced by almost all researchers in the field of optics—until other paradigms took over; first the concept of light as a wave and, in our century, the understanding of light as photons or quantum-mechanical entities that behave, in some ways, like waves and, in others, like particles (pp. 11–12).

When an achievement shares the two characteristics cited here—that is, if the achievement is sufficiently unprecedented to attract an enduring group of adherents away from competing modes of scientific activity and the work is sufficiently open-ended to leave enough problems for the new group of adherents to solve—Kuhn identifies it as a *paradigm*.[1] In the example of Newtonian optics, once the Newtonian paradigm took hold, the other options for conceptualizing light lost adherents. Researchers in optics thereafter conducted their inquiry as if light were comprised of material corpuscles. After Newtonian optics came to dominance, for example, researchers looked for evidence of the pressure exerted by these light particles on solid bodies—evidence that understandably was not sought earlier by those who considered light to be a wave (Kuhn, 1970, p. 12). In other words, some examples of scientific practice—which includes law, theory, application, and scientific instrumentation—provide models from which a particular, coherent tradition of scientific research grows (p. 10). Thereafter, those whose research is based on a shared paradigm will be committed to the same rules and standards for scientific practice. This commitment and con-sensus allow the genesis and continuation of a particular research tradi-tion: Acquisition of a paradigm is a sign of maturity in the development of a scientific field (p. 11). Once a paradigm becomes entrenched, there is a field of study and research. The parameters for research are estab-lished. Labs are set up. Courses can be offered. Textbooks are written. Periodicals can be published. Once an authoritative text is written, the next creative scientist can begin research where others have left off. This scientist's research can concentrate on the subtlest and most esoteric as-pects of the field (p. 20). Thus, a paradigm shapes the field of study. It sets the parameters for inquiry, identifies the focus of study, and even gives an identity to those who practice within the field.

A key idea of Kuhn's work is that the scientific enterprise moves forward by means of revolutionary shifts in paradigms rather than cumulatively. Normal science is the state of affairs between the cataclys-mic paradigm shifts. "[T]he successive transition from one paradigm to another via revolution is the usual developmental pattern of mature science" (Kuhn, 1970, p. 12). Before a new paradigm breaks into the field, or after a new paradigm is firmly established, there is a period of business as usual.

> Mopping-up operations are what engage most scientists throughout their careers. They constitute what I am here calling normal science. Closely examined, whether historically or in the contemporary laboratory, that enterprise seems an attempt to force nature into the preformed and rela-tively inflexible box that the paradigm supplies. No part of the aim of normal science is to call forth new sorts of phenomena; indeed those that will not fit the box are often not seen at all. Nor do scientists normally aim to invent new theories, and they are often intolerant of those invented by others. Instead, normal scientific research is directed to the articulation of those phenomena and theories that the paradigm already supplies.
>
> Perhaps these are defects. The areas investigated by normal science are, of course, minuscule; the enterprise now under discussion has drastically restricted vision. (Kuhn, 1970, p. 24)

Thus, the paradigm that is dominant during a particular period of normal science significantly shapes and restricts the inquiry—as well as making any inquiry possible at all.

Kuhn (1970) identifies three foci of normal or paradigm-based re-search. "First is that class of facts that the paradigm has shown to be particularly revealing of the nature of things. By employing them in solving problems, the paradigm had made them worth determining both with more precision and in a larger variety of situations" (p. 25). An example of this first focus, in astronomy, would be the charting of the location of stars, measuring their intensity and their color.

A second class of data gathered during the period of normal science consists of those facts that can be used to test the predictions generated by the paradigm's theory. Kuhn explains that there are few areas in which a scientific theory can be directly compared with nature. It often takes great ingenuity to design the experiments and the measuring apparatus that can test theory. The facts or measurements themselves are sometimes of interest solely for the purpose of testing the theory— for example, would there be any reason to build an enormously expensive superconducting supercollider to detect and measure subatomic particles other than to test a particular theory or theories? The nature of the paradigm has a critical effect on the data that are collected and examined.

A third category of research that is undertaken during a period of normal science is the "sort of experiment which aims to articulate a paradigm" (Kuhn, 1970, p. 29). In this third category, experiments are undertaken to determine whether the paradigm could be applied to a new area.

Thus, during a period of normal science the research is directed and driven by the prevailing paradigm. Attention is focused on certain areas of inquiry and on a limited class of phenomena—to the neglect of others. There is a single prevailing or dominant paradigm. However, there comes a time when the prevailing paradigm begins to fray. The period of revolution and a paradigm shift are not far behind.

A period of normal science does not gradually give way to the next period of normal science defined by a new paradigm, according to Kuhn. For example, Newtonian optics did not gradually evolve into wave theory optics, nor did the understanding of the earth being the center of the universe slowly give way to the heliocentric universe. Instead a crisis precipitates a paradigm shift.

Anomalies, Crisis, and the Breakdown of the Established Paradigm

How does a crisis develop? It is preceded by anomalies. The theories associated with the prevailing paradigm are no longer able to account for the data. The set of procedures, rules, and understandings no longer is capable of puzzle-solving activity. "Discovery commences with the awareness of anomaly, i.e., with the recognition that nature has somehow violated the paradigm-induced expectations that govern normal science" (Kuhn, 1970, pp. 52–53).

One famous example of a paradigm shift is the emergence of Copernican astronomy. The Ptolemaic system could successfully predict the positions of both stars and planets.[2] However useful these predictions were, they did not quite conform with the best observations.

One of the principal problems or tasks of this established system of astronomy was to reduce further the minor discrepancies between theory and observation. Further complexities were introduced into Ptolemaic astronomy in an attempt to reduce the discrepancies. "[T]he net result of the normal research effort of many astronomers [was that] astronomy's complexity was increasing far more rapidly than its accuracy and that a discrepancy corrected in one place was likely to show up in another" (Kuhn, 1970, p. 68). It appeared to Copernicus that the astronomical tradition he had inherited had created a monster. Other astronomers recognized that the prevailing astronomical paradigm could no longer be fruitfully applied to the traditional problems of the field. This led to Copernicus's rejection of the Ptolemaic paradigm and his search for a new one. Astronomy was in a state of crisis (Kuhn, 1970, p. 69).[3]

After citing other historical examples of a breakdown in the normal problem-solving activity, Kuhn notes that the role of the crisis is critical in allowing a new paradigm to take over. In each instance, including the crisis in Ptolemaic astronomy, the solution had been considered before, but, in the absence of a crisis, had been ignored. For example, a third-century B.C.E. Greek astronomer, Aristarchus, proposed a heliocentric system, just as did Copernicus many centuries later. Furthermore, the Copernican system was neither simpler nor more accurate than Ptolemy's system. Because Ptolemaic astronomy had failed to solve its problems, there was a crisis, and it was time to give a competitor a chance (Kuhn, 1970, p. 76).

Kuhn makes a very critical—and perhaps seemingly obvious—observation at this point in his discussion of the history of science: There is more than one perspective for any situation, and more than one theory can be applied to a particular set of data. However, as long as we have a perspective, a method, a theory that works, we are unlikely to invent another—or perhaps even try an existing alternative.

> Philosophers of science have repeatedly demonstrated that more than one theoretical construction can always be placed upon a given collection of data. History of science indicates that, particularly in the early developmental stages of a new paradigm, it is not even very difficult to invent such alternates. But that invention of alternates is just what scientists seldom undertake except during the pre-paradigm stage of their science's development and at very special occasions during its subsequent evolution. So long as the tools a paradigm supplies continue to prove capable of solving the problems it defines, science moves fastest and penetrates most deeply through confident employment of these tools. The reason is clear. As in manufacture so in science—retooling is an extravagance to be reserved for the occasion that demands it. The significance of crises is the indication they provide that an occasion for retooling has arrived. (Kuhn, 1970, p. 76)

Once the prevailing paradigm encounters a crisis, the period of normal science may be nearing an end. What we observe, from an historical perspective, is a shift to a new paradigm, a scientific revolution. However, although scientists may encounter "severe and prolonged anomalies," they do not automatically treat the anomalies as "counter instances" and "renounce the paradigm that has led them into crisis" (Kuhn, 1970, p. 77). According to Kuhn, once a scientific theory has achieved the status of a paradigm, it is declared invalid "only if an alternative candidate is available to take its place" (p. 77). Counterinstances or anomalies, by themselves, do not lead to rejection of a particular theory although they can help to create or reinforce a crisis.

> [T]he act of judgment that leads scientists to reject a previously accepted theory is always based on more than a comparison of that theory with the world. The decision to reject one paradigm is always simultaneously the decision to accept another, and the judgment leading to that decision involves the comparison of both paradigms with nature *and* with each other. (p. 77)

One manifestation of this resistance to abandoning paradigms in the presence of counterinstances is the fact that the defenders will "devise numerous articulations and *ad hoc* modifications of their theory in order to eliminate any apparent conflict" (p. 78).

Aside from helping to create or reinforcing a crisis already in existence with respect to the current paradigm, these anomalies also play another role in the new paradigm, a paradigm in which they are no longer anomalies. The former crisis-evoking anomalies are no longer simply facts that are in accord with the new way of viewing the situation, but they "seem very much like tautologies, statements of situations that could not conceivably have been otherwise" (Kuhn, 1970, p. 78). They become the center of attention.

But not every anomaly creates a crisis. There are always anomalies in trying to fit nature into a theoretical framework. Kuhn, admitting that there is no general answer to the question of what makes an anomaly worthy of closer scrutiny, offers some hints. Such a crisis-evoking anomaly may "clearly call into question explicit and fundamental generalizations of the paradigm," or "may evoke a crisis if the applications that it inhibits have a particular practical importance," for example, the failure of the pre-Copernican system to deal with astrology and calendar design. Sometimes the development of normal science will render critical an anomaly that previously was considered only pesky and inconvenient (Kuhn, 1970, p. 82). However the many factors combine—at some point the anomaly moves from the status of a puzzle of normal science to a center of attention. As many great minds in the field focus on the anomaly, it becomes *the* subject matter of the discipline.

Kuhn (1970) offers a narrative of the breakdown of a paradigm at this point in the discussion of the nature of paradigm shifts:

> For [the scientists focusing attention on the anomaly] the field will no longer look quite the same as it had earlier. Part of its different appearance results simply from the new fixation point of scientific scrutiny. An even more important source of change is the divergent nature of the numerous partial solutions that concerted attention to the problem has made available. The early attacks upon the resistant problem will have followed the paradigm rules quite closely. But with continuing resistance, more and more of the attacks upon it will have involved some minor or not so minor articulation of the paradigm, no two of them quite alike, each partially successful, but none sufficiently so to be accepted as paradigm by the group. Through this proliferation of divergent articulations (more and more frequently they will come to be described as *ad hoc* adjustments), the rules of normal science become increasingly blurred. Though there still is a paradigm, few practitioners prove to be entirely agreed about what it is. Even formerly standard solutions of solved problems are called into question. (p. 83)

Although Kuhn describes this transition stage in the objective language of a philosopher and historian, he gives us a brief insight into what it is like for a human being to live in the middle of a crumbling paradigm by quoting two of our century's most brilliant physicists, Wolfgang Pauli and Albert Einstein. Einstein wrote: "It was as if the ground had been pulled out from under one, with no firm foundation to be seen anywhere, upon which one could have built" (as quoted in Kuhn, 1970, p. 83). Wolfgang Pauli, writing prior to a significant paper on quantum mechanics by Werner Heisenberg, "At the moment physics is again terribly confused. In any case, it is too difficult for me, and I wish I had been a movie comedian or something of the sort and had never heard of physics." After the Heisenberg paper, Pauli responded in a different manner, "Heisenberg's type of mechanics has again given me hope and joy in life. To be sure, it does not supply the solution to the riddle, but I believe it is again possible to march forward" (as quoted in Kuhn, 1970, p. 84). It appears that when one's paradigm is in tatters, it is difficult to continue the inquiry. A paradigm shapes and directs inquiry and action, but the state of the paradigm also affects whether one will inquire or act at all. Indeed, "there is no such thing as research in the absence of any paradigm" (p. 79).

Once a paradigm is in crisis, there are three options that Kuhn identifies: The normal science proves able to handle the problem that precipitates the crisis; the problem is labeled as insoluble at the present time and shelved for a later generation of scientists; or a candidate for a new paradigm may emerge and win the battle for acceptance (Kuhn, 1970, p. 84). Kuhn, of course, focuses his attention on the third option in describing the nature of a scientific revolution or paradigm shift.

The Emergence of the New Paradigm

A critical observation for Kuhn (1970) is that the shift to a new paradigm is discontinuous, revolutionary, and extraordinary rather than cumulative, evolutionary, or developmental:

> The transition from a paradigm in crisis to a new one from which a new tradition of normal science can emerge is far from a cumulative process, one achieved by an articulation or extension of the old paradigm. Rather it is a reconstruction of the field from new fundamentals, a reconstruction that changes some of the field's most elementary theoretical generalizations as well as many of its paradigm methods and applications. During the transition period there will be a large but never complete overlap between the problems that can be solved by the old and by the new paradigm. But there will also be a decisive difference in the modes of solution. When the transition is complete, the profession will have changed its view of the field, its methods, and its goals. (pp. 84–85)

Kuhn explains that other historians have described this shift variously as "picking up the other end of the stick," that is, "handling the same bundle of data as before, but placing them in a new system of relations with one another by giving them a different framework" (Butterfield, 1949, pp. 1–7), or as a change in a visual gestalt, that is, the marks on the paper that were first seen as a goblet are now seen as two human silhouettes (Kuhn, 1970, p. 85). However, Kuhn finds these parallels misleading. "Scientists do not see something *as* something else; instead they simply see it. . . . In addition, the scientist does not preserve the gestalt subject's freedom to switch back and forth between ways of seeing" (p. 85).

Furthermore, Kuhn (1970) makes clear that the new paradigm is necessarily incompatible with the old (p. 92). A revolution in paradigms displaces "the conceptual network through which scientists view the world" (p. 102). Kuhn considers in detail the argument that the shift from Newtonian dynamics to relativistic (Einsteinian) dynamics does not really involve a revolutionary shift in understanding, that is, that Newtonian dynamics is merely a case of relativistic dynamics applied to the narrow range of values that most people encounter in everyday life. For example, it can be argued that engineers find Newtonian mechanics perfectly acceptable when they are building bridges or designing cars or solving other typical engineering problems as long as any velocities involved do not approach the speed of light, that is, as long as we stay within the normal range of everyday life. If an engineer used Einstein's rather complex relativity equations and added the restriction that all velocities are far less than the speed of light, these relativity equations would yield equations that would appear identical to the far simpler expressions of Newtonian laws of motion, gravity, and other scientific phenomena. However, Newtonian physics or mechanics is not just a special case of Einsteinian physics, because the basic concepts of mass, energy, and velocity are not the same for the two systems. In Newtonian physics, for example, mass is conserved; in Einsteinian physics mass is convertible with energy, that is, the familiar but revolutionary equation $E = mc^2$.

> For in the passage to the limit it is not only the forms of the laws that have changed. Simultaneously we have had to alter the fundamental structural elements of which the universe to which they apply is composed.
>
> This need to change the meaning of established and familiar concepts is central to the revolutionary impact of Einstein's theory. . . . Though subtler than the changes from geocentrism to heliocentrism . . . or from corpuscles to waves, the resulting conceptual transformation is no less decisively destructive of a previously established paradigm. . . . Just because it did not involve the introduction of additional objects or concepts, the transition from Newtonian to Einsteinian mechanics illustrates with particular clarity the scientific revolution as a displacement of the conceptual network through which scientists view the world. (p. 102)

Kuhn (1970) further explains how successive paradigms differ from each other. First,

> successive paradigms tell us different things about the population of the universe and about that population's behavior. They differ, that is, about such questions as the existence of subatomic particles, the materiality of light, and the conservation of heat or energy. (p. 103)

However, the successive paradigms differ not only in substance but also in their definition of the science that gave rise to them. "They are the source of the methods, problem-field, and the standards of solution" accepted by the mature scientific community (Kuhn, 1970, p. 103).

> Some old problems may be relegated to another science or declared entirely "unscientific." Others that were previously nonexistent or trivial may, with a new paradigm, become the very archetypes of significant scientific achievement. . . . The normal-scientific tradition that emerges from a scientific revolution is not only incompatible but often actually incommensurable with that which has gone before. (p. 103)

In other words,

Previously, we had principally examined the paradigm's role as a vehicle for scientific theory. In that role it functions by telling the scientist about the entities that nature does and does not contain and about the ways in which those entities behave. That information provides a map whose details are elucidated by mature scientific research. And since nature is too complex and varied to be explored at random, that map is as essential as observation and experiment to science's continuing development. Through the theories they embody, paradigms prove to be constitutive of the research activity. They are also, however, constitutive of science in other respects, and that is now the point. In particular, our most recent examples show that paradigms provide scientists not only with a map but also with some of the directions essential for map-making. In learning a paradigm the scientist acquires theory, methods, and standards together, usually in an inextricable mixture. Therefore, when paradigms change, there are usually significant shifts in the criteria determining the legitimacy both of problems and of proposed solutions. (p. 109)

Thus, a new paradigm not only offers a better idea about how the universe works but also provides a new set of concepts for describing the world, new methods for exploring that world, and even new standards for what is worth exploring, what problems are worth solving, and what is worth knowing. The new paradigm cannot be described in terms of the old. It sets its own terms. When the paradigm shifts, a new science is born.

HOW THE WORLD ITSELF CHANGES

We now finally examine how, as Kuhn describes it, not only the science changes, but the world itself changes when a paradigm shifts. When a new paradigm emerges, the scientist experiences a transformation somewhat like a gestalt shift. He sees the world in a radically different way. "Many readers will surely want to say that what changes with a paradigm is only the scientist's interpretation of observations that themselves are fixed once and for all by the nature of the environment and of the perceptual apparatus" (Kuhn, 1970, p. 120). But Kuhn argues that what "occurs during a scientific revolution is not fully reducible to a reinterpretation of individual and stable data" (p. 121).

Kuhn (1970) first suggests that "something like a paradigm is a prerequisite to perception itself. What a man sees depends both upon what he looks at and also upon what his previous visual-conceptual experience has taught him to see" (p. 113). Kuhn describes a particular type of psychological experiment that demonstrates that the size, color, and so on, that subjects perceive when shown various objects depends on their previous training and experience (p. 113). Experimental subjects were briefly shown a series of playing cards. Included among the standard playing cards were several anomalous ones, for example, a red six of spades or a black four of hearts. After the brief exposure to the series, subjects were asked to identify what they had seen. The anomalous cards were almost always identified, without hesitation or puzzlement, as normal. "Without any awareness of trouble, [the anomalous card] was immediately fitted to one of the conceptual categories prepared by prior experience" (p. 63). After longer exposure to the anomalous cards, subjects would begin to notice that something was not quite right, although they could not at first specify what was not right. "Even at forty times the average exposure [time] required to recognize normal cards for what they were, more than 10 per cent of the anomalous cards were not correctly identified" (p. 63). However, after the subjects identified two or three anomalous cards, that is, after they realized that they were being shown a red six of spades and after they added this new perceptual category to their experience, they had little difficulty in identifying other anomalous cards (pp. 63, 113).

In this type of psychological experiment or in the gestalt demonstration, the subject can be shown and persuaded that "regardless of what he *saw*, he was *looking at* a black five of hearts all the time" (Kuhn, 1970, p. 114). However, "[u]nless there were an *external standard* with respect to which a switch of vision could be demonstrated, no conclusion about alternate perceptual possibilities could be drawn" (p. 114, emphasis added). From our shared experience of playing cards, we all know that there really is no such thing as a black five of hearts. This is our external standard existing outside the psychology laboratory. However, in exploring our world afresh with a new paradigm, there is no external standard or a set of experiences that we all know. (There was a time, of course, when we all knew that the earth was the center of the universe.)

A scientist in the midst of a paradigm shift does not have the option of determining what she is really seeing.

> With scientific observation, however, the situation is exactly reversed. The scientist can have no recourse above or beyond what he sees with his eyes and instruments. If there were some higher authority by recourse to which vision might be shown to have shifted, then that authority would itself become the source of his data, and the behavior of his vision would become a source of problems (as that of the experimental subject is for the psychologist). The same sorts of problems would arise if the scientist could switch back and forth like the subject of the gestalt experiments. The period during which light was "sometimes a wave and sometimes a particle" was a period of crisis—a period when something was wrong—and it ended only with the development of wave mechanics and the realization that light was a self-consistent entity different from both waves and particles. In the sciences, therefore, if perceptual switches accompany paradigm

changes, we may not expect scientists to attest to these changes directly. Looking at the moon, the convert to Copernicanism does not say, "I used to see a planet, but now I see a satellite." That locution would imply a sense in which the Ptolemaic system had once been correct. Instead, a convert to the new astronomy says, "I once took the moon to be (or saw the moon as) a planet, but I was mistaken." That sort of statement does recur in the aftermath of scientific revolutions. If it ordinarily disguises a shift of scientific vision or some other mental transformation with the same effect, we may not expect direct testimony about that shift. Rather we must look for individual and behavioral evidence that the scientist with a new paradigm sees differently from the way he had seen before. (pp. 114–115)

Kuhn then uses the historical example of early observations of Uranus to bolster or demonstrate his claim that a scientist with a new paradigm sees differently than before, much like the psychological subject to whom the mystery of the anomalous cards has been explained. On numerous occasions during a period of over 90 years, a number of astronomers had seen a star in positions that we now conclude must have been occupied by the planet Uranus. One of the observers had actually seen the star on four successive evenings in 1769, but did not take note of the motion that would distinguish it from a star. Sir William Herschel, using an improved telescope, noticed an apparent disk-size that was unusual for a star. Knowing something was awry, Herschel scrutinized the object and discovered that it moved among the stars. He announced that he had seen a new comet. Only after another astronomer made fruitless attempts to fit this object into a cometary orbit did this astronomer suggest that the orbit was probably planetary (Kuhn, 1970, p. 115).

When that suggestion was accepted, there were several fewer stars and one more planet in the world of the professional astronomer. A celestial body that had been observed off and on for almost a century was seen differently after 1781 because, like an anomalous playing card, it could no longer be fitted to the perceptual categories (star or comet) provided by the paradigm that had previously prevailed. (Kuhn, 1970, pp. 115–116)

But it was not only the planet Uranus that was discovered. Perhaps because astronomers were now prepared to see planets, they discovered twenty minor planets or asteroids in the period 1800–1850, using standard instruments. Kuhn (1970) raises the question:

Can it conceivably be an accident, for example, that Western astronomers first saw change in the previously immutable heavens during the half-century after Copernicus' new paradigm was first proposed? The Chinese, whose cosmological beliefs did not preclude celestial change [as did the pre-Copernican paradigm], had recorded the appearance of many new stars in the heavens at a much earlier date. (p. 116)

Kuhn concludes:

> The very ease and rapidity with which astronomers saw new things when looking at old objects with old instruments may make us wish to say that, after Copernicus, astronomers lived in a different world. In any case, their research responded as though that were the case. (p. 117)

Kuhn (1970) offers additional examples from the history of science of "the shifts in scientific perception that accompany paradigm change" (p. 117). Of particular importance to Kuhn's contention, "What occurs during a scientific revolution is not fully reducible to a reinterpretation of individual and stable data," is Galileo's view of pendulums (p. 121). Throughout history human beings have, no doubt, taken notice of heavy objects swinging back and forth on a string or chain and finally coming to rest. The Aristotelians believed that the heavy body was "moved by its own nature from a higher position to a state of natural rest at a lower one" and that "the swinging body was simply falling with difficulty. Constrained by the chain, it could achieve rest at its low point only after tortuous motion and a considerable time" (p. 119). Galileo, however, "saw a pendulum, a body that almost succeeded in repeating the same motion over and over again ad infinitum" (p. 119). Galileo built much of his dynamics, including the independence of weight and rate of fall, that is, that heavier things do not fall faster, around his observation of the pendulum. "All these natural phenomena he saw differently from the way they had been seen before" (p. 119).

Kuhn attributes Galileo's shift of vision not only to his individual genius. "Rather, what seems to have been involved was the exploitation by genius of perceptual possibilities made available by a medieval paradigm shift. Galileo was not raised completely as an Aristotelian" (p. 119). Instead, Galileo was trained in the medieval impetus theory of motion, which held that "the continuing motion of a heavy body is due to an internal power implanted in it by the projector that initiated its motion" (p. 119). Two 14th-century scholastics used the impetus theory to describe a vibrating string as having impetus implanted in it when it is first struck.

> [T]he impetus is next consumed in displacing the string against the resistance of its tension; tension then carries the string back, implanting increasing impetus until the mid-point of motion is reached; after that the impetus displaces the string in the opposite direction, again against the string's tension, and so on in a symmetric process that may continue indefinitely. (p. 120)

Although this explanation may seem a bit awkward to readers today, it is a close description of the oscillatory motion that Galileo saw in the pendulum. "Until that scholastic paradigm was invented, there were no pendulums, but only swinging stones, for the scientist to see. Pendulums were brought into existence by something very like a paradigm-induced gestalt shift" (Kuhn, 1970, p. 120).

How then is Galileo different from Aristotle? Is it a transformation of vision? Did these men really *see* different things when *looking at* the same sorts of objects? Is there any legitimate sense in which we can say that they pursued their research in different worlds? . . . Many readers will surely want to say that what changes with a paradigm is only the scientist's interpretation of observations that themselves are fixed once and for all by the nature of the environment and of the perceptual apparatus. . . . Aristotle and Galileo both saw pendulums, but they differed in their interpretations of what they both had seen. (pp. 120–121)

Although the idea that Aristotle and Galileo differed only in their interpretation of what they saw is in accord with the current epistemological tradition, Kuhn (1970) is convinced that "[w]hat occurs during a scientific revolution is not fully reducible to a reinterpretation of individual and stable data" (p. 121). First, "the data are not unequivocally stable. A pendulum is not a falling stone" (p. 121). Second,

the process by which either the individual or the community makes the transition from the constrained fall to the pendulum . . . is not one that resembles interpretation. How could it do so in the absence of fixed data for the scientist to interpret? Rather than being an interpreter, the scientist who embraces a new paradigm is like the man wearing inverting lenses. Confronting the same constellation of objects as before and knowing that he does so, he nevertheless finds them transformed through and through in many of their details. (p. 122)

Kuhn acknowledges that scientists do interpret observations and data. Aristotle interpreted observations on falling stones, and Galileo interpreted observations on the pendulum. "But each of these interpretations presupposed a paradigm. They were parts of normal science, an enterprise that, as we have already seen, aims to refine, extend, and articulate a paradigm that is already in existence" (Kuhn, 1970, p. 122). This is what most scientists do. "Given a paradigm, interpretation is central to the enterprise that explores it" (p. 122). The accepted paradigm tells the scientist what the data are, the instruments that might be used to acquire the data, and the concepts that are to be used in interpreting the data.

The operations and measurements that a scientist undertakes in the laboratory are not "the given" of experience but rather "the collected with difficulty." They are not what the scientist sees—at least not before his research is well advanced and his attention focused. Rather, they are concrete indices to the content of the more elementary perceptions, and as such they are selected for the close scrutiny of normal research only because they promise opportunity for the fruitful elaboration of an accepted paradigm. Far more clearly than the immediate experience from which they in part derive, operations and measurements are paradigm-determined. As a result, scientists with different paradigms engage in different concrete laboratory manipulations. The measurements to be performed on a pendulum are not the ones relevant to a case of constrained fall. (Kuhn, 1970, p. 126)

Kuhn argues that there is no observation more elementary than a pendulum. There is no hypothetical fixed vision, only vision through another paradigm, one that makes the swinging stone something other than a pendulum (Kuhn, 1970, p. 128).

A further argument that what is involved in a paradigm shift is something other than a reinterpretation of previous data is that paradigms can never be corrected by normal science. Paradigm shifts are preceded by recognition of anomalies and crises. A new paradigm does not come into existence by deliberation and interpretation, but by "a relatively sudden and unstructured event like the gestalt shift. Scientists often speak of the 'scales falling from the eyes' or of the 'lightening flash' that 'inundates' a previously obscure puzzle" that allows its solution (Kuhn, 1970, p. 122). "No ordinary sense of the term 'interpretation' fits these flashes of intuition through which a new paradigm is born" (p. 123).

Finally, Kuhn argues that after a paradigm shift, even the data change. This assertion is beyond retinal impressions or the effect that the paradigm has on conceptually subdividing the world in a particular way. It is beyond the claim that many former measurements and manipulations are no longer relevant and are replaced by other measurements and manipulations. "Whatever he may then see, the scientist after a revolution is still looking at the same world" (Kuhn, 1970, p. 129). His language may sound the same as before, and his laboratory may look the same. He may continue to do many of the same manipulations and use the same terms to describe his work as before the paradigm shift.

If these enduring manipulations have been changed at all, the change must lie either in their relation to the paradigm or in their concrete results. I now suggest . . . that both these sorts of changes occur. . . . [O]ne and the same operation, when it attaches to nature through a different paradigm, can become an index to a quite different aspect of nature's regularity. In addition, we shall see that occasionally the old manipulation in its new role will yield different concrete results. (p. 130)

In support of this startling contention Kuhn cites the work of John Dalton that revolutionized chemistry in the 18th century. Prior to Dalton's work, there was a confusing line between physical mixtures and chemical compounds. If there had been some evidence of a chemical reaction—heat, light, effervescence, for example—when two substances were mixed, there was assumed to be a chemical bond between the two, rather than a mere affinity. If particles in a mixture could be physically separated or distinguished by sight, it was assumed to be a physical mixture rather than a chemical compound. However, for a large class of combinations—salt dissolved in water, glass, mixtures of gases, alloys, and so on—there was disagreement on whether a chemical compound had been formed. For material in this gray area, some chemists argued for considering them to be chemical compounds, citing, among other things, the homogeneity of a salt solution or the gases in the atmosphere. Why did the heavier gases in the atmosphere not sink to the bottom if air were only a mixture? Other chemists considered these combinations to be mere mixtures. Kuhn argues that the mixture-compound distinction was more than a matter of definitions, more than a conventional convenience. "The mixture-compound distinction was part of their paradigm—part of the way they viewed their whole field of research" (Kuhn, 1970, pp. 131–132).

Dalton was a meteorologist rather than a chemist and was interested in the physical absorption of gases by water and the absorption of water in the atmosphere. Interesting: *"Partly because his training was in a different specialty and partly because of his own work in that specialty,*[4] he approached these problems with a paradigm different from that of contemporary chemists" (Kuhn, 1970, p. 133, emphasis added). Dalton's law of fixed proportion was a tautology in which he assumed at the start, that at least for that class of combinations that were clearly the result of chemical reactions, the proportions must be fixed, that is, that atoms could combine with other atoms only in a one-to-one or other simple whole-number relation. If the ingredients did not combine in such ratios, Dalton considered the resulting combinations, by their very nature, not a chemical process. Starting with the combinations he knew to be chemical compounds—because of the production of heat, light, effervescence, and the like—Dalton was able to determine the relative sizes and weights of the constituent atomic particles.

A law that experiment could not have established before Dalton's work, became, once that work was accepted, a constitutive principle that no single set of chemical measurements could have upset. As a result of what is perhaps our fullest example of a scientific revolution, the same chemical manipulations assumed a relationship to chemical generalization very different from the one they had before. (Kuhn, 1970, p. 133)

Once Dalton's law of fixed proportion captured the field of chemistry, the data changed.

> If, for example, atoms could combine chemically only in simple whole-number ratios, the re-examination of existing chemical data should disclose examples of multiple as well as of fixed proportions. Chemists stopped writing that the two oxides of, say, carbon contained 56 per cent and 72 per cent of oxygen by weight; instead they wrote that one weight of carbon would combine either with 1.3 or with 2.6 weights of oxygen. When the results of the old manipulations were recorded in this way, a 2:1 ratio leaped to the eye; and this occurred in the analysis of many well-known reactions and of new ones besides. . . . As a result, chemists came to live in a world where reactions behaved quite differently from the way they had before. (Kuhn, 1970, p. 134)

PLEDGING ALLEGIANCE TO AN ALTERNATIVE PARADIGM

After discussing in detail the revolutionary nature of a paradigm shift, Kuhn (1970) considers the following question:

> What is the process by which a new candidate for paradigm replaces its predecessor? Any new interpretation of nature . . . emerges first in the mind of one or a few individuals. It is they who first learn to see science and the world differently, and their ability to make the transition is facilitated by two circumstances that are not common to most other members of their profession. Invariably their attention has been intensely concentrated upon the crisis-provoking problems; usually, in addition, they are men so young or so new to the crisis-ridden field that practice has committed them less deeply than most of their contemporaries to the worldview and rules determined by the old paradigm. How are they able, what must they do, to convert the entire profession or the relevant professional subgroup to their way of seeing science and the world? What causes the group to abandon one tradition of normal research in favor of another? (p. 144)

Although there are, at first, many attempts at solving the crisis-provoking problem, the attempts are made within the paradigm. Only after persistent attempts have failed is there a crisis that may evoke an alternative candidate for paradigm. "In the sciences the testing situation never consists, as puzzle-solving does, simply in the comparison of a single paradigm with nature. Instead, testing occurs as part of the competition between two rival paradigms for the allegiance of the scientific community" (Kuhn, 1970, p. 145).

The competition among paradigms is a community issue. There is no single objective criteria for the competition between or among paradigms. Although the ability of the new paradigm to solve problems might appear central,

> paradigm debates are not really about relative problem-solving ability, though for good reasons they are usually couched in those terms. Instead, the issue is which paradigm should in the future guide research on problems many of which neither competitor can claim to resolve completely. A decision between alternate ways of practicing science is called for, and in the circumstances that decision must be based less on past achievement than future promise. The man who embraces a new paradigm at an early stage must often do so in defiance of the evidence provided by problem-solving. He must, that is, have faith that the new paradigm will succeed with the many large problems that confront it, knowing only that the older paradigm has failed with a few. A decision of that kind can be made only on faith. (Kuhn, 1970, pp. 157–158)

A paradigm gains ascendance gradually as it attracts more followers. It becomes the dominant paradigm on the basis of its acceptance by the scientific community. In fact, according to Kuhn, the paradigm, if it wins, defines the boundaries of that scientific community.

> Rather than a single group conversion, what occurs is an increasing shift in the distribution of professional allegiances.
>
> At the start a new candidate for paradigm may have few supporters, and on occasions the supporters' motives may be suspect. Nevertheless, if they are competent, they will improve it, explore its possibilities, and show what it would be like to belong to the community guided by it. And as that goes on, if the paradigm is one destined to win its fight, the number and strength of the persuasive arguments in its favor will increase. More scientists will then be converted, and the exploration of the new paradigm will go on. Gradually the number of experiments, instruments, articles, and books based upon the paradigm will multiply. Still more men, convinced of the new view's fruitfulness, will adopt the new mode of practicing normal science, until at last only a few elderly hold-outs remain. And even they, we cannot say, are wrong. . . . [T]he man who continues to resist after his whole profession has been converted has *ipso facto* ceased to be a scientist. (Kuhn, 1970, pp. 158–159)

And then, after a sufficient period of normal science under the new paradigm, the cycle of anomalies, crisis, alternative paradigm, and scientific revolution begins again.

SUMMARY OF KUHN'S CONCEPT OF PARADIGM SHIFT

Before considering the role of metaphor in our thought and action in the next chapter, it may be helpful to summarize Kuhn's work.

1. Fundamental understandings and approaches in the field of natural science are overturned and overtaken by rival understandings by a process of paradigm shifts.

   • There is a period of normal science during which the prevailing paradigm shapes the field, setting parameters for inquiry, identifying the focus of study, and establishing standards of practice, including law, theory, application, and scientific instrumentation.
   • The accumulation of anomalies in the research conducted under the prevailing paradigm may lead to a crisis in the field.
   • The crisis may resolve itself, be postponed, or open the door to a new paradigm.
   • If there is both a crisis and an available alternative paradigm, there is a period of competition during which the alternative paradigm may gather sufficient adherents that it gradually becomes established as the prevailing paradigm that then shapes the field in a new way.

2. Neither the existence of anomalies nor an alternative paradigm, alone, will lead to a paradigm shift.

   • After a scientific theory has achieved the status of a paradigm, it is declared invalid only if an alternative candidate is available to take its place.
   • As long as practitioners have a perspective, a method, a theory that works, they are unlikely to invent another or even try an existing alternative.
   • There is more than one perspective for any situation, and more than one theory can be applied to a particular set of data.
   • There are always anomalies in trying to fit nature into a theoretical framework.

3. These shifts to an alternative paradigm are revolutionary, discontinuous, and extraordinary rather than cumulative, evolutionary, or developmental.

   • The new paradigm is a reconstruction of the field from new fundamentals.
   • The field's basic theoretical generalizations, methods, and applications will be different.
   • A new paradigm is necessarily incompatible and incommensurable with the old.
   • After a paradigm shift, a scientist sees the world in a radically different way.

4. The prevailing paradigm directs and constrains how the scientist perceives, inquires, values, thinks, and acts.

- There is no research without a paradigm.
- Paradigms are constitutive of the research activity.
- The state of the paradigm affects whether one will inquire or act at all.
- A paradigm is a prerequisite to perception itself.
- A paradigm tells the scientist what the data are, the instruments that might be used to acquire the data, and the concepts that are to be used in interpreting the data.
- The nature of the paradigm has a critical effect on the data that are collected and examined; attention is focused on certain areas of inquiry and on a limited class of phenomena, to the neglect of others.
- Operations and measurements are paradigm-determined.
- A paradigm includes theory, methods, and standards, intertwined with each other.
- A paradigm includes criteria for the legitimacy of problems and solutions.
- A new paradigm provides a new set of concepts for describing the world, new methods for exploring that world, and even new standards for what is worth exploring, what problems are worth solving, and what is worth knowing.

5. The scientist does not preserve the gestalt subject's freedom to switch back and forth between ways of seeing.

- Those who can envision the new paradigm are those whose attention has been intensely concentrated upon the crisis-provoking problems and are so young or so new to the field that they are less deeply committed to the worldview and rules determined by the old paradigm.
- Those who are so young or new to the field that they are less committed to the worldview of the old paradigm are also more likely to grasp and adopt a new worldview.

NOTES

1. Note that Kuhn here uses an achievement as the definition of a paradigm. Later writers such as Harman and others define paradigm as a set of assumptions, understandings, and the like. Although an achievement in Kuhn's terms may embody a set of assumptions and understandings, his use of the term *paradigm* is different than what seems to be the contemporary understanding that has been popularized in recent years.

Kuhn (1970) notes that (at least prior to 1970) the established use of *paradigm* was *an accepted model or pattern*, such as illustrated by Latin verbs whose regularity allows conjugation in a predictable manner: *amo, amas, amat* or *laudo, laudas, laudat*. Either *amo* or *laudo* could serve as the pattern or *paradigm* for conjugating verbs. "In a science, on the other hand, a paradigm is rarely an object for replication. Instead, like an accepted judicial decision in the common law, it is an object for further articulation and specification under new or more stringent conditions" (p. 23).

In Kuhn's *Postscript–1969* included in the 1970 edition of *The Structure of Scientific Revolutions*, the author notes that "one sympathetic reader . . . concluded that the term [paradigm] is used in at least twenty-two different ways" (p. 181). Kuhn then discusses and critiques several ways in which he has used the term. The referents of the term *paradigm* will be discussed later.

2. *Ptolemaic astronomy* refers to a particular approach to the movements of the planets. There are many variations. A common thread is that the movements of the planets are analyzed from the perspective of the earth-bound observer, that is, it is assumed that the earth is the center of the universe. When we earth creatures look at the motion of the sun or the moon, there is no major problem. The sun generally looks like it is revolving around the earth: It comes up in the morning in the east and sets in the evening in the west. A similar pattern holds for our observation of the moon. However, when the observer on earth views one of the planets (which we now know revolves around the sun in a simple elliptical fashion), it appears to move around the earth until it retrogresses or appears to move backward for a time (Kuhn, 1957, pp. 47–48). The motion of the planets with respect to the earth is far more complex than the motion of the sun and moon—with respect to the earth. The Ptolemaic system used variations on a complex curve called an epicycle to explain the motion of the planets. As an analogy, consider the motion of the tip of the pedal on your bicycle. As the rider, you know that you are making a circular motion with the pedal. However, to the observer on the curb, the tip of the pedal is tracing a rather complex curve rather than a circle. Today, we trace the motion of the planets as ellipses around the sun. The early astronomers saw something very complex when they assumed that the earth was the center (pp. 64 ff.).

3. Kuhn (1970) notes that the breakdown of the normal science puzzle-solving activity was not the only source of the crisis. "An extended crisis would also discuss the social pressure for calendar reform . . . [and] would consider medieval criticism of Aristotle, the rise of Renaissance Neoplatonism, and other significant historical elements besides." But the core of the crisis was a technical breakdown (p. 60). The old way just did not work anymore.

4. Kuhn notes later the "revolutionary effects of applying to chemistry a set of questions and concepts previously restricted to physics and meteorology. That is what Dalton did, and the result was a reorientation toward the field, a reorientation that taught chemists to ask new questions about and draw new conclusions from old data" (p. 139).

Lakoff and Johnson and the Function of Metaphors

Having considered how paradigms affect thinking, perception, inquiry, valuing, and action, we now shift our attention to the influence of metaphor on our interactions with the world about us.

METAPHORS: CENTRAL, BUT UNCONSCIOUS

George Lakoff and Mark Johnson (1980) outline the role of *metaphor* or *metaphorical concept* in their concise book, *Metaphors We Live By*, and argue that human thought processes are largely metaphorical (p. 6).

> Metaphor is for most people a device of the poetic imagination and the rhetorical flourish—a matter of extraordinary rather than ordinary language. . . . We have found, on the contrary, that metaphor is pervasive in everyday life, not just in language but in thought and action. Our ordinary conceptual system, in terms of which we both think and act, is fundamentally metaphorical in nature.
>
> The concepts that govern our thought are not just matters of the intellect. They also govern our everyday functioning, down to the most mundane details. Our concepts structure how we perceive, how we get around in the world, and how we relate to other people. Our conceptual system thus plays a central role in defining our everyday realities. If we are right in suggesting that our conceptual system is largely metaphorical, then the

way we think, what we experience, and what we do every day is very much a matter of metaphor. (p. 3)

Furthermore, although metaphors play a central role in how we perceive, how we think, what we experience, and what we do in everyday life, we are not normally conscious of our conceptual system. We take it for granted. "In most of the little things we do every day, we simply think and act more or less automatically along certain lines" (Lakoff & Johnson, 1980, p. 3). The authors contend that "[s]ince communication is based on the same conceptual system that we use in thinking and acting, language is an important source of evidence for what that system is like" (p. 3).

Identifying the warlike metaphor that pervades our vocabulary when referring to argument—for example, *attack a position, indefensible, strategy, new line of attack, win, gain ground*, and the like—Lakoff and Johnson use this particular metaphor to illustrate how our (often hidden) metaphors shape our thinking and acting. For example,

> arguments usually follow patterns; that is, there are certain things we typically do and do not do in arguing. The fact that we in part conceptualize arguments in terms of battle systematically influences the shape arguments take and the way we talk about what we do in arguing. (p. 7)

Because, in our culture, we typically conceptualize argument as war, many of the things we do in arguing are, in part, structured by this concept. Of course, there is no physical battle, but there are attack, defense, and counterattack.

> It is important to see that we don't just *talk* about arguments in terms of war. We can actually win or lose arguments. We see the person we are arguing with as an opponent. We attack his positions and defend our own. We gain and lose ground. We plan and use strategies. If we find a position indefensible, we can abandon it and take a new line of attack. . . . It is in this sense that the ARGUMENT IS WAR metaphor is one we live by in this culture; it structures the actions we perform in arguing. (p. 4)

The authors suggest that we contrast this taken-for-granted metaphor for arguments with an alternative metaphor.

> Try to imagine a culture where arguments are not viewed in terms of war, where no one wins or loses, where there is no sense of attacking or defending, gaining or losing ground. Imagine a culture where an argument is viewed as a dance, the participants are seen as performers, and the goal is to perform in a balanced and aesthetically pleasing way. In such a culture, people would view arguments differently, experience them differently, carry them out differently, and talk about them differently. . . . [W]e

have a discourse form structured in terms of battle and they have one structured in terms of dance. (pp. 4–5)

With an alternative metaphor, that culture's thinking and acting with regard to argument would be different—whether or not one considered it better. Our metaphorical concepts for everyday life activities have a profound effect on how we think and how we live. "The most important claim we have made so far is that metaphor is not just a matter of language, that is, of mere words" (p. 6). Furthermore,

> in all aspects of life . . . we define our reality in terms of metaphors and then proceed to act on the basis of the metaphors. We draw inferences, set goals, make commitments, and execute plans, all on the basis of how we in part structure our experience, consciously and unconsciously, by means of metaphor. (p. 158)

It is important to note here that we may not have consciously chosen these metaphorical concepts that so shape our life activities.

METAPHORS: A PARTIAL UNDERSTANDING

A further observation is that a metaphor necessarily provides only a partial understanding of the object or activity to which it is applied.[1] "The primary function of a metaphor is to provide a partial understanding of one kind of experience in terms of another. This may involve preexisting isolated similarities, the creation of new similarities, and more" (Lakoff & Johnson, 1980, p. 154). A metaphor highlights certain aspects of a concept and hides or downplays others. "It is important to see that the metaphorical structuring involved here is partial, not total. If it were total, one concept would actually *be* the other, not merely be understood in terms of it" (pp. 12–13). For example, previous examples have been offered to illustrate how argument is war. However, we know that it is not totally true that argument is war. For example, as stated before, there is no physical contact. Nobody bleeds. No one dies. "[P]art of a metaphorical concept does not and cannot fit" (p. 13).

METAPHORS AND VALUES

According to Lakoff and Johnson (1980), not only do the prevailing metaphors affect how we think and act, they also affect how we value. "The most fundamental values in a culture will be coherent with the metaphorical structures of the most fundamental concepts in the culture" (p. 22). For example, the authors identify certain dominant spacialization metaphors in our culture, that is, how we view the concepts *up* and *down*, and suggest how certain cultural values in our society are coherent with them and whose opposites are not.

> "More is better" is coherent with MORE IS UP and GOOD IS UP. "Less is better" is not coherent with them.
>
> "Bigger is better" is coherent with MORE IS UP and GOOD IS UP. "Smaller is better" is not coherent with them.
>
> "The future will be better" is coherent with THE FUTURE IS UP and GOOD IS UP. "The future will be worse" is not.
>
> "There will be more in the future" is coherent with MORE IS UP and THE FUTURE IS UP.
>
> "Your status should be higher in the future" is coherent with HIGH STATUS IS UP and THE FUTURE IS UP. . . .
>
> We are not claiming that all cultural values coherent with a metaphorical system actually exist, only that those that do exist and are deeply entrenched are consistent with the metaphorical system. (pp. 22–23)

Whether or not the reader finds persuasive Lakoff and Johnson's identification of particular values in our culture, the authors do offer support for the argument that dominant metaphors in a culture have some relationship to dominant values, if not actually shaping them.

CHANGING METAPHORS

The authors also consider the possibility of changing the metaphors that govern our life. Lakoff and Johnson contrast the easily recognized puzzle metaphor for dealing with problems with a new metaphor termed the chemical metaphor. This chemical metaphor was invented by an Iranian graduate student who understood the phrase "the solution of my problems" as "a large volume of liquid, bubbling and smoking, containing all your problems, either dissolved or in the form of precipitates, with catalysts constantly dissolving some problems (for the time being) and precipitating out others" (p. 143). The authors found this novel metaphor beautiful and insightful.

> It gives us a view of problems as things that never disappear utterly and that cannot be solved once and for all. All of your problems are always present, only they may be dissolved and in solution, or they may be in solid form. The best you can hope for is to find a catalyst that will make one problem dissolve without making another one precipitate out. And since you do not have complete control over what goes into the solution,

you are constantly finding old and new problems precipitating out and present problems dissolving, partly because of your efforts and partly despite anything you do.

The CHEMICAL metaphor gives us a new view of human problems. It is appropriate to the experience of finding that problems which we once thought were "solved" turn up again and again. The CHEMICAL metaphor says that problems are not the kind of things that can be made to disappear forever. To treat them as things that can be "solved" once and for all is pointless. To live by the CHEMICAL metaphor would be to accept it as a fact that no problem ever disappears forever. Rather than direct your energies toward solving your problems once and for all, you would direct your energies toward finding out what catalysts will dissolve your most pressing problems for the longest time without precipitating out worse ones. The reappearance of a problem is viewed as a natural occurrence rather than a failure on your part to find "the right way to solve it."

To live by the CHEMICAL metaphor would mean that your problems would have a different kind of reality for you. A temporary solution would be an accomplishment rather than a failure. Problems would be part of the natural order of things rather than disorders to be "cured." The way you would understand your everyday life and the way you would act in it would be different if you lived by the CHEMICAL metaphor.

We see this as a clear case of the power of metaphor to create a reality rather than simply to give us a way of conceptualizing a preexisting reality. . . . The PROBLEMS ARE PUZZLES metaphor characterizes our present reality. A shift to the CHEMICAL metaphor would characterize a new reality. (pp. 143–145)

The parallels between Lakoff and Johnson's view of the function of metaphor and Kuhn's understanding of the role of a paradigm are highlighted by this delightful story of an encounter with a new metaphor. First, both the paradigm and the metaphor in this case shape our thinking and acting. Second, both the paradigm and metaphor might be said to create a new reality. Kuhn used the image of the scientist living in a new world after a paradigm shift. Kuhn explained that a new paradigm involved more than a reinterpretation of old data. Lakoff and Johnson state here that the metaphor is creating a new reality rather than simply offering us a new way to conceptualize a preexisting reality. Lakoff and Johnson echo Kuhn in their identification of the radical effect of living out of a new metaphor.

Similarly, Lakoff and Johnson contend that "it is no easy matter to change the metaphors we live by," just as Kuhn pointed out that a scientist cannot easily shift back and forth between paradigms as can the one who experiences a visual gestalt shift (Lakoff & Johnson, 1980, p. 145; Kuhn, 1970, p. 85).

It is one thing to be aware of the possibilities inherent in the CHEMI-
CAL metaphor, but it is a very different and far more difficult thing to
live by it. Each of us has, consciously or unconsciously, identified
hundreds of problems, and we are constantly at work on solutions for
many of them—via the PUZZLE metaphor. So much of our unconscious
everyday activity is structured in terms of the PUZZLE metaphor that
we could not possibly make a quick or easy change to the CHEMICAL
metaphor on the basis of a conscious decision. (Lakoff & Johnson, 1980,
p. 145)

It is not, however, impossible for changes to occur. Lakoff and Johnson do not detail how one would intentionally introduce change into a
culture by means of a change in metaphor (although there is a suggestion here that one might first think in terms of this metaphor and then
begin to act in accord with it), but the authors do not doubt of the power
of metaphor.

New metaphors have the power to create a new reality. This can begin to
happen when we start to comprehend our experience in terms of a metaphor, and it becomes a deeper reality when we begin to act in terms of it.
If a new metaphor enters the conceptual system that we base our actions
on, it will alter that conceptual system and the perceptions and actions that
the system gives rise to. Much of cultural change arises from the introduction of new metaphorical concepts and the loss of old ones. For example,
the Westernization of cultures throughout the world is partly a matter of
introducing the TIME IS MONEY metaphor into those cultures.

The idea that metaphors can create realities goes against most traditional
views of metaphor. The reason is that metaphor has traditionally been
viewed as a matter of mere language rather than primarily as a means of
structuring our conceptual system and the kinds of everyday activities that
we perform. It is reasonable enough to assume that words alone don't
change reality. But changes in our conceptual system do change what is
real for us and affect how we perceive the world and act upon those
perceptions. (Lakoff & Johnson, 1980, pp. 145–146)

The authors begin to point to the implications of diverse cultures
having different metaphors or conceptual systems. "[P]eople with very
different conceptual systems than our own may understand the world
in a very different way than we do" (Lakoff & Johnson, 1980, p. 181).
There is also a suggestion that the physical surroundings, as well as
other factors, may play an important role in the development of metaphors that create our reality.

[T]he human aspects of reality are most of what matters to us, and these
vary from culture to culture, since different cultures have different conceptual systems. Cultures also exist within physical environments, some of

them radically different—jungles, deserts, islands, tundra, mountains, cities, etc. In each case there is a physical environment that we interact with, more or less successfully. The conceptual systems of various cultures partly depend on the physical environments they have developed in.

Each culture must provide a more or less successful way of dealing with its environment, both adapting to it and changing it. Moreover, each culture must define a social reality within which people have roles that make sense to them and in terms of which they can function socially. Not surprisingly, the social reality defined by a culture affects its conception of physical reality. . . . Since much of our social reality is understood in metaphorical terms, and since our conception of the physical world is partly metaphorical, metaphor plays a very significant role in determining what is real for us. (Lakoff & Johnson, 1980, p. 146)

METAPHOR AND SELF-UNDERSTANDING

Finally, although not the primary focus of the work, Lakoff and Johnson address the role of metaphor in self-understanding and in ritual.

Understanding of ourselves is not unlike other forms of understanding—it comes out of our constant interactions with our physical, cultural, and interpersonal environment. . . . Just as in mutual understanding we constantly search out commonalities of experience when we speak with other people, so in self-understanding we are always searching for what unifies our own diverse experiences in order to give coherence to our lives. Just as we seek out metaphors to highlight and make coherent what we have in common with someone else, so we seek out *personal* metaphors to highlight and make coherent our own pasts, our present activities, and our dreams, hopes, and goals as well. A large part of self-understanding is the search for appropriate personal metaphors that make sense of our lives. (Lakoff & Johnson, 1980, p. 232–233).

The authors define a process of self-understanding that includes developing an awareness of our own operating metaphors, including how and where they do and do not enter our life; having experiences that could form the basis for alternative metaphors; and engaging in a process of viewing our life through alternative metaphors (p. 233).

"We are constantly performing rituals," from the casual to the solemn (Lakoff & Johnson, 1980, p. 233). The authors contend that a ritual is a kind of experiential gestalt that is a coherent sequence of actions structured along the natural dimensions of experience. They suggest:

The metaphors we live by, whether cultural or personal, are partially preserved in ritual.

Cultural metaphors, and the values entailed by them, are propagated in ritual.

Ritual forms are an indispensable part of the experiential basis for our cultural metaphorical system. There can be no culture without ritual. (p. 234)

Neither can there be, according to the authors, a coherent view of the self without personal ritual. Our personal rituals are not random but are coherent with our view of the world and our system of personal metaphors. "Our implicit and typically unconscious conceptions of ourselves and the values that we live by are perhaps most strongly reflected in the little things we do over and over," that is, in our casual, daily rituals (p. 235).

SUMMARY: LAKOFF AND JOHNSON'S UNDERSTANDING OF METAPHOR

1. Metaphors shape how we perceive, think, experience, value, and act in everyday life.

   •Human conceptual processes are largely metaphorical.
   •A new metaphor creates a new reality for us rather than simply offering a new way to conceptualize a preexisting reality.
   •People with different conceptual systems from ours understand the world in a very different way than we do.
   •Different cultures have different conceptual systems.
   •Individually we seek out personal metaphors to highlight and make coherent our activities, dreams, hopes, and goals, that is, to make sense of our lives.
   •The metaphors we live by are partially preserved in ritual.
   •We draw inferences, set goals, make commitments, and execute plans, all on the basis of how we structure our experience, consciously and unconsciously, by means of metaphor.
2. We are not normally conscious of our conceptual system. Most of the time we act automatically, without considering the metaphors that give form to our thought and action.
3. A metaphor necessarily highlights certain aspects of a concept and hides or downplays others.
4. It is not easy to change the metaphors by which we live.
   •A new metaphor can begin to create a new reality when we start to comprehend our experience in terms of that metaphor.
   •A new metaphor can deepen a new reality when we act in terms of it.

NOTE

1. For a general discussion of the role of metaphor in shaping our thought and inquiry, see also Morgan, 1980.

Kenneth Boulding and the Function of Maps and Images

A third work describes how our maps of reality or images shape our thinking, inquiring, perceiving, valuing and acting.

IMAGES AND BEHAVIOR

Kenneth Boulding (1956), in his book *Images* (which predates the first edition of Thomas Kuhn's *The Structure of Scientific Revolutions* by several years), describes the images that form our internal knowledge structure and govern our behavior.

> As I sit at my desk, I know where I am. I see before me a window; beyond that some trees; beyond that the red roofs of the campus of Stanford University; . . . beyond them the bare hills of the Hamilton Range. I know, however, more than I see. . . . I know that beyond the mountains that close my present horizon, there is a broad valley; beyond that a still higher range of mountains; beyond that other mountains, range upon range, until we come to the Rockies; beyond that the Great Plains and the Mississippi; beyond that the Alleghenies; beyond that the eastern seaboard; beyond that the Atlantic Ocean; beyond that is Europe; beyond that is Asia. I know, furthermore, that if I go far enough I will come back to where I am now. In other words, I have a picture of the world as round. I visualize it as a globe. I am a little hazy on the details. . . . I probably could not draw a good

map of Indonesia, but I have a fair idea where everything is located on the face of this globe. Looking further, I visualize the globe as a small speck circling around a bright star which is the sun, in the company of many other similar specks, the planets. Looking still further, I see our sun as a member of millions upon millions of others in the Galaxy. Looking still further, I visualize the Galaxy as one of millions upon millions of others in the universe. (Boulding, 1956, pp. 3–4)

Boulding explains that we understand ourselves to be located not only in space, but in time, in a field of personal relationships, in a world of "subtle intimations and emotions" (pp. 4–5). He uses the term *image* to describe this subjective knowledge, that is, what an individual believes to be true, and identifies ten dimensions of an individual's operating image:

1. Spatial—the individual's location in space.
2. Temporal—the individual's place in time.
3. Relational—the picture of the universe as a system of regularities. This includes concepts of causality, randomness, and personal effectiveness.
4. Personal—the place of the individual in the universe of persons, roles, and organizations around him.
5. Value—the ordering by means of *better* or *worse* of the various parts of the whole image.
6. Affectional or emotional—the feeling or affect attached to various items in the image.
7. Consciousness—the division of the image into conscious, subconscious, and unconscious areas.
8. Certainty—the degree of certainty or uncertainty, clarity, or vagueness attached to the parts of the image.
9. Reality—the image of the correspondence of the image itself with some outside reality.
10. Public—the degree to which the image is shared by others or is peculiar to the individual (pp. 47–48).

This multifaceted image forms the basis for a human being's perceptions, thinking, inquiry, valuing, and actions.

It is this Image which governs my behavior. In about an hour I shall rise, leave my office, go to a car, drive down to my home, play with the children, have supper, go to bed. I can predict this behavior with a fair degree of accuracy because of the knowledge which I have; the knowledge that I have a home not far away, to which I am accustomed to go. . . . The prediction, of course, may not be fulfilled. There may be an earthquake, I may have an accident with the car on the way home, I may get home and find that my family has been suddenly called away. A hundred and one things may happen. As each event occurs, however, it alters my knowledge structure or my image. And as it alters my image, I behave accordingly. *The first proposition of this work, therefore, is that behavior depends on the image.* (pp. 5–6, emphasis in original)

INCOMING MESSAGES AND THE IMAGE

Boulding then considers how the image is formed and concludes that "[t]he image is built up as a result of all past experience of the possessor of the image" (Boulding, 1956, p. 6). The image develops from the moment of birth, initially as undifferentiated sights and sounds. Later the child's image of the world begins to develop and expand as he sees himself in his neighborhood, his city, the globe, and in a web of personal relationships. "Everytime a message reaches him his image is likely to be changed in some degree by it, and as his image is changed his behavior patterns will be changed likewise" (p. 7). For Boulding, "The meaning of a message is the change which it produces in the image" (p. 7).

There are several possible effects of a message on the image. First, the image may be completely unaffected. The message may be ignored or go unnoticed, for example, as background noise. Second, the message may change the image in a regular or well-defined way—for example, one looks at a world atlas and modifies one's image of where Indonesia is in relation to Papua New Guinea. The image will be modified, but the world will still generally fit the operating image. A third and related change is that the message will add to or diminish the degree of certainty with which one regards the image. For example, my watch says 5:00 p.m., but the expected rush hour traffic on the way home does not materialize. Is my watch correct? Is today a holiday? Is there something else awry (Boulding, 1956, pp. 7–10)?

Finally, a message can effect a revolutionary change in the image. "Sometimes a message hits some sort of nucleus or supporting structure in the image, and the whole thing changes in a quite radical way" (Boulding, 1956, p. 8). One returns home from work and discovers that one's spouse has moved out and taken the children and the furniture. The operating image of a happy family life is radically altered, not merely modified or reorganized.

A spectacular instance of such a change is conversion. A man, for instance, may think himself a pretty good fellow and then may hear a preacher who convinces him that, in fact, his life is worthless and shallow, as he is presently living it. The words of the preacher cause a radical reformulation of the man's image of himself in the world, and his behavior changes accordingly. (p. 8)

Our operating images are not easily changed. "The sudden and dramatic nature of these reorganizations is perhaps a result of the fact that our image is in itself resistant to change" (Boulding, 1956, p. 8). The values that are attached to our images, in varying degrees for various parts of our image of the world, will also affect the change that an incoming message has on our image. For example, we may feel strongly that "the University of Southern California is an outstanding university," but not care whether "Jupiter is a better planet than Venus." We may vigorously challenge an incoming message that suggests that the University of Southern California is second-rate: We might find ways to discount this information. However, information about Jupiter or Venus may be readily absorbed into our planetary map of reality or may even pass unnoticed.

> One of the most important propositions of this theory is that the value scales of any individual or organization are perhaps the most important single element determining the effect of the messages it receives on its image of the world. If a message is perceived that is neither good nor bad it may have little or no effect on the image. If it is perceived as bad or hostile to the image which is held, there will be resistance to accepting it. This resistance is usually not infinite. An often repeated message or a message which comes with unusual force or authority is able to penetrate the resistance and will be able to alter the image. (Boulding, 1956, p. 12)

The receiver of the message may resist the message by ignoring it or by meeting it with anger or hostility. On the other hand, messages that support and affirm the existing operating image are easily received, even if they result in minor modifications or accretions to the image (pp. 12–13). The degree of the image's resistance to change will also depend on its internal consistency, aesthetic relationships among the parts (e.g., elegance, beauty, and simplicity in mathematical arguments), and other nonlogical qualities (p. 13). Messages are mediated or filtered through a value system and are not merely facts. According to Boulding we often suspend belief not only in symbolic messages (e.g., language), but also in so-called factual or sensory data, that is, what our eyes (or other senses) are telling us. For example, our operating image tells us, contrary to the visual inp it, that the stick in the water is not really bent (p. 14).

SHARED IMAGES AND SOCIETAL BEHAVIOR

Boulding emphasizes that although all our messages are filtered through a value system and have varying effects on our individual operating image, our image is not purely subjective or private. This author introduces the concept of shared or common images.

Part of our image of the world is the belief that this image is shared by other people like ourselves who also are part of our image of the world. In common daily intercourse we all behave as if we possess roughly the same image of the world. If a group of people are in a room together, their behavior clearly shows that they all think they are in the same room. (Boulding, 1956, p. 14)

Boulding (1956) identifies conversation or discourse, the human ability not only to have an image of the world but also to talk about it, as the process that allows for these public or shared images.

A public image is a product of a universe of discourse, that is, a process of sharing messages and experiences. The shared messages which build up the public image come from both nature and from other men. A group of people talking around the table do not each receive the same messages. Indeed, each perceives the situation from his own position. Nevertheless, the image of the situation which is built up in each of the individuals is highly similar, at least in regard to the spatial and temporal image. In a group of close friends the personal and relational images may also be very similar. In a group of hostile or indifferent people they may not be. . . .

A subculture may be defined as a group of people sharing a public image. This need not be a conscious image, and the group need not be conscious that they are sharing it. If, however, there are basic similarities in the images of the different individuals in the group, the behavior of the group will reflect and will, in general, reinforce the similarities. (pp. 132–133)

For Boulding, there is a continuous process of an image shaping a society and society remaking the image. "The basic bond of any society, culture, subculture, or organization is a 'public image,' that is, an image the essential characteristics of which are shared by the individuals participating in the group" (p. 64). This public image includes that set of images regarding space, time, relations, evaluation, and so on, that is shared by the mass of its people (p. 64).

The public image produces a transcript that is handed down from generation to generation. In a primitive nonliterate society, the transcript may consist of verbal rituals, legends, poems, and ceremonials; in a literate society the transcript can be in the form of books, tapes, sound recordings, and the like, that can be transmitted independently of the transcriber. Some aspects of the image, however, such as touch, taste, or smell have not been able to be recorded (Boulding, 1956, pp. 64–65).

A geographic map is an example of an artifact of a society's image. We learn about our place in the world or the image of our ancestors' place in the world from a map.

When we look at the crudely constructed charts of the South Sea Islanders, they mean very little to us because we visualize the seas as a plain blue surface dotted with multicolored dots which we interpret as islands. The South Sea Islanders probably visualize their space in a somewhat different way in terms of the things you have to do to get from one place to another, the stars you have to observe, the directions you have to go, the courses you have to keep. Instead of being a plain blue surface, their space is a series of intersecting lines. The Romans had only vague ideas of the shape of their own empire. They knew pretty well, however, how far it was from Rome wherever they happened to be, and their maps indicate this spatial conception. The maps of the Middle Ages show the world centering in Jerusalem. The shapes were unimportant. The theological symbolism was the vital thing. . . . The gradual exploration of the globe leads to a closure of geography. This has profound effects upon all parts of the image. Primitive man lives in a world which has a spatial unknown, a dread frontier populated by the heated imagination. For modern man, the world is a closed and completely explored surface. This is a radical change in spatial viewpoint. It produces effects in all other spheres of life. (Boulding, 1956, p. 66)

Although there is a sharing of images among members of a culture or subculture, in a complex society, people have many roles and participate in various subcultures that may have different images. An individual may, for example, share one image with his coworkers and another with his family and yet another with his political party (Boulding, 1956, p. 135). With regard to academic disciplines, there is a "complex public image widely shared but characterized by specialization (p. 135). One has a sharp image of one's own specialty, but only a vague image of distant academic fields. "It can hardly be said, therefore, that there is a single public image uniting the intellectual subculture. Rather, there is a series of departmental and specialized images which form some kind of overlapping continuum" (p. 136). An image may grow strong in isolation from other images or when a particular subculture is isolated from others, but limited contact with other cultures frequently reinforces a value system (p. 147).

The role of images in directing a society—as well as the role of society in shaping images—is a focus of Boulding's (1956) *Image.*

Columbus would never have thought to set sail westward had he not had an image of the round world, and a high value in his system for spices. Similarly, the agricultural revolution itself marks the beginning of a period in which change became a welcome element in society instead of a feared and discordant one. The idea of progress always precedes development. In a society in which the image of progress does not exist, even if technological improvements are made accidentally or are made by mavericks and eccentrics of the society, they will be suppressed and not imitated. . . . The history of the technological revolution must be written largely in terms of the dynamics of the image—the image of change as a good and desirable thing introduced by the various religious reformations, and the image of an orderly universe whose secret relations might be explored by experiment and observation. (p. 122)

Although Boulding does not purport to know the processes by which certain images shape history, there are certain categories of understanding that seem to have a particularly important effect on a society's activities.

> In tracing the effect of images on the course of history, peculiar attention must be paid to the images of time and especially the images of the future. Curiously enough, it may not be so much the actual content of the image of the future which is important in its effect, but its general quality of optimism or pessimism, certainty or uncertainty, breadth or narrowness. The person or the nation that has a date with destiny goes somewhere, though not usually to the address on the label. The individual or the nation which has no sense of direction in time, no sense of a clear future ahead is likely to be vacillating, uncertain in behavior, and to have a poor chance of surviving. (Boulding, 1956, p. 125)

Thus, Boulding, offering insights from another intellectual perspective, joins Thomas Kuhn and Lakoff and Johnson in concluding that our most basic operating assumptions—whether embedded in paradigms, metaphors, or images—affect how we, as individuals and as a society, think, perceive, value, inquire, and act.

SUMMARY OF BOULDING'S CONCEPT OF IMAGE

1. A human being's perceptions, thinking, inquiry, valuing, and actions are dependent on the individual's operating image.

   - The operating image is multidimensional, including a person's orientation in space and time and in the web of human and organizational relationships.
   - The operating image includes a particular picture of the universe with regard to causality, randomness, and personal effectiveness.
   - There are values attached to various aspects of the image.
   - Various items in the image have an affect or emotion attached to them.
   - The various parts of the image are held with varying degrees of consciousness.
   - The parts of the image have varying degrees of clarity and certainty.
   - The individual's operating image includes the degree to which the image itself is understood to correspond with some outside reality.

• The image includes an apprehension of the degree to which the image is shared with others or is particular to the individual.

2. The image is changed by means of incoming messages.

3. An incoming message may have several effects: It may be ignored and have no effect; it may modify, correct, or clarify the image in a regular or well-defined way; it may add or detract from the certainty with which the image is held; or it may effect a radical change in the image.

4. Our image is resistant to change.

   • The greater value we attach to the image, the more difficult it will be to change the image.
   • Messages that threaten a valued image can be resisted or ignored.
   • Messages that support a valued image are easily received even if they result in some modification or accretion to the image.
   • All messages are filtered through a value system.
   • Messages that are repeated or are issued with authority are more likely to change the image.

5. A public image includes the set of images regarding space, time, relations, and the like, that is shared by the mass of a society's or subgroup's members.

   • The public image results in a transcript that may assume various forms handed down from generation to generation.
   • Although there is a sharing of images among members of a culture or subculture, in a complex society, people may participate in many roles or subcultures that may have different images.

Toward a Theory of Paradigms

We have now considered explorations of three intellectual constructs: paradigms, metaphors, and images. Each of these constructs
embodies in some manner our basic understandings or assumptions
about ourselves and the world about us. Each of the books surveyed
asserts that these assumptions, often unstated or unconscious, affect
how we think, perceive, inquire, value, and act. The corollary is that
a shift in operating paradigm, metaphor, or image will give rise to
different ways of thinking, perceiving, inquiring, valuing, or acting.
A next step here is to consider how thought, perception, inquiry,
valuing, and action in organizations are affected by the choice of
basic operating assumptions and perspectives. But before shifting
attention to the role of paradigm, image, and theory in organizations, it is necessary to pause, define key terminology, and begin to
outline a theory of paradigms.

PARADIGMS, METAPHORS, AND IMAGES:
DEFINITIONS

The first task is to distinguish between paradigm, metaphor, image,
and other related concepts and to offer some operating definitions. For
most purposes, this book uses *paradigm* to mean the most basic, fundamental set of assumptions and understandings forming our primary
view of reality, which assumptions and understandings can, of course,

be embedded in basic and fundamental metaphors, maps, images, and so on. But *paradigm* is used in a variety of ways here and in general discourse. It may be helpful to consider how the concept of *paradigm* has evolved over the decades.

Kuhn is said to have used the term *paradigm* twenty-two different ways in the earlier edition of *The Structure of Scientific Revolutions* (Kuhn, 1970, p. 181). Kuhn admits to using the term *paradigm* in a circular manner, that is, by first stating that a paradigm is what a scientific community shares and then defining a scientific community as those who share a paradigm (p. 176). That author then begins to sort through the constellation of group commitments that form a paradigm or the disciplinary matrix (pp. 181–182). This matrix includes symbolic generalizations or expressions such as f = ma or "elements combine in constant proportion by weight" or other generalizations that look like laws of nature (p. 183).[1] A second component of the disciplinary matrix is belief in the particular models.

> Though the strength of group commitment varies . . . along the spectrum from heuristic to ontological models, all models have similar functions. Among other things they supply the group with the preferred or permissible analogies and metaphors. By doing so they help to determine what will be accepted as an explanation and as a puzzle-solution; conversely, they assist in the determination of the roster of unsolved puzzles and in the evaluation of the importance of each. (p. 184)

The third component of the disciplinary matrix is values. For the natural sciences this may include values concerning predictions (e.g., accuracy), values to be used in judging whole theories (e.g., simplicity, self-consistency, plausibility, compatibility with existing theories), and values relating to the importance of social utility (p. 185). A fourth component of the disciplinary matrix for Kuhn is exemplars, the concrete problem-solutions that students first encounter at the start of their scientific educations and follow in other forms throughout their careers that "show them by example how their job is to be done" (p. 187).

Paul Davidson Reynolds (1971), in *A Primer on Theory Construction*, considers the role of worldviews and paradigms by examining how a scientist describes a new idea, particularly in the social sciences:

> At times this new idea is more than just a different way of describing the same data; it may include a unique "world view" or perspective that even the originator may not be completely aware of.
> . . . Basically, the newness of a new idea can only be appreciated if one is aware of the scope and quality of old ideas that prevailed before the new idea was introduced. It is convenient to classify "new ideas," according to

their degree of "newness" into three types: Kuhn paradigms, paradigms, and paradigm variations. (p. 21)

Reynolds describes and illustrates each of these three intellectual constructs.

Kuhn Paradigm

(1) It represents a radically new conceptualization of the phenomena;
(2) It suggests a new research strategy or methodological procedure for gathering empirical evidence to support the paradigm;
(3) It tends to suggest new problems for solutions;
(4) Application of the new paradigm frequently explains phenomena that previous paradigms were unable to explain. (Reynolds, 1971, p. 22)

Paradigms

(1) The conceptualization represents a unique description of the phenomena, but a *dramatic* new orientation or "world view" is absent;
(2) Although new research strategies may be suggested, dramatic new procedures or methodologies are absent;
(3) The new conceptualization may suggest new research questions;
(4) The new conceptualization may explain events previously unexplained. (Reynolds, 1971, p. 26)

Paradigm Variations

Once a conceptualization or orientation on the level of a paradigm or a Kuhn paradigm has been proposed, there are often a large number of details or refinements that are ambiguous or unspecified. Frequently there are several alternatives available in specifying details of the paradigm, each resulting in slightly different variations in the original conceptualization. (Reynolds, 1971, p. 32)

Reynolds explains that paradigms provide a different way of conceptualizing or describing certain phenomena, whereas Kuhn paradigms differ from paradigms only in degree. Paradigms introduce an orientation that is less than a scientific revolution (Reynolds, 1971, p. 26). "Paradigm variations are usually easy to identify because of rather direct and obvious links with existing paradigms, reflected in footnotes, bibliographies, and similarity of orientation" (p. 42). Thus, Reynolds views the paradigms discussed by Thomas Kuhn as the presentation of an idea. Where the idea (and the inquiry, method, and practice, and so on, associated with it) appears on the spectrum of Kuhn paradigm/ordinary paradigm/paradigm variation depends on how revolutionary or radical it is.

Gareth Morgan (1980), in "Paradigms, Metaphors, and Puzzle Solving in Organization Theory," explores the relationship among paradigms, metaphors, and puzzle solving as "specific modes of theorizing and research and the worldviews that they reflect" (p. 606). Morgan identifies three broad senses of the term paradigm, which are consistent with Kuhn's various uses of the concept:

(1) as a complete view of reality, or way of seeing;
(2) as relating to the social organization of science in terms of schools of thought connected with particular kinds of scientific achievements; and
(3) as relating to the concrete use of specific kinds of tools and texts for the process of scientific puzzle solving. (p. 606)

Morgan then proceeds to articulate a pyramid-type structure with paradigms as alternative realities at the top, metaphors as basis of schools of thought as the middle layer, and puzzle-solving activities as based on specific tools and texts as the bottom level (p. 606). (See Figure 5.1.)

Morgan (1980) carefully outlines the significance of Kuhn's concept of paradigm as an alternative reality:

Probably one of the most important implications of Kuhn's work stems from the identification of paradigms as alternative realities and the indiscriminate use of the paradigm concept in other ways tends to mask this basic insight. The term "paradigm" is therefore used here in its metatheoretical or philosophical sense to denote *an implicit or explicit view of reality*. Any adequate analysis of the role of paradigms must uncover the core assumptions that characterize and define any given world view, to make it possible to grasp what is common to the perspectives of theorists whose work may otherwise, at a more superficial level, appear diverse and wide ranging. (p. 607, emphasis added)

With respect to Kuhn's use of paradigm to denote the shared commitments of a scientific community, Morgan notes that the most fundamental bond rests on the shared worldview of the community of scientists (p. 606). The alternative reality or worldview may include different schools of thought, which may employ different metaphors as a basis for research. If a metaphor defines a particular school of thought, the *puzzle solving* level of the pyramid will include many kinds of research activities, textbooks, models, and research tools—described by Kuhn as normal science (p. 607).

Morgan (1980) focuses on social theory, and organization theory in particular, and defines four broad worldviews or paradigms,[2] which are reflected in different sets of metatheoretical assumptions (p. 607). Thus, Morgan begins to articulate a paradigm in terms of basic assumptions about reality.

Figure 5–1
Morgan's Pyramid

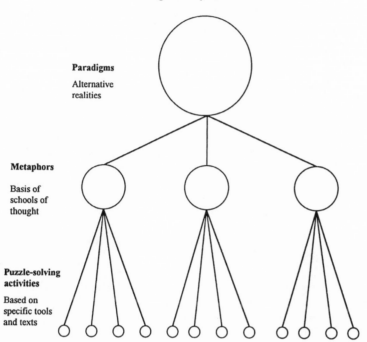

Paradigms

Alternative
realities

Metaphors

Basis of
schools of
thought

Puzzle-solving
activities

Based on
specific tools
and texts

Source: Gareth Morgan, Paradigms, metaphors, and puzzle solving in organization theory, *Administrative Science Quarterly*, Vol. 25, 1980, pp. 605–622. By permission of Administrative Science Quarterly, copyright 1980, all rights reserved, Cornell University.

The concepts of *paradigm* and *paradigm shift* have been applied beyond the realms of natural and social sciences to society as a whole, particularly in reference to various aspects of cultural transformation.[3] For example, Fritjof Capra (1982), in *The Turning Point*, outlines three cultural transitions over a period of five thousand years and uses the concept of paradigm shift to describe broad societal change. He describes a paradigm shift as "a profound change in the thoughts, perceptions, and values that form a particular vision of reality" (p. 30). The current paradigm has been dominant for several hundred years, shaping not only Western society but the whole world. The ideas and values that make up this paradigm, often associated with the scientific and industrial revolutions or the Enlightenment, differ from those that were dominant during the medieval era (pp. 30–31).

Some of the thoughts, perceptions, and values that form this paradigm include the scientific method, the mechanical view of the universe, the concept of matter being made of building blocks, the value of competition, and the belief in unlimited progress achieved through economic and technical advancements (Capra, 1982, pp. 30–31).

Willis Harman (1988), in *Global Mind Change,* in adapting Kuhn's concept of paradigm to speak of societal transformation, offers a succinct definition of the dominant paradigm of a society: "The basic ways of perceiving, thinking, valuing, and doing, associated with a particular view of reality" (p. 10). He explains:

> Every society ever known rests on some set of largely tacit basic assumptions about *who we are, what kind of universe we are in, and what is ultimately important to us.* Some such set of assumptions can be found to underlie the institutions and mores, patterns of thought and systems of value, that characterize a society. They are typically not formulated or taught because they don't need to be—they are absorbed by each person born into society as though by osmosis. They are accepted as given, as obviously true—and throughout most of history, by most people, never questioned. (p. 10)

To illustrate, Harman cites the paradigm shift accompanying Copernicus's revolutionary ideas:

> What was so earth-shaking about the Copernican revolution was that the *fundamental view of reality* was shifting; with that shift came major changes in "the basic ways of perceiving, thinking, valuing, and doing"—changes that heralded the modern era. (p. 10)

For the purposes of this book, *paradigm* is defined as the most basic, fundamental set of assumptions forming our primary view of reality. The current dominant paradigm is the most basic, fundamental set of assumptions operating in our time and would include the most basic images and rules of the game that form the backbone of Western contemporary culture.

A THEORY OF PARADIGMS

Up to this point, the discussion has focused on the role of paradigms, images, metaphors, maps of reality, and other intellectual constructs that direct and shape the thinking, perception, valuing, inquiry, and action of every human being in the course of daily life. Before considering the role of paradigms, and other intellectual constructs, in organizational life, the following theory of paradigms is offered as a basis for the argument that an alternative paradigm—that is, the contemplative paradigm—would give rise to alternative ways of thinking, perceiving, valuing, inquiring, and acting that might be brought to bear on society's wicked problems.

1. **Every human lives out of a set of fundamental assumptions about life that are not provable.** These constitute a worldview or paradigm. This paradigm or worldview may include assumptions concerning change, causality, randomness, determinism, control, and personal effectiveness; the type of knowledge one can acquire and how one acquires knowledge; the role and value of human beings; freedom, limits, and possibilities; and a variety of other areas beyond the basic location of oneself in space and time.

2. **This paradigm or set of fundamental assumptions gives rise to a particular means of perceiving, thinking, valuing, action, and inquiry.** It shapes a "default mode" or standard operating procedure, that is, a person's primary and usual mode of participating in life and relating to the universe.

3. **A paradigm obscures or downplays some aspects of reality and discloses or highlights other aspects.** Just as a metaphor or model is not identical to its referent, so a paradigm, as a view of reality, is only a view and necessarily obscures certain aspects of reality that another paradigm might highlight, and vice versa. (Comparisons can be made only with other paradigms and not with reality itself.)

4. **The operating paradigm is the context in which theories, models, metaphors and problem-solving techniques are embedded.** It is possible for a variety of mutually incompatible theories, models, metaphors, and methods of inquiry to exist within a certain paradigm, but these theories, metaphors, models, and problem-solving techniques must, by definition, be compatible with the assumptions of the operating paradigm. Otherwise, one is operating out of another paradigm. The assumptions of the operating paradigm are the most basic assumptions. Certain theories or models of the universe and society are excluded by the assumptions of a particular paradigm. These theories or models would be nonsense with respect to the operating paradigm. The basic assumptions of the operating paradigm set the parameters for the metaphors, theories, and problem-solving strategies that are within that particular paradigm.

5. **Members of a particular culture share a common paradigm.** There may be some variation within the culture, but every member has a grasp of the elements of the shared or dominant paradigm and can cite it as common sense, that is, the shared or common understanding of the universe. Members of the culture may set aside these assumptions and shift to another set of assumptions under special conditions. One may also participate simultaneously in other subcultures, with their unique operating assumptions, for

particular purposes. Different cultures may have different paradigms. This is true both when contemporaneous cultures exist side
by side and also in cultures separated by time and distance.

6. **The operating paradigm is usually taken for granted and is rarely
examined.** There is usually little interest in discussing one's paradigm. "What is there to talk about? That is just common sense."
The presentation of an alternative paradigm can throw the dominant paradigm into relief and bring it to consciousness, much like
swimming underwater highlights the importance of the air that is
ordinarily taken for granted.

7. **From the broad perspective of human history, fundamental
paradigms are, in effect, *temporary expediencies* that enable
people to relate to particular conditions of time and place, and
can be challenged and eclipsed as new circumstances emerge.**
Paradigms can shift to meet the demands of a new situation.
But the dominant paradigm is well-entrenched and difficult to
change.

8. **It is possible to shift to another paradigm and perceive, act, value,
inquire, and think in a different manner.** An alternative paradigm will make available alternative ways of thinking, perceiving,
valuing, acting and inquiring. This requires setting aside or relin-
quishing the current paradigm.

REFLECTIONS ON A SHIFT TO AN ALTERNATIVE
PARADIGM

Kuhn's concept of paradigm shift, and particularly the importance he
attaches to the paradigm's role in shaping and affecting perception,
inquiry, thinking, valuing, and action, forms this book's theoretical
underpinnings. The suggestion that an alternative paradigm may provide alternative ways of thinking, perceiving, inquiring, valuing, and
acting that may be brought to bear on society's wicked problems,
however, is challenged, limited, or clarified by certain elements of
Kuhn's discussion of paradigm shift, as well as by Lakoff and Johnson
and Boulding.

First, the existence of an alternative paradigm, according to Kuhn,
does not necessarily lead to its acceptance. There must be a crisis in the
prevailing paradigm. This combination of a crisis and an alternative
paradigm may lead to a battle for acceptance of one or the other
paradigm among the community of practitioners. Although the existence of wicked problems could arguably be evidence of a crisis, the
mere existence of another, alternative, paradigm would not necessarily
lead to its acceptance.

Second, Kuhn emphasizes that it is not easy to shift from one paradigm to another. Lakoff and Johnson make similar statements with regard to a shift in metaphor, as does Boulding with respect to images. Not only does a paradigm shift involve expensive retooling, in thought and action, it is difficult for a scientist to make the gestalt shift back and forth between alternative paradigms. Thus, Kuhn's work challenges the suggestion that having an alternative paradigm or paradigms would make available additional ways of thinking, perceiving, inquiring, valuing, and acting. Kuhn may be suggesting that scientists can handle just one paradigm at a time. Even Wolfgang Pauli and Albert Einstein had difficulty in the midst of a paradigm shift (Kuhn, 1970, pp. 83–84). However, this shift may be easier for persons who have not yet been firmly entrenched in the prevailing paradigm.

Third, Kuhn underscores the incommensurability of paradigms. At one point in the development of this book, it was suggested that the physics student's use of different kinds of graph paper—ordinary Cartesian graph paper, semi-log paper, log-log paper, or other specialized graph paper—might be analogous to using various alternative paradigms to make available new ways of thinking and acting. For example, when data from certain simple mechanics lab experiments are plotted on ordinary graph paper (before the advent of hand-held computers), the data points appear to form a curve—for which it is difficult for a beginning student to state an equation. However, if those same data points are plotted on semi-log paper, that is, graph paper in which the x axis is laid out in the usual, linear, equally-spaced manner and the y axis is displayed logarithmically—the data points form a straight line from which the student can easily discern a simple equation. In this example of a simple physics experiment, use of a different kind of graph paper reveals relationships that are not obvious with the use of ordinary graph paper. It seemed, at one point, as if the use of different paradigms would be analogous—the alternative paradigm might reveal alternative understandings and ways of acting or inquiring. However, in the case of alternative graph paper, the two ways of viewing reality are commensurable and easily translatable (with a simple exponential equation) one to the other. Kuhn asserts that paradigms are incommensurable; the concepts and understandings are not translatable one to the other. The difference in paradigms is far more profound than the difference in graph paper.

Finally, it is necessary to consider whether and to what extent Kuhn's discussion of the history of the natural sciences is applicable to other fields, or to organizations in general. Kuhn himself, while discussing the question of why the fields of science considered earlier in the book seem to move steadily ahead in a manner that other enterprises such as art, political theory, or philosophy do not, notes that debates about whether one or the other of the social sciences is really a science have parallels in the pre-paradigm periods of fields now unhesitatingly recognized as sciences (Kuhn, 1970, p. 160). His first insight into this issue is that "members of a mature scientific community work from a single paradigm or from a closely related set" (p. 162). In other, nonscientific, fields, Kuhn suggests, there are always competing paradigms or schools that constantly question the foundations of the others. In addition, it appears that only during periods of normal science does progress seem obvious and assured (pp. 162–163).

> [O]nce the reception of a common paradigm has freed the scientific community from the need constantly to re-examine its first principles, the members of the community can concentrate exclusively upon the subtlest and most esoteric of the phenomena that concern it. (p. 165)

In addition to challenging implicitly the notion that the introduction of yet another paradigm into organizational life would be helpful, Kuhn's ideas induce the organizational leader to ask whether there is a common paradigm for organizations or leadership or perhaps even for one of the many component fields or whether organizational theory or leadership is in a pre-paradigm stage.

An additional observation grows out of Kuhn's argument that a paradigm is accepted by a particular community, which in Kuhn's work is a natural science community, for example, the communities of chemists, physicists, or astronomers. He does not directly address, as later authors do, the nature of the general population's paradigm. However, the field of organizational development or organizational theory have very permeable boundaries. The wicked problems identified earlier—poverty, balancing of work and family life, racial and ethnic conflicts—are of personal concern to and are addressed by a large population of individuals who may or may not identify themselves with any particular field of knowledge, for example, police officers, parents, employees, elected officials, stockholders. Whereas the community of physicists or chemists—and their particular paradigms—are fairly easy to identify and define,[4] the community of those concerned with the wicked problems are not. Thus, the community to be offered the contemplative paradigm as an alternative may be rather large and heterogeneous, and some of Kuhn's observations regarding paradigm shifts may not be directly applicable.

Keeping these difficulties in mind, we now shift the focus specifically to organizational life and consider how the choice of paradigm, image, and theory affects thinking, perception, inquiry, valuing, and action.

NOTES

1. Kuhn makes a distinction here between laws and definitions, but that discussion is not essential for our purposes.

2. These four paradigms in organization theory are termed the *radical humanist, radical structuralist, interpretative,* and *functionalist* paradigms.

3. See, for example, Harman, 1988; Schaef and Fassel, 1988; Eisler, 1987; Theobald, 1987; Lenz and Myerhoff, 1985; Harman and Rheingold, 1984; Beam and Simpson, 1984; Fox, 1983; Capra, 1982; Thayer, 1981; Ferguson, 1980.

4. Few of us who are not employed as natural scientists concern ourselves with the emerging issues in genetics or astronomy or geology—beyond reading the Tuesday science section of the *New York Times.*

PART II

Paradigms, Images, and Theories in Organizational Life

Up to this point the focus has not been on organizations. Kuhn, Lakoff and Johnson, and Boulding explore, in their particular fields, how our thinking, perceiving, acting, valuing, and inquiry are affected by the operating paradigms, theories, metaphors, and other maps of reality. In the following three chapters we consider specific works within the realm of organizational theory that reveal how paradigms, images, or theories direct thought, inquiry, valuing, perception, and action in that field.

Chapter 6 examines Burrell and Morgan's *Sociological Paradigms and Organisational Analysis* and explores how paradigms affect analysis and inquiry in sociology and organizational theory. These authors define four separate and distinct paradigms in the field of sociology by articulating the specific assumptions underlying each paradigm. They then explicate how analysis and inquiry in each of the four sociological paradigms is shaped by the respective underlying assumptions.

Gareth Morgan's *Images of Organization* is the subject of chapter 7. In a manner similar to his earlier work with Burrell, outlined earlier, Morgan reviews eight distinct images or metaphors for organizations and illustrates how the choice of image affects and directs the possibilities for thought and action in an organization.

Chapter 8 completes the journey from paradigm to image to theory and surveys Harmon and Mayer's *Organizational Theory for Public Administration*. Michael M. Harmon and Richard T. Mayer identify the basic assumptions underlying six different schools of organizational theory and explore how the underlying assumptions affect the range of approaches to the wicked problems confronting public administrators.

6

Burrell and Morgan

Sociological Paradigms

The first of the three works in organization theory to be considered is Burrell and Morgan's (1979) *Sociological Paradigms and Organisational Analysis*. This classic addresses the question of how paradigms affect organizational analysis and inquiry. The authors define four separate and distinct paradigms in the field of sociology by articulating the specific assumptions underlying each of these paradigms and then explicate how analysis and inquiry in each of the four sociological paradigms are shaped by the respective underlying assumptions. *Sociological Paradigms and Organisational Analysis* is of interest here less for the specific content of its analysis than for its insight into the importance of paradigms and the manner in which the four paradigms are defined by sets of metatheoretical assumptions about the nature of society and the nature of social science. This method of articulating and distinguishing a paradigm provides guidance for articulating the contemplative paradigm in later chapters. Burrell and Morgan (1979) state their thesis:

> Our proposition is that social theory can usefully be conceived in terms of four key paradigms based upon different sets of metatheoretical assumptions about the nature of social science and the nature of society. The four paradigms are founded upon mutually exclusive views of the social world.

Each stands in its own right and generates its own distinctive analyses of social life. With regard to the study of organisations, for example, each paradigm generates theories or perspectives which are in fundamental opposition to those generated in other paradigms.

Such an analysis of social theory brings us face to face with the nature of the assumptions which underwrite different approaches to social science. It cuts through the surface detail which dresses many social theories to what is fundamental in determining the way in which we see the world which we are purporting to analyse. It stresses the crucial role played by the scientist's frame of reference in the generation of social theory and research. (p. vii)

FOUR SOCIOLOGICAL PARADIGMS

Burrell and Morgan (1979) argue that social scientists approach their research with implicit or explicit assumptions about the nature of social science and the nature of society. In constructing a framework for social science, the authors use these two dimensions—assumptions about the nature of society and assumptions about the nature of social science—to construct a two-dimensional, four-cell array corresponding to four distinct sociological paradigms: radical humanist, radical structuralist, interpretive, and functionalist. (See Figure 6.1.)

Assumptions About the Nature of Society

For the dimension of the framework concerned with the nature of society, Burrell and Morgan (1979) identify two contrasting models for

Figure 6.1
Burrell and Morgan's Sociological Paradigms

The Sociology of Radical Change
(Assumptions about the nature of society)

	Radical Humanist	Radical Structuralist	
Subjective (Assumptions about the nature of social science)			Objective (Assumptions about the nature of social science)
	Interpretive	Functionalist	

The Sociology of Regulation
(Assumptions about the nature of society)

Source: Gibson Burrell and Gareth Morgan, *Sociological Paradigms and Organisational Analysis* (Portsmouth, NH: Heinemann, 1979), p. 22.

the analysis of social processes termed the *sociology of regulation* and the *sociology of radical change*. This dimension is then termed the regulation-radical change dimension and forms the vertical axis for the four-cell framework.

> We introduce the term *"sociology of regulation"* to refer to the writings of theorists who are primarily concerned to provide explanations of society in terms which emphasise its underlying unity and cohesiveness. It is a sociology which is essentially concerned with the need for regulation in human affairs; the basic questions which it asks tend to focus upon the need to understand why society is maintained as an entity. It attempts to explain why society tends to hold together rather than fall apart. It is interested in understanding the social forces which prevent the Hobbesian vision of "war of all against all" becoming a reality. The work of Durkheim with its emphasis upon the nature of social cohesion and solidarity, for example, provides a clear and comprehensive illustration of a concern for the sociology of regulation.
>
> The *"sociology of radical change"* stands in stark contrast to the "sociology of regulation," in that its basic concern is to find explanations for the radical change, deep-seated structural conflict, modes of domination and structural contradiction which its theorists see as characterising modern society. It is a sociology which is essentially concerned with man's emancipation from the structures which limit and stunt his potential for development. The basic questions which it asks focus upon the deprivation of man, both material and psychic. It is often visionary and Utopian, in that it looks toward potentiality as much as actuality; it is concerned with what is possible rather than with what is; with alternatives rather than with acceptance of the *status quo*. In these respects it is as widely separate and distant from the sociology of regulation as the sociology of Marx is separated and distant from the sociology of Durkheim. (p. 17)

The authors outline the regulation-radical change dimension with the following contrasting concerns (p. 18):

The sociology of REGULATION is concerned with:
- (a) The status quo
- (b) Social order
- (c) Consensus
- (d) Social integration and cohesion
- (e) Solidarity
- (f) Need satisfaction
- (g) Actuality

The sociology of RADICAL CHANGE is concerned with:
- (a) Radical change
- (b) Structural conflict
- (c) Modes of domination
- (d) Contradiction
- (e) Emancipation
- (f) Deprivation
- (g) Potentiality

Assumptions About the Nature of Social Science

The second dimension, or horizontal axis, for the framework for the four sociological paradigms is concerned with contrasting assumptions regarding the nature of social science. There are contrasting sets of assumptions regarding ontology, epistemology, human nature, and methodology that form this axis, termed the *subjective-objective dimension* (Burrell & Morgan, 1979, p. 1). Figure 6.2 summarizes the subjective-objective dimension of the framework for sociological paradigms.

Burrell and Morgan (1979) first outline the ontological issues:

> All social scientists approach their subject via explicit or implicit assumptions about the nature of the social world and the way in which it may be investigated. First, there are assumptions of an *ontological* nature—assumptions which concern the very essence of the phenomena under investigation. Social scientists, for example are faced with a basic ontological question: whether the 'reality' to be investigated is external to the individual—imposing itself on individual consciousness from without—or the product of individual consciousness; whether "reality" is of an "objective" nature, or the product of individual cognition; whether "reality" is a given "out there" in the world, or the product of one's mind. (p. 1)

Burrell and Morgan (1979) identify this set of opposite approaches as the "ontological debate" between nominalism and realism. The nominalist assumes that the social world "external to individual cognition is made up of nothing more than names, concepts and labels which are used to structure reality" (p. 4). For the nominalist, there is no "'real' structure to the world which these concepts are used to describe" (p. 4).

Figure 6.2
Subjective-Objective Framework of Sociological Paradigms
[Assumptions about the nature of society]

The subjective-objective dimension

The subjectivist approach to social science		The objectivist approach to social science
Nominalism	ontology	Realism
Anti-positivism	epistemology	Positivism
Voluntarism	human nature	Determinism
Ideographic	methodology	Nomothetic

Source: Gibson Burrell and Gareth Morgan, *Sociological Paradigms and Organizational Analysis* (Portsmouth, NH: Heinemann, 1979), p. 3.

For the realist, however, the social world has a hard, concrete reality of its own. The social world is made up of tangible, immutable structures. "Whether or not we label and perceive these structures . . . they still exist as empirical entities. We may not even be aware of the existence of certain crucial structures and therefore have no 'names' or concepts to articulate them" (p. 4).

The second pair of opposing assumptions that are included in the subjective–objective axis of Burrell and Morgan's (1979) framework of four sociological paradigms is the *antipositivism-positivism* dichotomy of the *epistemological debate*:

> These are assumptions about the grounds of knowledge—about how one might begin to understand the world and communicate this as knowledge to fellow human beings. These assumptions entail ideas, for example, about what forms of knowledge can be obtained, and how one can sort out what is regarded to be "true" from what is to be regarded as "false." [This dichotomy] . . . is predicated upon a view of the nature of knowledge itself: whether, for example, it is possible to identify and communicate the nature of knowledge as being hard, real and capable of being transmitted in tangible form, or whether "knowledge" is of a softer, more subjective, spiritual or even transcendental kind, based on experience and insight of a unique and essentially personal nature. (pp. 1–2)

"Positivist" is used in this dichotomy to "characterise epistemologies that seek to explain and predict what happens in the social world by searching for regularities and causal relationships between its constituent elements" (Burrell & Morgan, 1979, p. 5). This is the predominant view in the natural sciences today. Antipositivism, however, views the social world as relativistic. It can be understood "from the point of view of the individuals who are directly involved in the activities to be studied" (p. 5). There is no detached observer or vantage point for understanding human activities. "Anti-positivists tend to reject the notion that science can generate objective knowledge of any kind" (p. 5).

The third pair of assumptions on the objective-subjective axis concerns human nature. The debate is between voluntarism and determinism.

> [W]e can identify perspectives in social science which entail a view of human beings responding in a mechanistic or even deterministic fashion to the situations encountered in their external world. This view [determinism] tends to be one in which human beings and their experiences are regarded as products of the environment; one in which humans are conditioned by their external circumstances. This extreme perspective can be contrasted with one which attributes to human beings a much more

creative role: with a perspective where "free will" occupies the centre of the stage; where man is regarded as the creator of his environment, the controller as opposed to the controlled, the master rather than the marionette. In these two extreme views of the relationship between human beings and their environment we are identifying a great philosophical debate between the advocates of determinism on the one hand and voluntarism on the other. Whilst there are social theories which adhere to each of these extremes, as we shall see, the assumptions of many social scientists are pitched somewhere in the range between. (p. 2)

The fourth and final pair of contrasting assumptions that form the objective-subjective axis of the paradigmatic framework is the nomothetic-deographic dichotomy. The other three sets of assumptions have important consequences for the methodological debate between the nomothetic and ideographic approaches. "Different ontologies, epistemologies and models of human nature are likely to incline social scientists toward different methodologies" (Burrell & Morgan, 1979, p. 2).

The ideographic approach to social science is based on the view that one can only understand the social world by obtaining firsthand knowledge of the subject under investigation. It thus places considerable stress upon getting close to one's subject and exploring its detailed background and life history. The ideographic approach emphasises the analysis of the subjective accounts which one generates by "getting inside" situations and involving oneself in the everyday flow of life—the detailed analysis of the insights generated by such encounters with one's subject and the insights revealed in impressionistic accounts found in diaries, biographies and journalistic records. The ideographic method stresses the importance of letting one's subject unfold its nature and characteristics during the process of investigation.

The nomothetic approach to social science lays emphasis on the importance of basing research upon systematic protocol and technique. It is epitomised in the approach and methods employed in the natural sciences, which focus upon the process of testing hypotheses in accordance with the canons of scientific rigour. It is preoccupied with the construction of scientific tests and the use of quantitative techniques for the analysis of data. Surveys, questionnaires, personality tests and standardised research instruments of all kinds are prominent among the tools which comprise nomothetic methodology. (pp. 6–7)

The subjective-objective dimension forms the horizontal axis of the framework of sociological paradigms, and the regulation-radical change dimension forms the vertical axis to yield four distinct sociological paradigms: the radical humanist, the radical structuralist, the interpretive, and the functionalist paradigms. (Refer to Figure 6–1.)

MUTUAL EXCLUSIVITY OF PARADIGMS

These four distinct paradigms, while encompassing a range of intellectual territory, are mutually exclusive.

Given the overall meta-theoretical assumptions which distinguish one paradigm from another, there is room for much variation within them. Within the context of the "functionalist" paradigm, for example, certain theorists adopt more extreme positions in terms of one or both of the two dimensions than others. Such differences often account for the internal debate which goes on between theorists engaged in the activities of "normal science" within the context of the same paradigm. . . .

[T]he four paradigms are mutually exclusive. They offer alternative views of social reality, and to understand the nature of all four is to understand four different views of society. They offer different ways of seeing. A synthesis is not possible, since in their pure forms they are contradictory, being based on at least one set of opposing meta-theoretical assumptions. They are alternative, in the sense that one *can* operate in different paradigms sequentially over time, but mutually exclusive, in the sense that one cannot operate in more than one paradigm at any given point in time, since in accepting the assumptions of one, we defy the assumption of all others. (Burrell & Morgan, 1979, pp. 24–25)

After detailing the four-cell framework of sociological paradigms, the authors apply this framework to the field of organizational analysis and locate a variety of theorists and schools of organizational theory within each of the four paradigms. For example, phenomenology is located within the interpretive quadrant, whereas critical theory is placed in the radical humanist quadrant.

The authors then observe, "The functionalist paradigm has provided the dominant framework for academic sociology in the twentieth century and accounts for by far the largest proportion of theory and research in the field of organisation studies" (Burrell & Morgan, 1979, p. 48). The functionalist paradigm is currently the dominant paradigm for sociology and organizational theory. The functionalist paradigm includes the celebrated traditions of F. W. Taylor, Henri Fayol, the Hawthorne studies, Chester Barnard, Herbert Simon, action research, systems theory, and other schools of thought that form the core curriculum for a student of organizational theory (pp. 121–220). Following the framework of Burrell and Morgan set forth earlier, the assumptions underlying this dominant, functionalist, paradigm include the following:

- •Realist: The external social world exists independently of the perceiver.
- •Positivist: The social world can be predicted and explained experimentally through searching for regularities and causal relationships.

•Determinist: Human beings and their activities are determined by the environment.

•Nomothetic: The social world is understood by attention to rigorous protocol in constructing and testing hypotheses.

•Sociology of regulation: A concern for providing explanations of the status quo, social order, consensus, social integration, solidarity, need satisfaction, and actuality (p. 26).

However, although the functionalist paradigm is the dominant paradigm in the field of organization theory, Burrell and Morgan (1979) recognize the importance of the other three, alternative, paradigms in generating new ideas and opening new areas of inquiry.

Viewing social theory and the literature on organisational analysis from the perspective of the functionalist paradigm, one has the impression that there is a dominant orthodoxy which is surrounded by critical perspectives, each of which seeks to adopt some form of "radical" stance. Such a view is unduly narrow; it assumes that the perspectives are satellites which take their principal point of reference from the orthodoxy itself; it assumes that their aim and function is critique and exposure of the limitations reflected in the orthodoxy. They tend to be considered and, if possible, rebuffed or incorporated within the context of the dominant orthodoxy. Such a view favours fusion and incorporation as the natural line of intellectual development. (p. 396)

The model of a dominant paradigm surrounded by lesser, satellite, variations is not adopted by Burrell and Morgan (1979); neither is the concept of a steadily developing consensus within the field that would constitute an orthodoxy. The authors recognize the value of alternative paradigms.

[T]he fusion [of the points of view of other, non-functionalist paradigms] has not by any means done full justice to the respective problematics from which these elements derive. Indeed, it has been at the cost of their complete emasculation and a misunderstanding of their very nature. (p. 396)

Instead, the authors favor the conscious use of separate and distinct paradigms, each having its own separate, distinct, and mutually exclusive assumptions about the nature of human beings and the world in which they live. Burrell and Morgan (1979) recommend that theorists in other paradigms than the dominant functionalist paradigm

ground their perspective in the philosophical traditions from which [their paradigm] derives; to start from first principles; to have the philosophical and sociological concerns by which the paradigm is defined at the forefront of their analysis; to develop a systematic and coherent perspective within the guidelines which each paradigm offers, rather than taking the tenets of a competing paradigm as critical points of reference. Each paradigm needs to be developed in its own terms.

In essence, what we are advocating in relation to developments within these paradigms amounts to a form of isolationism. . . . Contrary to the widely held belief that synthesis and mediation between paradigms is what is required, we argue that the real need is for paradigmatic closure. (pp. 397–398)

The purpose, for Burrell and Morgan, of conducting such research in separate and distinct paradigms is to open new avenues of inquiry and expand the field of organizational theory. "Only by grounding itself [organizational theory] in a knowledge of its past and of the alternative avenues for development can it realise its full potential in the years ahead" (p. 402).

This foundational work of Burrell and Morgan invites organizational theorists to consider the possibility of consciously adopting another, distinct, alternative paradigm in which to operate. The authors suggest that these alternative paradigms may give birth to new insights and avenues of research that might be neglected by the current dominant paradigm. Burrell and Morgan (1979) also encourage the organizational theorists to investigate and identify one's underlying assumptions, to start from first principles, to ground his or her perspective in the philosophical principles from which it derives, to keep the underlying assumptions and concerns at the forefront of the analysis (p. 397). This book accepts that invitation and attempts to define and make explicit the underlying assumptions of our culture's dominant paradigm and offer an alternative paradigm with alternative underlying assumptions. It then explores the alternative method and means of organizational leadership to which the alternative, contemplative, paradigm gives birth.

7

Morgan and Organizational Images

EIGHT ORGANIZATIONAL IMAGES

We now turn to Gareth Morgan's *Images of Organization* which, in a manner similar to his earlier work with Burrell, outlined in Chapter 6, illustrates how images or metaphors affect and direct how we think about and act with respect to organizations.

> The basic premise on which the book builds is that our theories and explanations of organizational life are based on metaphors that lead us to see and understand organizations in distinctive yet partial ways. Metaphor is often just regarded as a device for embellishing discourse, but its significance is much greater than this. For the use of metaphor implies *a way of thinking* and *a way of seeing* that pervade how we understand our world generally. For example, research in a wide variety of fields has demonstrated that metaphor exerts a formative influence on science, on our language and how we think, as well as how we express ourselves on a day-to-day basis. (Morgan, 1986, pp. 12–13)

Morgan (1986) identifies the value of managers' using a variety of metaphors in reading the situations they are organizing or managing:

> [Managers and professionals who are skilled in *reading* organizations] have a capacity to remain open and flexible, suspending immediate judg-

ments whenever possible, until a more comprehensive view of the situation merges. They are aware of the fact that new insights often arise as one reads a situation from "new angles," and that a wide and varied reading can create a wide and varied range of action possibilities. Less effective managers and problem solvers, on the other hand, seem to interpret everything from a fixed standpoint. As a result, they frequently hit blocks that they can't get around; their actions and behaviors are often rigid and inflexible and a source of conflict. When problems and differences of opinion arise, they usually have no alternative but to hammer at issues in the same old way and to create consensus by convincing others to "buy into" their particular view of the situation. (p. 12)

For Morgan, a new way of viewing a situation, that is, seeing a situation in terms of an alternative metaphor or image, opens up new possibilities for both thinking and acting when strategies arising from the usual metaphor have failed.

This conclusion is in accord with the fundamental nature of a metaphor, that is, that a metaphor is not identical to the situation itself and necessarily highlights certain aspects and downplays others.

We use metaphor whenever we attempt to understand one element of experience in terms of another. Thus, metaphor proceeds through implicit or explicit assertions that A *is* (or is like) B. When we say "the man is a lion," we use the image of a lion to draw attention to the lionlike aspects of the man. The metaphor frames our understanding of the man in a distinctive yet partial way.

One of the interesting aspects of metaphor rests in the fact that it always produces this kind of one-sided insight. In highlighting certain interpretations it tends to force others into a background role. Thus in drawing attention to lionlike bravery, strength, or ferocity of the man, the metaphor glosses the fact that the same person may well also be a chauvinist pig, a devil, a saint, a bore, or a recluse. Our ability to achieve a comprehensive "reading" of the man depends on an ability to see how these different aspects of the person may coexist in a complementary or even a paradoxical way. (Morgan, 1986, p. 13)

Because of this one-sided nature of metaphors, our metaphors, conscious or unconscious, for organizations or other phenomena in organizational life direct and shape our thinking, closing off certain avenues for action and opening others.

Many of our taken-for-granted ideas about organizations are metaphorical, even though we may not recognize them as such. For example, we frequently talk about organizations *as if* they were machines designed to achieve predetermined goals and objectives, and which should operate smoothly and efficiently. And as result of this kind of thinking we often attempt to organize and manage them in a mechanistic way, forcing their human qualities into a background role.

By using different metaphors to understand the complex and paradoxical character of organizational life, we are able to manage and design organizations in ways that we may not have thought possible before. (Morgan, 1986, p. 13)

The bulk of the book is Morgan's exploration of eight different metaphors or images of organization: organizations as machines, organisms, brains, cultures, political systems, psychic prisons, flux and transformation, and instruments of domination. For each metaphor of organization, Morgan identifies the tradition or authors using the metaphor and the strengths and limitations of that particular metaphor. Figure 7.1 outlines and compares the focus, strengths, weaknesses, and action orientation of each of the eight organizational images or metaphors as well as listing representative authors who use these metaphors.

COMPARISON OF TWO ORGANIZATIONAL IMAGES

The Organization as Machine

For the sake of illustrating how Morgan differentiates the various metaphors, one of the most popular metaphors, the organization as machine, is contrasted here with the metaphor of the organization as a political system.

The machine metaphor has entrenched itself in the popular culture of the 20th century. We have applied it to ourselves, our society, and especially to organizations, according to Morgan. (See also Henri Fayol, 1978; Frederick Winslow Taylor, 1978; and Max Weber, 1978.)

Consider, for example, the mechanical precision with which many of our institutions are expected to operate. Organizational life is often routinized with the precision demanded of clockwork. People are frequently expected to arrive at work at a given time, perform a predetermined set of activities, rest at appointed hours, then resume their tasks until work is over. In many organizations one shift of workers replaces another in methodical fashion so that work can continue uninterrupted twenty-four hours a day, every day of the year. Often the work is very mechanical and repetitive. Anyone who has observed work in the mass-production factory, or in any of the large "office factories" processing paper forms such as insurance claims, tax returns, or bank checks, will have noticed the machinelike way in which such organizations operate. They are designed like machines, and their employees are in essence expected to behave as if they were parts of machines. (Morgan, 1986, p. 20)

Figure 7.1
Images of Organization

Image	Focus	Strengths	Weaknesses	Authors	Guide to:
Machine	Bureaucratic structure; *Classical management theory*	Works well under stable, predictable, uniform conditions	Resistant to change; Subgoals subvert primary goals; Dehumanizing	Fayol Taylor The Classics	Mechanistic approach
Organism	Environment; Survival and health; Organization life cycles; Organization effectiveness	Used by most modern theorists; Emphasizes environment, internal needs, and variety of species	Too concrete; Too materialistic; Leads to assumption that unity and harmony can be achieved	Argyris Hertzberg McGregor Systems theorists Contingency theorists	Organizing to meet environmental demands
Brain	Information processing; Learning; Self-organization	Insight into organizational learning; Innovation, change	Overlooks conflicts between learning and reality of power	Simon March Argyris Schon	Organizing for learning and innovation
Culture	Meaning; Values; Symbols; Myths	Points to symbolic significance of *rational* aspects of organization	Manipulation of culture in a mechanistic or political way	Deal and Kennedy Peters and Waterman Weick, Schein Bennis and Nanus	Managing meaning
Political Systems	Organizations as systems of government; Interests; Conflict; Power	Takes account of political realities; Explodes myth of rationality	Encourages cynicism and distrust; Pluralist perspective may be superficial	Weber Aristotle Burns Burrell and Morgan	Acting politically
Psychic Prison	Being trapped by illusions; The unconscious	Uncovers unconscious processes, ethics	Ignores ideological considerations	Burrell and Morgan Jung Freud	Escaping cognitive traps
Flux and Transforma-tion	Hidden processes below the surface of reality; Change	Understanding of how organizations can influence change	Too idealistic; Too complex; Logics of change seen retrospectively	Bateson Bohm Prigogine	Influencing change
Instruments of Domination	Ugly face of organizations: multinationals, worker exploitation, workaholism, and stress	Provides radical critique; Questions rationality of actions: for whom?	Tends to divide by focusing blame; Organizations need not be instruments of domination	Weber Marx Michels	Highlighting and marshaling resistance to processes of societal domination

Source: Gareth Morgan, *Images of Organization* (Beverly Hills: Sage, 1986), passim.

This is the familiar *bureaucracy*. It assumes orderly, mechanical relations between well-defined parts. We expect mechanical behavior from this familiar organization, that is, routinized, efficient, reliable, predictable behavior (p. 22).

The focus of the machine metaphor. When organizations are viewed as machines, attention is focused on certain aspects of the organization. The familiar hierarchical organization chart includes precisely defined and titled jobs, arranged in the chain of command, with carefully considered lines of communication and spans of responsibility. It is important to know how one job interlocks with the next, how one department networks with the others. The classical theorists, who pioneered in defining the machine metaphor, focused on patterns of authority and responsibility, division of work, the general process of directing work, discipline, subordination of the individual's interests to the organization's interest, and the achievement of precisely determined objectives or effects.

"Set goals and objectives and go for them."
"Organize rationally, efficiently, and clearly."
"Specify every detail so that everyone will be sure of the jobs that they have to perform."
"Plan, organize, and control, control, control."

These and other similar ideas are often ingrained in our way of thinking about organization and in the way we read and evaluate organizational practice. For many people it is almost second nature to organize by setting up a structure of clearly defined activities linked by clear lines of command, communication, coordination, and control. Thus when a manager designs an organization he or she frequently designs a formal structure of jobs into which people can then be fitted. Or if the people are available first, it is a question of finding everyone a clearly defined role to play. When a vacancy arises in an organization, managers frequently talk about having "a slot" to fill. (Morgan, 1986, p. 33)

These concerns are the concerns of those operating out of the machine metaphor.

The strengths of the machine metaphor. Each of the organizational metaphors Morgan (1986) considers has strengths and weaknesses that are reflected in the organizations that are shaped by the individual metaphor.

The strengths [of the machine metaphor] can be stated very simply. For mechanistic approaches to organization work well only under conditions where machines work well: (a) when there is a straightforward task to perform; (b) when the environment is stable enough to ensure that the products produced will be appropriate ones; (c) when one wishes to produce exactly the same product time and again; (d) when precision is at a premium; and (e) when the human "machine" parts are compliant and behave as they have been designed to do. (p. 34)

Morgan gives examples of organizations in which the machine metaphor may function well—such as franchising systems, where centrally designed products and services are implemented in a decentralized but highly controlled way, or organizations such as surgical wards, aircraft maintenance departments, finance offices, or courier firms, where clear accountability is especially important (pp. 34–35).

The weaknesses of the machine metaphor. Morgan (1986) identifies the limitations of the mechanistic approach.

> [T]hey: (a) can create organizational forms that have great difficulty in adapting to changing circumstances; (b) can result in mindless and unquestioning bureaucracy; (c) can have unanticipated and undesirable consequences as the interests of those working in the organization take precedence over the goals the organization was designed to achieve; and (d) can have dehumanizing effects upon employees, especially those at the lower levels of the organizational hierarchy.
>
> Mechanistically structured organizations have great difficulty adapting to changing circumstances because they are designed to achieve predetermined goals; they are not designed for innovation. (p. 35)

The Organization as Political System

Although the machine metaphor is one of the most popular ways of thinking about organizations today, it is not the only way to think about organizations. Morgan (1986) explores the metaphor of organizations as political systems.

> I live in a democratic society. Why should I have to obey the orders of my boss eight hours a day? He acts like a bloody dictator, ordering us around and telling us what we should be doing. What right does he have to act in this way? The company pays our wages, but does this mean it has the right to command all our beliefs and feelings? It certainly has no right to reduce us to robots who must obey every command. (p. 141)

Morgan uses this angry comment of a factory worker to introduce the political aspect of organizations. Although it is an extreme situation, this worker's plight brings to our attention the authoritarian or democratic nature of an organization, the means by which order and direction are created in the midst of diverse interests and the process of creating legitimacy. The worker's complaints raise political issues.

> [P]olitics and politicking may be an essential aspect of organizational life, and not necessarily an optional or dysfunctional extra. . . . [T]he idea of politics stems from the view that, where interests are divergent, society should provide a means of allowing individuals to reconcile their differences through consultation and negotiation. For example, in ancient Greece, Aristotle advocated politics as a means of reconciling the need for unity in the Greek *polis* (city-state) with the fact that the *polis* was an

"aggregate of many members." Politics, for him, provided a means of creating order out of diversity while avoiding forms of totalitarian rule. . . .

By attempting to understand organizations as systems of government, and by attempting to unravel the detailed politics of organizational life, we are able to grasp important qualities of organization that are often glossed over or ignored. (Morgan, 1986, pp. 142–143)

Thus, by applying the political system metaphor rather than the machine metaphor to an organization, new and different aspects of organizational life are highlighted—and others are ignored or downplayed.

The focus of the political system metaphor. Morgan (1986) identifies interests, conflict, and power as the three foci of the political systems metaphor.

Organizational politics arise when people think differently and want to act differently. This diversity creates a tension that must be resolved through political means. . . . [T]here are many ways in which this can be done: autocratically ("We'll do it this way."); bureaucratically ("We're supposed to do it this way."); technocratically ("It's best to do it this way."); or democratically ("How shall we do it?"). In each case the choice between alternative paths of action usually hinges on the power relations between the actors involved. By focusing on how divergent interests give rise to conflicts, visible and invisible, that are resolved or perpetuated by various kinds of power play, we can make the analysis of organizational politics as rigorous as the analysis of any other aspect of organizational life. (p. 148)

Thus, when the organizational leader adopts the political systems metaphor, inquiry will be focused on interests, conflict, and power. Data will be collected in these three categories. Questions will be formulated in terms of these concepts. Morgan includes here issues of control of scarce resources, control of knowledge and information, control of decision processes, gender and the management of gender relations, formal authority, information organization, and a host of other organizational concerns. "Organizational goals, structure, technology, job design, leadership style, and other seemingly formal aspects of organizational functioning have a political dimension, as well as the more obvious power plays and conflicts" (Morgan, 1986, p. 195). When a manager is operating out of the political system metaphor, thinking will be directed and constrained by the concepts of interests, conflict, and power. She will view the organization in these terms. They will shape the administrator's inquiry.

The strengths of the political system metaphor. The political systems metaphor encourages the leader to take into account the oft-ignored political dimension of organizational life. This metaphor also confronts the myth of organizational rationality.

> Organizations may pursue goals and stress the importance of rational, efficient, and effective management. But rational, efficient and effective for whom? Whose goals are being pursued? What interests are being served? Who benefits? The political metaphor emphasizes that organizational goals may be rational for some people's interests, but not for others. An organization embraces many rationalities, since rationality is always interest-based and thus changes according to the perspective from which it is viewed. Rationality is always political. No one is neutral in the management of organizations—even managers! (Morgan, 1986, p. 195)

Another strength of the political system metaphor for organizations is that it overcomes the limitations of viewing organizations as functionally integrated systems. Much of organization theory is grounded in the assumption that "organizations, like machines or organisms, are unified systems that bind part and whole in a quest for survival" (Morgan, 1986, p. 196). The political system metaphor, however, highlights the disintegrative forces that arise from diverse interests.

A further strength of the political system metaphor is its politicization of the way human beings behave in organizations:

> [W]e are obliged to recognize that tensions between private and organizational interests provide an incentive for individuals to act politically. Whereas some people view such action as a manifestation of the selfish or "dark" side of human personality, the analysis presented here suggests that there is usually a structural as well as a motivational basis. Even the most altruistic persons may find their action following a political script in the sense that their orientation to organizational life is influenced by the conflicting sets of interests that they bring to issues of immediate concern. . . . The political metaphor encourages us to recognize how and why the organizational actor is a political actor, and to understand the political significance of the patterns of meaning enacted in corporate culture and subculture. (Morgan, 1986, pp. 196–197)

Finally, Morgan notes that this metaphor encourages organizational participants to recognize the sociopolitical implications of the different types of organizations we encounter and the role they play in society (Morgan, 1986, p. 197).

The weaknesses of the political system metaphor. According to Morgan (1986), the political system's primary weakness is in the generation of cynicism and mistrust that arises from seeing hidden agendas where there are none:

Under the influence of a political mode of understanding everything becomes political. The analysis of interests, conflicts, and power easily gives rise to a Machiavellian interpretation that suggests that everyone is trying to outwit and outmaneuver everyone else. Rather than use the political metaphor to generate new insights and understandings that can help us deal with divergent interests, we often reduce the metaphor to a tool to be used to advance our own personal interests. (p. 197)

Thought this may reflect a somewhat jaundiced and limited definition of politics, Morgan has given his view of one weakness of the use of a political systems metaphor.

An additional weakness relates to the concept of plurality of interests that is encompassed in this metaphor. This approach may blind the organizational theorist to the fundamental class antagonisms present in society.

Is it realistic to presume a plurality of interests and a plurality of power holders, or are more radical organizational theorists correct in seeing fundamental class antagonisms between structures of interest and power? A strong case can be made for the idea that the interests of the individuals or small coalitions may best be served if they recognize the affinities of a "class" kind and act in a unified manner. Such is the logic of trade unionism. . . . [P]luralist politics may be restricted to the resolution of marginal, narrow and superficial issues and may fail to take account of the structural forces that shape the nature of those issues. As a result, the political metaphor may overstate the power and importance of the individual and underplay the system dynamics that determines what becomes political and how politics occurs. (Morgan, 1986, p. 198)

METAPHOR AND ACTION

Morgan uses the eight different organizational metaphors to offer a variety of options not only for thinking about organizations but also for acting within organizations. "Images and metaphors are not only interpretive constructs or ways of seeing; they also provide frameworks for action" (Morgan, 1986, p. 343). "[T]here is a close relationship between the way we think and the way we act" (p. 335). The metaphors offer prescriptive as well as diagnostic and evaluative options.

Whether by critic or by consultant, the important point is that the insights of all the metaphors *can* be used prescriptively. As we understand an organization through the lens provided by a particular metaphor we are shown a way of managing and designing the organization in accordance with a particular image. The machine metaphor suggests a mechanistic approach. The organismic metaphor suggests how we can best organize to meet environmental demands. The brain metaphor shows us how we can manage meaning. The political metaphor teaches us how to act polit-ically. The psychic prison metaphor shows a way of escaping from cogni-tive traps. The flux metaphor shows how we can influence change. The domination metaphor shows us a way of highlighting and marshaling resistance to processes of societal domination. And so on. Each metaphor has its own injunction or directive: a mode of understanding suggests a mode of action. (p. 334)

Morgan's analysis of the various images of organizations begins to suggest how the options available to the organizational leader for dealing with wicked problems would be broadened by lessening one's grip on favorite ways of thinking about organizations and allowing other assumptions and metaphors to expand the imagination.

8

Harmon and Mayer and Organizational Theories

The final work to be considered, *Organizational Theory for Public Administration,* focuses on the assumptions upon which a particular theory is based and the relation of the multiple variety of theories to the wicked problems confronting public administrators. Michael M. Harmon and Richard T. Mayer use an approach similar to that used by Gareth Morgan in *Images of Organization* to emphasize the strengths and weaknesses of each metaphor for organization and the possibilities for action that each metaphor provides: However, Harmon and Mayer consider the variety of organizational theory rather than the variety of organizational images. Harmon and Mayer consider six perspectives on organization theory, that is, six alternative sets of theories of public organizations. The six perspectives include neoclassical theory, systems theory, later human relations theory, market theories, interpretive and critical theories, and theories of emergence. Again, we are less concerned with the substance of each theoretical school than with the ways in which the underlying assumptions affect the range of options available to adherents of a particular school in addressing wicked problems.

SIX ALTERNATIVE THEORETICAL PERSPECTIVES

These theories are alternative in the sense of differing from what Harmon and Mayer first identify as the baseline for organization theory and public administration, that is, the concepts and orientations toward organizational life presented by Max Weber, Frederick Winslow Taylor, the work of the early human relations movement, and Chester Barnard (Harmon & Mayer, 1986 p. 67).

In a manner similar to the authors reviewed earlier, Harmon and Mayer (1986) observe, "Each perspective addresses only certain aspects of the public administrator's world, while ignoring, deemphasizing or even skewing other parts of it" (p. 119). The six perspectives are roughly distinguished initially by their individual focus: organizations as decision sets (neoclassical theory), organizations as purposive entities (systems theory), integrating individuals and organizations (later human relations theory), organizing as revealed self-interest (market theories), organizing as social action (interpretive and critical theories), and organizing as discovered rationality (theories of emergence). (See Figure 8.1.) Harmon and Mayer (1986) further define these theoretical perspectives along six dimensions: the differing cognitive interests supported by the theory, the dominant metaphor, the primary unit of analysis, the relation of the individual to the organization, the meaning of rationality, and the primary values embodied in that theoretical perspective (pp. 17–20).

> Each of these dimensions carries with it implications for the way in which a theoretical perspective will view particular problems, offer unique solutions and generally approach the question of how humans organize themselves for collective activity over time. (p. 20)

THE UNDERLYING ASSUMPTIONS

The two authors explain the types of assumptions underlying each of the various dimensions of a theoretical perspective. The differing cognitive interests supported by the theory refer to "the type of practical purpose that is potentially served by a theory"—for example, explicating cause and effect for the purpose of social control, providing a means for interpreting problem situations as understood by those involved in them, or providing a reasoned basis for normative criticism (Harmon & Mayer, 1986, pp. 18–19). This dimension is concerned with why the public administrator wants to know about theory and what practical purpose it is to serve (p. 404).

Of special interest is the second dimension of a theoretical perspective, its dominant metaphor:

> Metaphors are indispensable both to our everyday comprehension of the social world, as well as to theoretical understanding. Differences in theoretical perspectives are to a great extent reducible to differences in their dominant metaphors. A metaphor provides the theorist with an overall

Figure 8.1
Comparison of Theoretical Perspectives

Theoretical Perspective/ Dimension	Neoclassical Theories	Systems Theories	Later Human Relations Theories	Market Theories	Interpretive/ Critical Theories	Theories of Emergence
Focus	Organizations as decision sets	Organizations as purposive entities	Integrating individuals and organizations	Organizing as revealed self–interest	Organizing as social action	Organizing as discovered rationality
Cognitive Interests (generally)	Technical	Technical	Unclear, technical, or emancipatory	Technical	Interpretive and emancipatory	Interpretive and emancipatory
Dominant Metaphor	Decision set	Biological organism	Integration	Marketplace	Language	Emergence
Primary Unit of Analysis	Decision	System viewed holistically	Self-actualizing individual	Self-interested individual	Face-to-face encounter; the alienated individual	Human and/or intrapsychic encounter; shared social experience
Relation of Individual to Organization	Organization	Organization	Individual	Individual	Individual	Individual
Meaning of Rationality	Thought precedes action.	Thought precedes action at individual level.	Thought and action are interactive.	Thought, i.e., decisions about ends precedes action.	Action mainly precedes thought.	Action precedes thought.
Primary Values	Efficiency, rational goal attainment	Organizational survival and adaptation to environment; Achieving collective purpose through democratic means	Achieving organizational goals by promoting individual self-actualization	Free individual choice and maximizing aggregate utility; Ameliorating known social ills; Responding to diverse organizational and environmental interests	Promoting noncoercive discourse and processes of decision making; Reducing individual alienation	Discovering shared purposes through humane, noncoercive social processes; Facilitating reflexive self-awareness to enable responsible personal action

Source: Michael M. Harmon and Richard T. Mayer, *Organization Theory for Public Administration* (Boston: Little, Brown, 1986), *passim.*

image of his or her subject matter that affects both methodologies for research and normative evaluation. (Harmon & Mayer, 1986, p. 19)

The question is which images might be helpful in ordering one's understanding of organizations (p. 404).

The third dimension of the theoretical perspective, the primary unit of analysis, makes reference to the starting point for the investigation, that is, what is most real about, most basic to an understanding of the subject of inquiry, for that theoretical perspective. A primary unit may differ in the level of analysis, for example, the organization as a whole, the small group, the individual, to which attention is directed or to what is presumed to be their motives or purposes (Harmon & Mayer, 1986, pp. 19–20). "Whose point of view should you take: that of an external, disinterested observer; a concerned citizen; top management; an ordinary worker? How broadly or narrowly, given your present interests or circumstances, should you focus your attention?" (p. 404).

The fourth dimension, the relation of the individual to the organization, includes assumptions about human nature and the social order. "A given combination of assumptions, in turn, influences the theorist's beliefs about whether organizations are fundamentally instruments of domination or benign associations of cooperative activity" (Harmon & Mayer, 1986, p. 20). Should people be integrated into organizations, protected from them or enabled to transcend them (p. 404)?

The fifth dimension, the meaning of rationality, considers whether it is assumed that thought precedes and informs action or that action precedes and gives rise to thought (Harmon & Mayer, 1986, p. 20). To what extent can we know why we do things or what the consequences of these actions will be? Do our goals emerge from our experience or do we first set goals and objectives and then act (p. 404)?

The sixth and last dimension, primary values, is not independent of the other five dimensions of the theoretical perspectives:

> [V]alues are products of the particular manner in which theorists grapple with each of the five preceding dimensions. Values, for theorists, are embodied in their particular stances toward cognitive interests, dominant metaphors, primary units of analysis, the relation of the individual to the organization, and the meaning of rationality. (Harmon & Mayer, 1986, p. 20)

Is it more important to achieve goals, be efficient, be faithful to certain principles, understand what is happening, promote social processes, be left alone, and the like (p. 404)?

Harmon and Mayer are particularly helpful in identifying the various kinds of assumptions implicit in the many theoretical perspectives. Each perspective (or perhaps even each theory within a perspective) represents a particular approach to life and to inquiry, that is, an understanding of why one theorizes, a particular image or metaphor of organizations, a set of important values, and the like. Whereas Thomas Kuhn pointed to the fact that there are distinctive paradigms or sets of basic assumptions that direct and shape scientific inquiry, his work does not focus on identifying the specific assumptions that comprise individual paradigms. Harmon and Mayer begin to outline the types of assumptions that are important in shaping thought, inquiry, and action.

MULTIPLE PERSPECTIVES AND WICKED PROBLEMS

Harmon and Mayer (1986) also explain how the multiplicity of theoretical perspectives can be helpful to a leader who must deal with wicked problems. The authors define tame and wicked problems as being at different ends of a spectrum. Tame problems are "malleable problems, the ones that could be attacked with common sense and ingenuity"—for example, "the kinds of problems that professionals in government were traditionally hired to deal with [that] have in large part been solved—the roads are paved, the houses built, the sewers connected." "Tame problems can be solved because they can be readily defined and separated from other problems and from their environment." The tame problems may be difficult, time-consuming, or complex—for example, the moon landing—but their solution is primarily technical (p. 9).

Wicked problems, as defined by Harmon and Mayer (1986), on the other hand are "the problems with no solutions, only temporary and imperfect resolutions. They deal with the location of a freeway, the development of school curriculum, the confrontation with crime" (p. 9). Drawing on the description offered by Horst W. J. Rittel and Melvin Webber, they are described as wicked in the sense of being malignant, vicious, tricky, or aggressive.

> We are calling them "wicked" not because these problems are themselves ethically deplorable. We use the term "wicked" in a meaning akin to that of "malignant" (in contrast to "benign") or "vicious" (like a circle) or "tricky" (like a leprechaun) or "aggressive" (like a lion, in contrast to the docility of a lamb). (p. 9)

Wicked problems are difficult to define, have no agreed-upon solution to determine when a solution has been found, and, in fact, have no clear definition of what the problems is (p. 9). "Moreover, because of their uniqueness, wicked problems are not amenable to standardized routines for analysis and evaluation. Therefore, to the extent that it is possible to list solutions beforehand to a wicked problem, these solutions are unlikely to be mutually exclusive" (p. 11). However, wicked problems are not hopeless, nor are they impossible to define.

Public administrators and other organizational leaders are called upon to tame these wicked problems, to define and frame the issues. How a leader thinks about these problems, frames the issue for further investigation, and finally acts upon them is dependent on the theoretical approach that is used. "Various theoretical approaches frame the same situations in different ways, ask differing questions about them, and thereby suggest differing solutions or preferred modes of action for contending with them" (Harmon & Mayer, 1986, p. 12). Thus, alternative theoretical perspectives—just as, it is argued, alternative paradigms—offer a leader additional and alternative means of acting on wicked problems.

[T]hought and action . . . are not merely related, but are actually constitutive of one another. . . . [T]heory is not to be valued for the definitive answers that it offers, but for the basis it provides for self-reflexive conversations about potentially sensible ways to understand and act in the world. (p. 392)

PART III

The Shape of the Contemplative Paradigm

An Alternative for Addressing Wicked Problems

Part I reviewed the work of a variety of authors concerning the relationship between intellectual constructs, that is, images, theories, metaphors, paradigms, and the ways of thinking, inquiring, perceiving, valuing, and acting that arise from those constructs, and has organized their contributions into a general theory of paradigms. Other contributors in Part II have illustrated how paradigms, metaphors, and images have shaped range of thinking, inquiring, perceiving, valuing and acting in the field of organization theory in particular. In addition, Harmon and Mayer have developed the concept of wicked problems and have pointed to the importance of the choice of intellectual constructs in developing approaches to tame these problems.

Part III now shifts the focus to a particular intellectual construct, the contemplative paradigm. The task now is to articulate the underlying assumptions of this paradigm. In articulating the four sociological paradigms, Burrell and Morgan used two dimensions: assumptions about the nature of society and assumptions about the nature of social science. The assumptions about the nature of society (the sociology of radical change/sociology of regulation axis) were outlined as contrasting concerns. The assumptions about the nature of social science (the subjective/objective axis) were organized as assumptions about ontology, epistemology, human nature, and methodology. Part III is inspired by Burrell and Morgan's method of articulating and defining a paradigm in terms of its underlying assumptions.

However, this book adopts a different framework of assumptions than Burrell and Morgan used. As detailed in Part IV, the assumptions underlying the contemplative paradigm are organized in terms of the fourfold path derived by Matthew Fox from the writings of the 14th–century German mystic Meister Eckhart. Finally, Part IV includes, in chapter 15, a restatement of the contemplative paradigm in terms of contemporary images and themes.

As a prelude to the fourfold path framework and as a means of introducing the contemplative paradigm, chapters 9 and 10 examine, respectively, the current dominant paradigm and the nature of the contemplative experience itself. Chapter 9 surveys the work of several contemporary authors to build a baseline, an articulation of our current paradigm, a statement of the common sense of our time to be contrasted later with an alternative, that is, the contemplative paradigm. Borrowing from the method of Morgan's *Images of Organization* as well as Harmon and Mayer's *Organization Theory for Public Administration*, chapter 10 examines the central metaphor of the contemplative paradigm, that is, the contemplative experience itself, as a first step into the contemplative paradigm.

Finally, Part V further explores some of the thinking, perceiving, inquiring, valuing, and action that arise from the contemplative paradigm by outlining the style of contemplative leadership. The final chapter suggests further areas for exploration.

9

The Dominant Paradigm

A paradigm, as used in this and the following chapters, is the most basic, fundamental set of assumptions forming our primary view of reality. The alternative paradigm is defined in terms of the most basic, fundamental set of assumptions that form the view of reality for an ordinary human being rather than in terms of the assumptions that are of concern to organizational theorists or social scientists alone. In much the same manner as swimming underwater enhances one's awareness of the nature and importance of air, an understanding of the nature and significance of the currently dominant paradigm may be enhanced by immersing oneself in the alternative contemplative paradigm. However, we begin by examining the dominant paradigm, the cultural atmosphere we take for granted, and identify the set of basic and almost invisible assumptions in which Western contemporary society is immersed.

THE DOMINANT PARADIGM: CONTEMPORARY PERSPECTIVES

A variety of contemporary authors have articulated, reflected upon, and critiqued our culture's current dominant paradigm. This literary genre includes Ferguson (1980), *The Aquarian Conspiracy*; Capra (1982),

The Turning Point; Schaef (1985), *Women's Reality*; Harman (1988), *Global Mind Change*; Lenz and Myerhoff (1985), *The Feminization of America*; Elgin (1981), *Voluntary Simplicity*; Theobald (1987), *The Rapids of Change: Social Entrepreneurship in Turbulent Times*; Yankelovich (1981), *New Rules: Searching for Self-fulfillment in a World Turned Upside Down*; Thayer (1981), *An End to Hierarchy and Competition*; Peters and Waterman (1982), *In Search of Excellence*; and many others. Some of these authors, such as Thayer, are more deeply rooted in the social sciences; others, such as Ferguson, seek to address a more general population. Many of these authors are proposing or predicting some form of alternative paradigm and articulate our existing dominant paradigm in contrast.

It would be unusual to articulate the status quo unless one were proposing something different.

> A "common sense" is the utterly ordinary. It is so ordinary that it becomes a frame of reference for entire communities. It is a shared knowing that does not need to be expressed as it is already a part of the common sensing of how things are. (Elgin, 1981, p. 220)

> Every society ever known rests on some set of largely tacit basic assumptions about *who we are, what kind of universe we are in, and what is ultimately important to us*. Some such set of assumptions can be found to underlie the institutions and mores, patterns of thought and systems of value, that characterize a society. They are typically not formulated or taught because they don't need to be—they are absorbed by each person born in society as through osmosis. They are accepted as given, as obviously true—and throughout most of history, by most people, never questioned. (Harman, 1988, p. 10)

Because the existing paradigm is ordinarily outlined as part of a critique, it is not surprising then, that many of these authors highlight the worst aspects of the existing paradigm. Their description of the status quo may seem somewhat skewed. In addition, as suggested earlier, there are probably times and places in our lives, often in extreme or exceptional circumstances, when we do not apply the usual operating assumptions. There exist, of course, edge thinkers, who have left the dominant assumptions behind and no longer operate out of the dominant paradigm. But these individuals are, by definition, the exception. When judging the accuracy of the description of the prevailing paradigm, we might consider the person we meet at the bus stop downtown and ask ourselves whether the following dominant paradigm is his or her version of common sense. Is there a nod of recognition? The picture of the dominant paradigm is intended to be a rough idea of what we usually take for granted. In view of these caveats, the following descriptions of the dominant paradigm are offered as a means of identifying what has generally been the norm, the usual, the commonplace, in contemporary society, that is, the usually unstated, often unconscious, assumptions that underlie our thinking, perceiving, inquiring, valuing, and acting.

Fritjof Capra

The first articulation of the dominant paradigm to be presented here is that offered by Fritjof Capra, a physicist who has examined ancient Chinese thought as a counterpoint to our current ways of thinking. Capra is one of many who attempt to identify the historical roots of the status quo. Identifying the paradigm that has dominated and shaped Western society for the last several hundred years, and which is distinctly different from the thinking and values of the Middle Ages, Capra points to the scientific revolution, the Enlightenment, and the industrial revolution and the values and ideas that these historical forces have shaped.

> They include the belief in the scientific method as the only valid approach to knowledge; the view of the universe as a mechanical system composed of elementary building blocks, the view of life in society as a competitive struggle for existence; and the belief in unlimited material progress to be achieved through economic and technological growth. (Capra, 1982, pp. 30–31; see also, Capra, 1984, pp. 5–10)

Capra identifies several themes of our inherited paradigm:

1. *Rational Knowledge.* Our society favors rational knowledge over intuitive wisdom. "Our culture takes pride in being scientific; our time is referred to as the Scientific Age. It is dominated by rational thought, and scientific knowledge is often considered the only acceptable kind of knowledge" (Capra, 1982, p. 39). Rational thinking is characterized as being linear, focused, and analytic; it is part of the intellectual functions of discriminating, measuring, and categorizing. Rational knowledge tends to be fragmented. Intuitive knowledge is not generally recognized in the dominant paradigm (pp. 38, 39).
2. *Division of mind and matter.* Westernized people tend to equate their identity with the rational mind. Thinking is seen as a function of the brain rather than the entire body. (Descartes, of course, is a significant contributor to this view and a major force in shaping the dominant paradigm.) There is a body-mind dichotomy and a separation of human beings from the natural environment. Although people see a need to care for the environment and refrain

from pollution or extermination of other species, our rational mind sets us apart from everything else in the universe. The Biblical mandate of human beings having dominion over the natural world is taken literally. Natural resources are to be developed and used. Raw materials are turned into usable items (pp. 40–41).

3. *Mechanistic Conception of the World.* The universe is viewed as a mechanical system consisting of separate building blocks whose properties and interactions completely determine all natural phenomena. Living organisms are also regarded as complex machines constructed from separate parts. Our technology is based on control, mass production, standardization, and centralized management (p. 44). Elements of this mechanistic, reductionistic approach include the breaking of complex phenomena into their basic parts and the search for the mechanisms connecting these basic parts. "Like human-made machines, the cosmic machine was thought to consist of elementary parts" (p. 47). This mechanistic and reductionistic approach, pioneered in classical physics, became so ingrained in our view of reality that social scientists turned to this model when they sought to be scientific.

4. *Determinism.* The universe follows certain laws of nature. Although we may not have yet discovered them, these laws determine a predictable, orderly universe, where interactions between the various parts result in certain outcomes, much as colliding billiard balls fall into the right pocket if the player is sufficiently skilled (p. 69).

5. *Knowability.* The universe can be a mysterious place—until we finally figure out what is happening. A beautiful sunset inspires awe, but we know, of course, that it is a result of the atmosphere bending the light rays in a particular way, and so on. The dominant paradigm includes the assumption that we can know everything about the universe as our tools become more sophisticated, for example, as we send better telescopes into space, as we build superconducting supercolliders, as we develop machines better than a magnetic resonance imager, or perhaps as we invent more-accurate survey techniques. Many things we once assumed to be unknowable—for example, why we share certain characteristics with our ancestors—are the subject of *Readers Digest* articles. The universe is ultimately knowable in this paradigm, although it may yield its secrets grudgingly.

6. *Competition.* "Promotion of competitive behavior over cooperation is one of the principal manifestations of the self-assertive tendency in our society" (p. 44). Capra traces this emphasis on competition to the Social Darwinists of the 19th century who held

that life in society is a struggle for existence, ordered by the maxim "survival of the fittest" (p. 44). Competition is the default mode for ordering in our society.

7. *Power and Control*. Power and control, as well as domination of others, are a pattern of behavior in our culture. Power and control are sought in a variety of forms—technological, economic, political. There are, of course, restraints on the acquisition and exercise of power and control, but the assumption is that individuals act in a manner that increases their power and control. A corporation or country with great economic strength is expected to increase that strength and acquire more influence or a greater market share. Powerful politicians are expected to increase their power. People are not ordinarily rewarded for giving up power or control. Individuals with political, economic, or technological power are held up as models. There is, in fact, an expectation that human beings will expand their control to the extent possible. Power and control are linked to responsibility. Parents are expected to control the behavior of their children; managers are expected to control the behavior of their employees, at least to the extent that the employees accomplish the goals of the organization; presidents are expected to control the economy (p. 44).

Willis Harman

Willis Harman, an electrical engineer and systems analyst with an interest in humanistic psychology, takes a slightly different perspective on the dominant paradigm than Capra does, but still echoes the basic themes identified by Capra. In *Global Mind Change*, Harman (1988) argues that a transformation comparable to the scientific revolution begun in Western Europe is underway today. Tracing the roots of the current dominant paradigm to Copernicus's 16th-century geocentric heresy, Harman (1988) articulates the "unspoken assumptions of conventional science" with a list of premises.

It is humbling to the educated Westerner to realize that to an undeterminable extent science, like the traditional belief system of "primitive" cultures, described a world that is shaped by its built-in assumptions. To illustrate this, consider the following set of ten premises which, if encountered in a textbook a few decades ago, would hardly have aroused question:

A Rational Set of Premises for a Scientific Age

1. The only conceivable ways in which we can acquire knowledge are through our physical senses, and perhaps by some sort of information transmission through the genes. The sole way in which we extend our

understanding of the nature of the universe is through empirical science—that is, the exploration of the measurable world through instrumentation which augments our physical senses.

2. All qualitative properties (at least the ones we can talk about scientifically) are ultimately reducible to quantitative ones (for example, color is reduced to wavelength, thought to measurable brain waves, hate and love to the chemical composition of glandular secretions).

3. There is a clear demarcation between the objective world, which can be perceived by anyone, and subjective experience which is perceived by the individual alone, in the privacy of his/her own mind. Scientific knowledge deals with the former; the latter may be important to the individual, but its exploration does not lead to the same kind of publicly verifiable knowledge.

4. The concept of free will is a prescientific attempt to explain behavior which scientific analysis reveals is due to a combination of forces impinging on the individual from the outside, together with pressures and tensions internal to the organism.

5. What we know as consciousness or awareness of our thoughts and feelings is a secondary phenomenon arising from physical and biochemical processes in the brain.

6. What we know as memory is strictly a matter of stored data in the central nervous system, somewhat analogous to the storage of information in a digital computer.

7. The nature of time being what it is, there is obviously no way in which we can obtain knowledge of future events, other than by rational prediction from known causes and past regularities.

8. Since mental activity is simply a matter of dynamically varying states in the physical organism (primarily in the brain), it is completely impossible for this mental activity to exert any effect directly on the physical world outside the organism.

9. The evolution of the universe and of man has come through physical causes (such as random mutation, natural selection), and there is no justification for any concept of universal purpose in this evolution, or in the development of consciousness, or in the strivings of the individual.

10. Individual consciousness does not survive the death of the organism; or if there is any meaningful sense in which the individual consciousness persists after death of the physical body we can neither comprehend it in this life nor in any way obtain knowledge about it. (pp. 29–31)

Harman's definition of the dominant paradigm reflects his concern with issues of human consciousness. Although Harman's and Capra's outlines are not identical, neither are they contradictory. Offering several perspectives on the current common sense may lend a fullness to an outline of the dominant paradigm. Duane Elgin offers yet another view.

Duane Elgin

Elgin (1981) identifies the Western scientific view of reality as that which historically developed in Western European nations, exemplified by the Greek philosophical traditions and the Judeo-Christian religious traditions (p. 222). He identifies six characteristics of the current view of reality:

1. *Materialistic.* The universe is made up of elementary particles that interact in a predictable manner. This is often termed the billiard ball model of the universe (p. 222).
2. *Dualistic.* In the Judeo-Christian religious tradition God is separated from the creation. God is the force that created the machine-like universe, set it in motion, and then let it go. God is as much apart from this complex and predictable universe as a watchmaker who crafts and winds his creation and then sets it on the shelf or otherwise separates himself and moves on (p. 222).
3. *Lifeless.* Because the universe is comprised of inanimate building blocks of elementary particles, the universe is fundamentally non-living. "The universe is seen as an inanimate machine wherein humankind occupies a unique and elevated position among the sparse life-forms that do exist. . . . [I]t is only rational for humanity to exploit the rest of the universe" (pp. 222–223).
4. *Rational.* Rationality and the intellect are given the highest place among our human faculties. "[I]t was felt that humankind could discover the natural laws governing the vast machine-universe and thereby acquire growing mastery over nature" (p. 223).
5. *Progress-oriented.* There is a potential for material change and progress as well as for social progress (p. 223).
6. *Physical.* Our individuality is equated with our physical existence. "The individual, then, is both unique and alone—apart from others and apart from the Divine. The knowing faculty, or consciousness, is viewed as little more than the product of biochemical activity in the brain. Thus, consciousness is not viewed as a bridge beyond physical separateness" (p. 223).

Burrell and Morgan

Burrell and Morgan (1979), as previously explained, have identified four sociological paradigms. According to these authors, the functionalist paradigm is currently dominant. Four of the assumptions (concerning the nature of social science) are arguably in accord with Capra, Harman, and Elgin:

1. *Realist.* The external social world exists independently of the perceiver.
2. *Positivist.* The social world can be predicted and explained experimentally through searching for regularities and causal relationships.
3. *Determinist.* Human beings and their activities are determined by the environment.
4. *Nomothetic.* The social world is understood by attention to rigorous protocol in constructing and testing hypotheses (p. 26).

Again, Burrell and Morgan's articulation of the dominant paradigm differs from those outlined here, but it is consonant with them.

THE DOMINANT PARADIGM: ORGANIZATIONAL MANIFESTATIONS

To this point the dominant paradigm has generally been described in terms that could be applied to any field of inquiry. We now turn to two descriptions of the dominant paradigm, which focus on the embodiment of these assumptions in an organization.

Peters and Waterman

The first description is from a popular critique of business management practices, Peters and Waterman's (1982) *In Search of Excellence.* Although aimed at the for-profit sector (and possessing a style that is somewhat polemical), the book may provide a general sense of how the dominant paradigm affects management practices, whether in the public or private sector.

Peters and Waterman (1982), as do many of the other critics of the dominant paradigm, cite the Copernican revolution as the source of the old rationality that needs to be replaced by a "new, different, and more useful one" (p. 42).

> The old rationality is, in our opinion, a direct descendent of Frederick Taylor's school of scientific management and has ceased to be a useful discipline. Judging from the actions of managers who seem to operate under this paradigm, some of the shared beliefs include:
>
> • Big is better because you can always get economies of scale. . . . Incidentally, as you get big, make sure everything is carefully and formally coordinated.
> • Low-cost producers are the only sure-fire winners. . . . Survivors always make it cheaper.

- Analyze everything. . . . Use budgeting as a model for long-range planning. Make forecasts. Set hard numerical targets on the basis of those forecasts. Produce fat planning volumes whose main content is numbers. (Incidentally, forget the fact that most long-range forecasts are bound to be wrong the day they are made. Forget that the course of invention is, by definition, unpredictable.)
- Get rid of the disturbers of the peace—i.e., fanatical champions. After all, we've got a plan. . . .
- Control everything. A manager's job is to keep things tidy and under control. Specify the organization structure in great detail. Write long job descriptions. Develop complicated matrix organizations to ensure that every possible contingency is accounted for. Make black and white decisions. Treat people as factors of production.
- Get the incentives right and productivity will follow. . . .
- Inspect to control quality. Quality is like everything else; order it done. . . .
- It's all over if we stop growing. When we run out of opportunity in our industry, buy into industries we don't understand. At least we can continue growing. (pp. 43–44)

Again, whether the account of the beliefs predominant in business organizations given by Peters and Waterman is completely accurate or fair is less important than the ability of this brief account to throw into relief an alternative view.

Four Themes of the Dominant Paradigm Applied to Organizations

The following four themes are yet another attempt to outline the Enlightenment or rational-scientific paradigm that is currently dominant, from the perspective of contemporary organizational life, particularly in the public sector. (See Eggert, 1990, pp. 34–35.)

Control. Control is the central theme in the dominant understanding of organizations. A good manager is one who has the situation under control. Budgeting is one manifestation of the need for control of financial resources. Strategic planning is another form of control. An administrator is expected to control her area of responsibility to the extent that goals and objectives are met. It is not appropriate for a manager—or a nonsupervisory employee—to name uncontrollable situations, such as the truck that broke down, the check that was not in the mail, or the technician who was late, as excuses for missed deadlines. An able leader is expected to plan for such contingencies and control the specific outcomes. Implicit in this expectation is the assumption that there is a causal connection between what an administrator does and the outcomes for the organization. Although it may not be clear at the moment what action could be taken to achieve the desired outcome, it is understood that there exists a chain of causation that would give the result being sought.

Good managers (like a good quarterback) make things happen. They are proactive. They get things done by sheer force of will. Watching and waiting is a sign of a reactive manager. There are timelines that dictate action. Situations must be squeezed and pushed to fit the predetermined schedule. If work is behind schedule, it is the manager's job to determine what has gone wrong, correct the problem, and ensure that everything is on schedule. Managers do not have the luxury of waiting to see how a situation evolves; they must take control. One must set limits on the gestation period for an idea or project.

Although personnel cannot be controlled in the same manner as trucks and computers, they are nevertheless to be controlled—for example, to be motivated to get to work on time, to meet performance expectations, and to refrain from any behavior that might have a negative effect on the organization. Human beings, it is presumed, also follow basic laws of nature although the laws seem to be very complex and difficult to discern. It is contrary to the purpose of an organization for individuals to follow their own agendas. A manager or executive is usually judged and evaluated, at least in part, on how well the people under his supervision meet expectations. The management literature today overflows with techniques to control people and make them more productive. The hallmarks of a good bureaucracy are written rules and procedures and a hierarchical structure in which someone is always in charge of other workers and has a span of control.

Managers rely on coercion and power over to get things done. Sometimes the coercion is as subtle as withholding approval or allowing an individual to assume that there will be negative consequences. Power in the organization is distributed from the top down: People have power because someone with more authority granted them power or allowed them to exercise it. Empowerment of lower-level individuals, or allowing them to discover their own power, can be dangerous because the situation could become uncontrollable and the outcomes unpredictable.

As with any other individual within the dominant paradigm, a member of an organization is expected to increase his power and control. It is unusual for anyone willingly to give up power or take a position with less authority. The assumption is that the person is actually being demoted or perhaps has family problems that prevent him from continuing in the more powerful position. The ladder of success goes in one direction only. Individuals who leave the fast track and engage in pursuits that tend to result in diminished power and control are the subject of newspaper articles because of the novelty of their decision.

Power and control in an organization are not limited to the authority to hire and fire. Control over information, decisions, agendas, processes, purchasing, budgeting, public image, and rule making would also be included.

Technology within an organization is often geared toward increasing power and control. Various evaluation techniques are intended to give managers better information and the ability to change important outcomes. New computer technology is often geared toward providing more-accurate information and a greater variety of information, helping an executive discover problem areas more quickly, predicting outcomes for alternative strategies, and generally offering an administrator more power and control within the organization.

A subtheme of the dominant paradigm that is related to the search for more power and control is the need for definition and clarity rather than ambiguity and uncertainty. Data need to be hard, accurate, and timely. It is assumed that hard, accurate data can be acquired if one has the proper tools, whether they be survey methods, reporting procedures, or data-processing equipment. A way can be found to measure accurately whatever is important to the organization. Goals are specific and measurable.

The mystery of organizational life is squeezed out. Managers look for theories that will fit their specific situation, explain exactly what is going on, and accurately predict what will happen next. Whether or not an administrator is successful in finding such theories, the assumption is that there is a theory that will fit the situation—in a book, in a business magazine, or in the manager's own imagination. Surprises and aberrations are nuisances. Chaos and disorder are signs of failure.

Attachment. Managers in the dominant paradigm take actions that give security. The successful administrator acquires roles, positions, ideas, principles, powers, theories, and relationships that provide meaning and experience—and adhere to them with tenacity. Good leaders (as would any individual operating within the dominant paradigm) develop their own theories from personal experience, but may become attached to their particular way of looking at the world and may ardently (and perhaps blindly) defend their perspective as the right one. When any of these previously listed possessions are threatened, managers suffer anxiety and insecurity and take reasonable steps to defend these foundational pillars of personal identity. A good manager carefully protects and nurtures her sources of power.

Appearances are important in maintaining power and other elements of personal identity. Some elements of appearance are obvious. A successful manager dresses like a successful manager in order to maintain the necessary power and respect. Similarly, the corner office is assigned to the manager with a higher position than the individual with an inside office. The sense that not everything is quite nailed down or under control fuels the desire to possess more, to fix one's desire on a specific object (like a new theory, bigger budget, better people) that will help secure the manager's place in the organization. A successful executive is never satisfied. Within certain bounds, the overriding emphasis is to take care of one's own interests.

Competition is the default operating mode in the dominant paradigm and undergirds time-honored principles in the workplace such as hiring or promotion on the basis of merit. In fact, elaborate mechanisms and rules—such as annual performance reviews, affirmative action, standardized tests, ethical guidelines, and the like—are devised in an attempt to ensure fairness of competition. Competition ordinarily presumes a focus on individuality. Although there is a strong countertheme of teamwork in organizations in recent years, organization members are ordinarily evaluated and rewarded on the basis of individual performance—even if "ability to work as a team" is one of the evaluative criteria.

Efficiency. According to the rules of the dominant paradigm, organizations have clearly defined purposes. Most organizations have a mission statement. The manager's job is to see that the purpose is achieved in the most efficient way. Neither time nor money nor personnel should be wasted, waste being defined as activities that do not have a direct relationship to goals. Utility is the keynote of action. Resources should be used in the most cost-effective manner—whether the resources expended are tax dollars or stockholder investments. Human beings are valued on the basis of what they contribute to achieving the mission. They have no intrinsic worth outside their role in the organization. Unless employees have some unique skill, they can be replaced. "Hurry up! Get it done! Just do it!" are the watchwords of the dominant paradigm.

Rationality. Rationality includes not only the valuing of a machinelike logic over other mental processes but a preference for the objective, the measurable, the predictable. Logical positivism, empiricism, and the scientific method occupy a central position in the methodology of organization. Causality is the assumed model for explaining how and why things happen. Rules and procedures undergird the desire for certainty and safety. Although it is easy to ridicule voluminous procedural manuals, the intent of making operating procedure explicit is to ensure logical, rational, objective decisionmaking.

Managers are expected to make decisions on the basis of rational deliberation rather than whims or emotions. Spontaneity and chaos are considered dangerous. Observable phenomena are the focus of attention, and inner, subjective workings are ignored. Time is a limited commodity that can be budgeted and parceled out. Human resources are finite quantities measured in "full-time employee equivalents" or "person-hours" that are budgeted in the same manner as dollars and cents. Action is motivated by purpose. Questions are to be answered. Ambiguity must be lessened or removed.

THE DOMINANT PARADIGM: STRENGTHS AND WEAKNESSES

As is apparent from the descriptions of the dominant paradigm given here, as with any paradigm or metaphor, certain aspects of reality are highlighted and developed while other aspects are neglected and underdeveloped. The rational-scientific paradigm has been successful, for example, in material and social development.

> This includes not only more goods and services, but also the development of highly efficient modes of organization—economic, legal, political—designed to promote and support the material development of society. . . . Western cultures have also cultivated the development of autonomous individuals capable of relatively high levels of self-regulating behavior. Although personal material gain has often been the motivating force for self regulation, the Western setting has pushed the individual to learn to take charge of his or her own life, particularly with regard to personal and social concerns. Thus, the principal contributions of the Western world view are, I think, twofold: sociomaterial growth and psychological maturation. (Elgin, 1981, p. 224)

Because most of the descriptions of the current paradigm were drawn from critiques of this paradigm, the weaknesses have not been hidden from the reader. Nevertheless, the purpose of the foregoing is not to judge or condemn the dominant paradigm—or any other paradigm—but to set the stage for describing a contrasting paradigm—the contemplative paradigm—and to explore the additional and alternative ways of thinking, perceiving, inquiring, valuing, and acting that might be made available within the contemplative paradigm. Thus, we now turn from the status quo, the currently dominant, rational-scientific paradigm, to the alternative, contemplative paradigm.

10

The Contemplative Experience

To explore how an alternative set of operating assumptions, that is, an alternative to the dominant paradigm, would result in additional modes of thinking, perceiving, inquiring, valuing, and acting, it is helpful first to choose a particular alternative set of assumptions, that is, a specific alternative paradigm, for examination. What follows is an attempt to delineate and articulate a distinctly contemplative view of reality, a contemplative paradigm, that is recognizably different from the currently dominant, rational-scientific, paradigm. This alternative paradigm would then, arguably, provide alternative or additional modes of thinking, perceiving, inquiring, valuing and acting.

The term *contemplative paradigm* is not chosen at random. The naming of this set of assumptions as the contemplative paradigm is first a claim that there is an extant tradition that embodies this alternative view of reality, and second, an admission of the contributions of others, an acknowledgment that this alternative paradigm is not my own invention. Although it is not essential to the core argument, that is, that alternative paradigms yield alternative ways of thinking, inquiring, perceiving, valuing, and acting, thereby providing a broader range of tools for responding to wicked problems, it is suggested that what is termed here the contemplative paradigm is the set of assumptions that the Western (Christian) contemplatives could claim as their own. In other words, the contemplative paradigm arguably has some relation to what is known generally as the contemplative tradition.

There are, of course, the same pitfalls in articulating the contemplative paradigm as there are in spelling out the dominant paradigm. There are always exceptional circumstances and exceptional individuals who seem to have other operating assumptions—who still might be identified as contemplatives. In addition, there is the additional unclarity about who would be encompassed by the term *contemplative*. Nevertheless, this project forges ahead and attempts to articulate the broad outlines of the contemplative paradigm.[1]

ALTERNATIVE METHODS AND A CONTEMPLATIVE WORLDVIEW

It might be helpful to recall also that, in my own journey into this area of inquiry, my experience with the alternative management methods preceded the recognition that these might be contemplative methods. There seemed to be other assumptions than those of the dominant paradigm underlying these alternative methods; only later did I tentatively recognize them as the operating assumptions of the contemplatives. A glimpse into these alternative methods may provide an entrée into the contemplative paradigm (see Eggert, 1990, pp. 31–32).

Often these nontraditional methods were used in the midst of planning processes with businesses, community groups, or nonprofit organizations. In one example, representatives from various community projects were attempting to understand the root causes of persistent problems they had encountered and to formulate strategies to address those issues. In a traditional meeting, there might be a formal agenda, driven to completion by the particular interests (or hidden agendas) of the participants. But in this situation there was a large wall filled with clusters of index cards, each with a short phrase, written in letters large enough to be read from a distance, describing some aspect of the situation. All participants stared intently and silently at the cards for a period of time. This attentiveness stemmed in part from the collaborative conversation and individual effort that had generated the cards. By the time the group was staring silently at the cards, the individual ideas had become the collective creativity, represented by the clusters of cards on the wall. After a few minutes, brief comments emerged from the silence: "I see something there about . . ."; "There seems to be a relationship between . . . ." After more periods of silence, there would be a burst of creativity. One participant would stand up and blurt out a full sentence describing the underlying issue. The group received her idea, and the conversation began to explode like a bag of microwave popcorn. Eventually, from the configuration of the data symbolized by the clusters of index cards, a consensus emerged regarding the meaning and implications of the issues that had brought the group together.

This group process was completed in a relatively short period of time and resulted in a group consensus that had a comparatively long half-life. Anyone coming into the group with a pet idea would soon find his or her favorite insight becoming lost in a sea of index cards. Rationality joined hands with intuition to break loose creativity and insight. In comparison to many other group processes or meetings, there was more watching and waiting and less talking. There was a strong sense that something would emerge from the group wisdom if the participants listened to each other and trusted the process.

A second example of what later seemed like contemplative methods occurred on a New Year's weekend in an old mansion. A service organization had gathered for its quarterly celebration and planning retreat. There was a 10-foot strip of white wrapping paper on the wall of the parlor. Old magazines, rubber cement, and scissors were dispersed around the room. There was the expected celebrative chatter as partygoers renewed acquaintances and began to build the Wall of Wonder. Each participant recalled some significant event from the past year, which he then symbolized by cutting a suitable picture from a magazine and adding it to the collective montage on white wrapping paper.

This Wall of Wonder served as a focus of attention later in the evening as the group gathered to celebrate the experiences of the past year. Although the previous year's planning retreat articulated specific plans for the coming year, the question at the current gathering was not whether all goals had been reached. The focus was what had been accomplished, how the direction of the organization had changed, and what the present circumstances revealed about the next steps. The Wall of Wonder helped the group listen to each other, absorb the significance of the past year's events, and move beyond linear, rational, verbal processes to prepare the group for the next day's planning session.

There was a different sense, a different feel, even a different scent, in these encounters from what I had noticed during more-traditional meetings. Later, in exploring the contemplative approach to life—whether in reading about others' accounts or in reflecting on my own experience, I recognized the scent again and wondered about the relationship between these nontraditional group events and the contemplative tradition.

CENTRAL METAPHOR OF THE CONTEMPLATIVE PARADIGM

Although it requires more than a metaphor to articulate a paradigm, a metaphor may be a good starting point. The universe as a machine is often cited in articulations of the dominant, Enlightenment or rational-scientific, paradigm. For example, this machine metaphor implies that the universe is made up of separate parts that are linked together in a particular way with predictable outcomes, that is, that determinism, causality, knowability, rationality, and the like, are part of the rules of the game.

In a similar manner, the contemplative experience itself serves as a unifying metaphor for the contemplative paradigm. However, the contemplative experience may not enjoy the easy and immediate recognition that the machine does. This new metaphor may require further explanation and definition.

Psychiatrist Gerald May not only provides a description and identifying criteria for the contemplative experience but also contributes a number of pertinent observations about the contemplative experience. According to May there are many states of awareness—intensely focused attention, deep trance, distracted anxiety, and so on. We pass in and out of these states, often without even noticing that we are doing so. The contemplative state of awareness can be described as an open, available, attentive presence to what is going on both internally and externally. The contemplative state of awareness is also something that ordinary people, who may not define themselves as contemplatives, experience, even if for brief moments. It is neither shutting out the world nor focusing intently. May (1987) describes it as a "direct, immediate, open-eyed encounter with life as-it-is. . . . It is a specific psychological state characterized by alert and open qualities of awareness" (p. 28).

Gerald May further characterizes the contemplative state as involving a loss of self-definition. This is in contrast to a variety of other experiences that he terms self-defining inasmuch as they are characterized by a retention of the sense of self during the experience (G. May, 1983, p. 53). Self-definition, according to May, is a creation of a dualistic state of mind, that is, "'I' creates 'You,' self creates other, and subject makes object." If one side of a duality disappears, so does the other (p. 103).

People of other times and cultures have often defined themselves largely in terms of genealogy, social caste, or geographic origins. In our era, self-definition tends to occur on the basis of more personal, individualistic factors. The most common of these are our names, body-images, accomplishments, aspirations, likes and dislikes, and the kinds of relationships we establish. These can all be considered bases for self-definition. The act of self-definition constantly creates self-image, which has four fundamental components:

body: the image we have of our physiques, combined with the sense of being "in" our bodies and the perception of our geographical location in relation to "other" people and things

will: the sense of volition, how we manage ourselves and our lives; our perceptions of what we can and cannot control in ourselves and in the environment

desire: what characteristically attracts and repels us; the things we hope for and the things we fear; what gives us pleasure and pain

relationship: our basic sense of alone-ness or together-ness; our confidence and fear with others; our sense of relatedness to other people, society, and the world and cosmos around us.

These four components, with various refinements and elaborations, make up that complicated and intricate mental production called self-image. (p. 104)

Thus, when the contemplative experience is described in terms of loss of self-definition, reference is being made to these four elements loosening, relaxing, becoming more ambiguous. What a person once thought was solid and concrete simply begins to appear as empty space. Experiences that increase or strengthen or even change one's sense of these four elements are termed self-defining.

These self-defining experiences, which are *not* within May's definition of the contemplative state, range from "conversion experiences in which people feel immediately and dramatically transformed" to visionary experiences in which certain revelations are made to the subject. (Self-defining experiences also include the mundane and ordinary, of course.) Neither are "psychic experiences, associated with extrasensory perception, astral projection, spirit communication" or possession experiences included in the definition of the contemplative state (G. May, 1983, p. 52). Even the more common event of having a hunch, an experience that involves more activity, interpretation, and self-definition than what May cites as true intuition, is excluded from the definition of contemplative state. Peak experiences, such as those studied by Abraham Maslow, may be similar, but not identical to, the contemplative experience. Gerald May points out that he encouraged people to recall unitive or contemplative experiences by asking them for experiences characterized by being "at one," "caught up in time," or "immediately present." May (1983) sometimes asked individuals to try to recall "a time when you were wide awake, very clear and open, and yet so caught up that you forgot yourself" (p. 58). Maslow, however, in documenting peak experiences, would ask questions like, "What was the most ecstatic moment of your life?" (G. May, 1983, p. 58).

The contemplative state, in contrast to these somewhat unusual, self-defining, experiences, "occurs much more commonly than the others, seems to be universal among different cultures and environments, and is characterized by a *loss* of self-definition" (G. May, 1983, p. 53). This unitive experience involving loss of self "is the fundamental, paradigmatic experience of consciousness, mystery and being. It constitutes true intuition and radical spontaneity" (p. 53).

> In spontaneously occurring unitive experiences, one feels suddenly "swept up" by life, "caught" in a suspended moment where time seems to stand still and awareness peaks in both of its dimensions, becoming at once totally wide awake and open. Everything in the immediate environment is experienced with awesome clarity, and the vast panorama of consciousness lies open. For the duration of the experience—which is usually not long—mental activity seems to be suspended. Preoccupations, misgivings, worries and desires all seem to evaporate, leaving everything "perfect, just as it is." Usually there are some reactive feelings that occur toward the end of the experience, feelings such as awe, wonder, expansiveness, freedom, warmth, love, and a sense of total truth or "rightness." After the experience is over, there is an almost invariable recollection of having been *at one.* (pp. 53–54)

May offers three qualities as identifying characteristics of the contemplative experience. First, the experience is characterized as being-at-one. May does not use the words feeling or sensing oneness, because "during the experience itself, all self-defining activities cease" (G. May, 1983, p. 59). Feeling or sensing oneness may occur, but only after the experience has passed and one is reflecting on it. "[I]t is not the addition of a unitive feeling but the subtraction of self-definition that characterizes true unitive experiences" (p. 59).

> This cessation of self-defining activities includes many things that we generally take for granted. In full realization of union there is, for example, no idea of controlling, accomplishing, or even of *doing* anything. There is no intent, no memory, no aspiration, and no conscious fear. Time seems to stop—and actually does, for time is a way of defining and locating oneself in terms of past, present and future. Thus, in looking back upon unitive experiences, people are given to say that they were suspended in the "eternal present," immersed in immediacy.
>
> All the things we use to maintain our sense of "me" are suspended for the duration. Usually, though not always, thinking stops. On rare occasions thoughts that are not self-defining can continue during unitive experience. But if they do, there is no sense of anyone thinking them, nor of what they might signify or where they might lead. . . .
>
> While self-other distinctions disappear from awareness during unitive experience, body-sense is preserved at a physical level. Thus, people do not walk into trees or walls because of the self-forgetfulness of union. Actions can be performed, words said, demands met. All these capabilities

> are preserved, but absent from them is any consideration of self. There is
> no sense of intention or expectation in them. (p. 60)

Second, awareness is radically opened. During the unitive experience
there is a change in awareness. "All focusing of attention ceases, for this
too is almost inevitably a self-defining activity. Wakefulness, alertness,
and sharpness of awareness are at the maximum, and awareness is
opened radically" (G. May, 1983, p. 61). The senses are acute, but there
is no need for the labeling or judging of the sensory input. There is no
need to comment, internally or externally, "That is a bird singing
outside my window," or "The flower is so beautiful." But May remarks,
"[I]t is my guess that there is some variability in the degree to which
awareness opens" in a unitive experience, that is, that one is never
completely open (p. 61). Preoccupation or restriction of attention pre-
cludes a full unitive experience (p. 62).

> There does seem to be, however, a difference between the degree of
> opening of awareness that happens when "normal" people encounter
> unitive experience and that characterizes the experience of the so-called
> masters. As we shall see, this may in part be due to the masters having
> been enabled to overcome their fear of self-loss, and it may be that this is
> why they are masters. (p. 62)

Third, reactive sensations commonly include wonder, awe, beauty,
reverence, and truth or *rightness*. These are reactions occurring only
after the experience or while reflecting on it. There are many variations
on the reaction, but the preceding are the most common.

> One is left with the feeling that what has just been experienced is the way
> things really are. Often there is a sense of completion or fulfillment and of
> warmth and love. As we shall see, there is usually some sense of fear or
> anxiety as well, though this may not be allowed into awareness fully. Some
> people find themselves trying to perpetuate the experience, to hold on to
> it and make it last. When this happens, a feeling of frustration and poi-
> gnancy is added to the mix, because the attempt to hold on never works.
> Such clinging is, of course, such a strongly self-defining act that it could
> never be successful. (G. May, 1983, p. 62)

These three qualities help delimit the range of unitive or contemplative experiences. Although "presumptive evidence exists that experiences having unitive characteristics may be associated with human
brainwave patterns that are synchronous with the alpha range of eight
to twelve cycles per second or slower," brainwave patterns are not a
useful or definitive criterion for a contemplative experience. "The conclusion that must be drawn from a scientific standpoint here is that

although unitive experiences *may* be associated with slow, synchronous brainwave patterns, these experiences are by no means always associated with unitive experience" (G. May, 1983, p. 56).

Although May (1983) observes that unitive or contemplative experiences seem to occur quite naturally without regard to age, culture, personality, or historical era, they seem quite special in our culture perhaps because of "our modern Western preoccupations with willful thinking, planning and doing" that make us less open or available to these common experiences (p. 55). Another reason these contemplative experiences, although universally experienced, are not often discussed or noted is that they tend to be forgotten. (Perhaps they tend to be forgotten because our culture does not place much value in them.)

> Ironically, the most frequent final reaction to a unitive experience is to forget it, to put it out of one's mind and "get back to business." Sometimes this returning to self-defining activity occurs so abruptly that one feels shocked by the transition. When this happens there is little chance of the experience being integrated meaningfully into one's subsequent attitudes toward life. It is simply a moment, experienced and forgotten, leaving only a hint of longing at levels that are barely conscious. (p. 62)

Sometimes individuals need the assistance of others in recognizing a contemplative experience. It may be an issue of perception, somewhat akin to a city dweller's first encounter with deer in the woods. A companion experienced in the ways of the outdoors may see numerous deer on a hike together, while the city dweller sees nothing—until the outdoorsperson says, "Look! Over there . . . three feet to the left of that big rock. Do you see its white tail in the air?" Then the city dweller utters the cry of recognition, "Yes, I see it now!" With someone to spot and identify the deer, the city dweller begins to see those large but camouflaged animals that had been abundant in the woods all along. The category of deer-experience is added to the perceptual repertoire of that individual, just as the category of black four of hearts was added to the universe of possible playing-card experiences for the subject of the psychological experiment described by Thomas Kuhn or the category of sun-circling planets to the list of possible celestial bodies for the early observers of Uranus (Kuhn, 1970, pp. 114–115). Enabling someone to recognize his or her own contemplative experiences can be as simple as asking a few questions, as Gerald May did with his subjects, or having others relate their experiences.

Despite the tendency to forget contemplative experiences or perhaps to fail to notice them in the first place, and because this experience serves as the primary metaphor for the contemplative paradigm, it may be helpful for the reader to recognize and remember his or her own contemplative experiences in order for the metaphor to be most effective in communicating the contemplative paradigm. For example, when Gareth Morgan used machine, organism, brain, and political system as metaphors for organization, little or no explanation was needed. A reader from our culture understands what Morgan means—because of shared experience with machines, organisms, brains, and political systems. His use of the metaphor *psychic prison* did, however, require a retelling of Plato's cave allegory for those who did not recognize or recall this story.[2] Otherwise, the metaphor would have been useless and even confusing (Morgan, 1986, passim). Here it cannot be assumed that all readers readily recognize or remember the contemplative or unitive experience. Accordingly, a retelling may be necessary. But whether or not the reader experiences the *aha* of recognition during the retelling, the retelling will also serve to describe the metaphor.

> Unitive experiences are usually quite transient and frequently seem to be associated with certain specific situations. Most people, for example, can recall having had unitive experiences in relationship to nature. Seeing the sun rising over mountains or watching it set beyond the horizon of the sea, walking through the woods and coming upon an unexpected waterfall, standing in the rain and feeling its rhythm, or gazing into the starry infinity of a winter night—moments such as these are perhaps the most common. In a similar way, unitive experiences sometimes occur in aesthetic settings, as in being swept away by a symphony or caught up in a great painting or an especially touching poem.
>
> Often people report such experiences in moments of close, loving intimacy with other people: in sex or in times of deep sharing or reconciliation. Similarly, they may occur during major life events such as the birth of a child, the death of someone close, a serious illness, or a significant crisis. Both great stress and relief from stress can seem to act as triggers for unitive experiences. Soldiers, for instance, have reported such experiences while under heavy fire, and also after a battle had stopped. (G. May, 1983, p. 54)

It may be helpful to include several accounts of ordinary unitive experiences to illustrate what May (1983) has described. The first is from a young woman who spoke in terms of love—about her experience washing dishes:

> I was standing at the kitchen sink, doing the dishes. The suds foamed up over the water, over my hands. The house was still. For some reason—I'll never know why—I just stopped for a moment and looked at the suds on my hands. Thousands upon thousands of bubbles, making that little gentle crackling sound bubbles make. Suddenly the world opened up. The sun through the windows, the shadows on the floor. A bird singing outside.

The breeze. The world had a kind of humming sound to it, so incredibly alive. And I had this exquisite romance. I was falling in love—literally "falling" and literally "in"—totally in love with the world. (pp. 82–83)

Sometimes religious terminology is used to describe the experience, as did the corporate lawyer in the second illustration:

I was on vacation in the mountains. Two friends and I had hiked most of the morning and we were very tired. I lay down by a tree stump and slept. When I awoke it was late afternoon and everything had become quiet. The crickets and cicadas had silenced their chirping, and even the breeze stopped. All I can say is that moment was an eternity, and it was the moment of my birth. I was forty-five years old, but in those few minutes I was born. I had no reaction except for a deep quiet and peace. This is hard for me to say, but at some point I remember thinking "There is a God, there is a God." And my life has not been the same since then. I still practice law, and I keep the same friends. I still worry about money and politics. I still snap at my wife when I've had a hard day, but I'm different. Somewhere deep down something has changed. Now I look for God—I seek the wonder of life, and while I appreciate being here on the face of this earth more than ever before, I also fear death less. I sit alone sometimes, and now and then I enter that moment again. (p. 69)

Although contemplative moments are often stereotyped in the popular culture as occurring when one is alone, in the peaceful stillness of a starry night, or on a beautiful mountain top (and these certainly can be occasions for unitive experiences), these experiences can occur in a group setting, during times of great stress, and in situations that are not pretty. The third example retells such an experience:

Everyone is right there, awake to the moment just as it is, somehow freed for a time from psychological and social agendas, enabled to be directly, consciously, immediately open. . . . I tried to think of other situations where such clear open attentiveness happens in a sustained way in groups of people. I was shocked by the example that came to my mind.

The most perfect instance I could think of was the way soldiers can be when they are together on patrol or awaiting attack at a base perimeter. My mind went back to the brief time I had spent in Viet Nam with the Air Force. It is not something I like to think about, but I vividly recalled the quality of contemplative awareness that human beings can achieve together when their lives depend upon it. You are immediately, panoramically alert. You notice every sound, every sight, every subtle movement or change. Any action you might take entails a risk of diminished attentiveness. To think of home, to shift your body to a more comfortable position, to whisper a word to your buddy— any such activity risks focusing your attention on one thing instead of being open to everything, and in that moment you might miss the thing that is coming to kill you. (G. May, 1991, p. 5)

At this point, whether or not the reader has identified in his or her own life what May has identified as the contemplative or unitive experience, we will move beyond the identifying characteristics and anecdotal illustrations of the central metaphor of the contemplative paradigm, that is, the contemplative experience itself, and flesh out this central metaphor by describing it in more detail and offering additional generalizations about the contemplative experience.

CHARACTERISTICS OF THE CONTEMPLATIVE EXPERIENCE[3]

There Is No Cause-Effect Relationship in a Contemplative Experience

[Y]ou cannot do it, you cannot make it happen, you cannot achieve it. . . . [T]hough we may incline ourselves in the direction of such experiences, it is impossible to make them happen. (G. May, 1983, p. 57)

It is somewhat like standing in the middle of a golf course during a thunderstorm: We cannot control the lightning, but we can place ourselves under conditions that seem to increase the likelihood of being struck by lightning. Similarly, although some contemplative experiences seem to be triggered by environmental or psychological situations, for example, sitting on a mountain top watching the sun set, chanting a mantra, or being very relaxed, it is not possible to *achieve* a unitive or contemplative experience (G. May, 1983, p. 58).

This observation makes it almost impossible for us *not* to jump to the conclusion that some cause-effect relationship does exist and that we could master and control it if we only knew how. To date, however, such attempts have at best succeeded in achieving only pieces of unitive experience. The full thing has not been, and the contemplatives would say *cannot* be, achieved. (p. 58)

Furthermore, any attempt to accomplish anything contemplative is self-defeating. "Unitive experiences are associated not with doing anything extra to one's self, but with doing less" (G. May, 1983, p. 65). "Trying dilutes the basic disposition of receptivity that is necessary" (Keating, 1986, p. 72). It is, however, possible to foster a willingness for something to happen. Certain contemplative disciplines can foster this willingness and sensitize one to the contemplative experience so that it can be recognized when it does happen (G. May, 1983, p. 58).

Contemplative practice may also nurture a sort of wide-awake gentleness so that unitive experiences are not brushed off so abruptly and forgotten so readily. But that is all. Nothing in the contemplative practice of any tradition establishes a cause-effect relationship in which some activity on the part of the person makes unitive experiences happen. (G. May, 1983, p. 58)

One Does Not Have Control in the Midst of a Contemplative Experience

It is not possible to control the contemplative experience—for example, make it last longer. There is, instead, a sense of being vulnerable and out of control.

One is neither controlling anything nor feeling controlled by any other person or thing. Actions and behavior take place, but they "just seem to happen." There is an impeccable spontaneity, unfettered by arbitrary planning, judging, or ambivalence.

Planning may occur during the experience, but it creates no sense of difficulty because it too is part of the flow, it too "just happens." (G. May, 1983, p. 106)

The contemplative experience requires a hands-off approach. Simply let it be. A contemplative experience will unfold and reveal itself. Contemplation is an exercise in letting go (Keating, 1986, pp. 74, 99).

The Contemplative Experience Can Be Accompanied by an Indifference

"Desire disappears entirely. Whatever is given in any situation is totally sufficient. There may be pain, experienced as a pure sensation, but there is no suffering" (G. May, 1983, p. 106). (See also Keating, 1986, pp. 76–77.) Nothing else needs to happen. There is a sense of being at peace. This indifference is not the result of a dulled awareness or passivity. It is no longer necessary to have one's own way. This surrender of will is a letting go of our attachments.

The Contemplative Experience Often Occurs as a *Breakthrough* Experience

In most instances, it appears that the ego is *surprised* by the [unitive] experience, caught off guard while it is either occupied with something else or simply resting from its self-defining activities. In part, this explains why unitive experiences are common in moments of crisis or fatigue or in sudden environmental changes. Walking though the woods, in a relatively tranquil and receptive state of mind, one comes *suddenly* upon a waterfall, and then it happens. If one were planning to come upon such a scene and were thinking about it, there would be far less likelihood of such an experience happening.

It is this quality of totally unintended surprise that causes people to say they were "caught," "swept up," or "captured." . . . There are times, as we have noted, when no predisposing circumstances can be seen to exist. The experience very literally "just happens." . . . Sometimes—and maybe really always—one is *broken through unto.* (G. May, 1983, p. 113)

This spontaneity can be threatening to our self-definition. "Wide-awake spontaneity is always a potential prelude to union, and unitive experiences always constitute the acme of human spontaneity" (p. 216). It is transformative in that, suddenly, everything seems different.

The Contemplative Experience Is a Gift

The contemplative experience is simply received. One cannot say, "I earned it," or boast, "Look what I have." It does not make one special. No competition is involved.

May (1983) identifies a backlash that the ego can employ when it is threatened with the willingness (cf. willfulness) that can accompany unitive experience: spiritual narcissism.

Simply stated, spiritual narcissism is the unconscious use of spiritual practice, experience and insight to increase rather than decrease self-importance. . . .

The gentlest form of spiritual narcissism is the idea that one can accomplish one's own spiritual growth. . . . The belief that "I can do it" is intimately associated with the assumption that "it is my idea, my desire, to do it." . . .

. . . In order for spiritual narcissism to work, it must take possession of the entire spiritual process. It has to take personal responsibility for the journey in order to sabotage it. . . . First, I may feel that the search is my doing. . . . I make it happen. If I feel successful, I can pat myself on the back. If I fail, I have only my personal lack of diligence and discipline to blame. . . . I aggrandize myself for being specially selected above other human beings, or I wallow in self-deprecation because I have not been so chosen. Thus it can be seen that no matter how spiritual narcissism comes to be applied, whether through accomplishment or failure, receiving special gifts or being denied them, the result is the same. One uses spirituality to become increasingly self-engrossed. (pp. 115–116)

A Contemplative Experience Can Involve Mystery

One is satisfied not to know exactly what is happening. Ambiguity is accepted. There is an appreciation for what is. "[O]rdinary things become more wonder-filled" (G. May 1983, p. 114).

When consciousness is perceived directly, with or without content, it is inevitably accompanied by a sense of mystery. Consciousness seems vast and spacious, with dimensions and limits that are unfathomable if they exist at all. . . . At the same time that consciousness seems very much alive and active, it appears to reflect a supreme constancy, an abiding solidity that is totally uninfluenced by any of its contents. As such, it can feel like bedrock, a ground upon which all of life's experiences and activities are founded. And yet, even so, it seems to have no true substance. (pp. 45–46)

The first requirement for even partial encounter with mystery . . . is to be willing to surrender one's habitual tendencies to either solve or ignore mystery. Secondly, one must be willing to risk some degree of fear. These two conditions combine to make up what . . . is the essence of contemplative spirituality; the willingness and the courage to open oneself to mystery. (p. 32)

Contemplatives Experience Increased Clarity

Gerald May (1987) contends that, over time, the state of contemplation results in changes in human brain function. The first category of changes includes increased clarity and breadth of awareness.

Instead of the usual shifting of focused attention back and forth among different objects and tasks, the experienced contemplative develops a capacity for more panoramic, all-inclusive awareness. This is accompanied by less "habituation" or "tuning out" of stimuli that would normally be considered distracting or irrelevant. Thus, more information, both external and internal, is available. (pp. 28–29)

The Contemplative Experience Can Result in More-Direct and Incisive Responsiveness

May (1987) identifies a second category of effects of contemplation that relates to how the information is used.

Since more perceptions are immediately available on a moment-by-moment basis, the contemplative tends to be more present-centered and capable of responding to the unexpected. In addition, experienced contemplatives develop an increased confidence in the natural or "intuitive" abilities of their minds to respond to the majority of incoming stimuli. Thus, while they have more perceptive information available, they also have less need to consciously "think about" what to do with it. This combination of increased information and decreased mental effort enable more immediate and efficient reactions to all situations. (p. 29)

There Is an Increase in Knowledge of the Mind's Activities

May (1987) identifies this knowledge as a third effect of contemplative practice. In contemplation one "directly notices the mind's activities" (p. 29).

> This leads to increased knowledge of the nature and substance of thoughts, sensations, emotions, memories, images and all other mental functions. Mental activities that were previously unnoticed become observable; material that had been 'unconscious' becomes "conscious." Intuitive sensibilities become more refined. Personal abilities and vulnerabilities are better identified. Most significantly, the insubstantiality of one's self-image is recognized and, as a result, one becomes less vulnerable to a variety of existential anxieties. (p. 29)

A Contemplative State Can Be Used for Good or Ill

There is often a tendency to associate contemplative experience with moral, holy, purposes or to assume that contemplatives are necessarily religious. However, as described by May (1987), the contemplative state is simply an objective reality that can be used for a broad spectrum of purposes.

> [A] contemplative state can be used for good or ill. Great athletes and artists are often in such states at times of peak performance. Contemplation was also central to training for ninjitsu, the ancient Japanese art of assassination. . . .
>
> It should be obvious that effects [of contemplative practice] such as these, when well developed, constitute a capacity for massive personal power. A person with heightened perceptions, more direct responsiveness, enhanced self-knowledge and freedom from fear can be a formidable agent for good or for ill. One can expect contemplative practice to lead to personal power; *one cannot, however, automatically assume that it will be used for good.* (pp. 28–29, emphasis added)

THE CENTRALITY OF THE CONTEMPLATIVE EXPERIENCE FOR THE CONTEMPLATIVE PARADIGM

Up to this point the contemplative experience has been described in contemporary terms borrowing heavily from the observations of psychiatrist Gerald May (who, one can surmise on the basis of his many writings, values the contemplative state and contemplative practice). The contemplative experience has been portrayed here as an ordinary human experience. All human beings have experienced aggression, anxiety, suffering, comfort—and the contemplative state. The articulation of the contemplative paradigm is a description of a worldview (or perhaps a culture) that pays attention to the contemplative experience. This worldview includes certain assumptions about human beings and the world around us, assumptions about causality, knowability, means of interacting with the world and other human beings, and so on. The contemplative state itself informs and shapes these assumptions.

There are analogous situations in which other basic human experiences have been highlighted by a culture. For example, the life of the Yanomamo Indians of southern Venezuela and northern Brazil—the fierce people studied by anthropologist Napoleon A. Chagnon, has been characterized as regulated violence. The Yanomamo value a capacity for rage, a quick temper, and little hesitation for using violent means to achieve one's ends (Chagnon, 1968, p. viii).

> Much of the behavior of the Yanomamo can be described as brutal, cruel and treacherous, in the value-laden terms of our own vocabulary. . . .
>
> The Yanomamo appear to be constantly on the verge of extranormal behavior. . . . Life in their villages is noisy, punctuated by outbursts of violence, threatened by destruction by enemies. . . .
>
> This is a study of a fierce people who engage in chronic warfare. It is also a study of a system of controls that usually hold in check the drive toward annihilation. Conflict among the Yanomamo is regulated through a series of graded escalations, from chest-pounding and side-slapping duels, through club fighting, spear throwing, to raiding in a state of war, to the ultimate—*nomoboni*—massacre by treachery. . . .
>
> The Yanomamo goad each other, within their own villages, to the brink of an explosion. . . . This hostility is projected on a larger scale in the negotiating of alliances between villages. Each principal must establish the credibility of his own threats, as well as discover the point at which the opposite party's bluffing will dissolve into action. It is . . . a politics of brinksmanship. (pp. vii–viii)

The author of this anthropological study describes the Yanomamo myth of the origin of the people in which the Spirit of the Moon is hit with an arrow, causing profuse bleeding. The blood spills to Earth and changes into men as it hits the earth. The Yanomamo people today are descended of the blood of the Spirit of the Moon.

> *Because they have their origin in blood, they are fierce and continuously making war on each other.* This myth seems to be the "charter" of Yanomamo society.
>
> Where the blood was thickest, in the areas directly underneath the spot where [the Spirit of the Moon] was shot, the wars were so intense that the Yanomamo terminated themselves. Where the blood had an opportunity to thin out, the Yanomamo were less fierce and therefore did not become extinct, although they too fought continuously. (Chagnon, 1968, pp. 47–48, emphasis in original)

Chagnon notes that "the Yanomamo explain the nature of man's ferocity and origin in myth and legend" (p. 53). One might consider that the Yanomamo culture pays great attention to aggression and develops basic assumptions about life that revolve around aggression, for example, that the basic way one interacts with the world is through violence and aggression.

In a parallel manner, the contemplative culture could be seen as paying great attention to the contemplative state and developing assumptions about life that grow out of or revolve around the contemplative experience as described here. The myths that give rise to the Western contemplative assumptions may also assist our understanding of that worldview just as the Yanomamo myths give a context for their culture.

NOTES

1. If the reader is more comfortable with a term other than *contemplative* for this alternative worldview, the reader would be most welcome to use it. In fact, upon review of what is termed here the contemplative paradigm, the reader might remark, "That sounds like Zen." I do not have the background to affirm or deny that conclusion. It is best left to those with experience in Eastern spirituality. (However, considering Kuhn's comments on the incommensurability of paradigms, one might make such comparisons cautiously. See Kuhn, 1970, pp. 101 ff.). This book does not attempt to review the Eastern contemplative tradition, although occasionally reference may be made to those contributions.

2. Plato's *Republic* presents the allegory of an underground cave with a blazing fire at its mouth. The inhabitants of the cave are chained and can see only the cave wall directly in front of them, on which the fire's light throws shadows. The cavedwellers take the shadows for reality. Thus, the cave represents a psychic prison, our being trapped by illusions. (See Morgan, 1986, 199–231.)

3. See also Benson (1975), *The Relaxation Response*, especially pp. 104–140, and Garfield and Bennett, 1984, *Peak Performance*, especially pages 158–160. Although both Benson and Garfield and Bennett are concerned with physiological or athletic implications of meditation or similar experiences, their descriptions of altered states are similar to those described by May and set a context for the characteristics listed here.

PART IV

The Fourfold Path

A Description of the Contemplative Paradigm

The task of articulating the contemplative paradigm for contemporary leaders shifts now from an examination of the current dominant paradigm and the nature of the contemplative experience to a tour of the Western contemplative mind. How do the Western contemplatives understand themselves, the world about them, and their place in the universe? Rather than attempting a comprehensive overview of contemplative thought, this segment of the journey uses contemporary historian and theologian Matthew Fox's (1981) construct of the fourfold path, and particularly his unique interpretation of Meister Eckhart, a German contemplative living from about 1260 to 1329 (p. 1), as a vehicle for exploring contemplative thought. After describing each of the four paths, this segment of the journey closes by restating the fourfold-path in contemporary language.

MEISTER ECKHART AND WESTERN CONTEMPLATIVE SPIRITUALITY

Although Eckhart does not represent each and every branch of Western contemplative spirituality (no individual contemplative could fulfill that role adequately), he stands squarely in the midst of the contemplative tradition and is held in high regard by both Western and Eastern contemplatives.[1]

In Germany, [Eckhart's] disciples and brothers Dominicans Henry Suso and John Tauler drew extensively from his thinking even after his condemnation [by papal decree posthumously in 1329]. Nicholas of Cusa in the fifteenth century commented on Meister Eckhart's works and Martin Luther in the sixteenth century drew heavily from Eckhart by way of John Tauler, whom, as Hoffman points out, . . . Luther admired unwaveringly from his youth to his final days [Hoffman, 1976, pp. 124, 154, 41 ff., and passim]. Lutheran mystic Jakob Boehme (1575–1629) owed much to Eckhart, as did the radical mystic-politician Thomas Munzer. . . . In England, the anonymous author of *The Cloud of Unknowing* as well as Walter Hilton and especially Julian of Norwich demonstrate a significant debt to Meister Eckhart. The work of seventeenth-century Polish mystic-poet Angelus Silesius has been called a "seventeenth-century edition of Eckhart" and the fourteenth-century Flemish mystic Jan van Ruysbroeck was influenced by him. "We can be sure," says scholar Jeanne Ancelet-Hustache, "that through the intermediary of the Flemish mystics, Eckhart's thought had anonymously found its way even to Teresa of Avila and Saint John of the Cross" since the Spanish dominated the Netherlands and the exchange of ideas was a regular one between the two countries. Ignatius of Loyola is recognized to have known Eckhart's theology and his brother Jesuit Peter Canisius, who edited John Tauler's works in 1543, also was indebted to Eckhart. Saint Paul of the Cross, founder of the Passionist Order in the eighteenth century, owed much to Eckhart's spirituality. . . . Asian scholars like D.T. Suzuki speak of the "closeness of Meister Eckhart's way of thinking to that of Mahayana Buddhism, especially of Zen Buddhism" and Professor S. Ueda in Kyoto, Japan, says that Eckhart breaks "the sound barrier of the normal intellectual world of Christianity and thereby enters into the world of Zen." Catholic monk Thomas Merton agrees, saying that "whatever Zen may be, however you define it, it is somehow there in Eckhart." Merton confesses to having been "entranced" by Meister Eckhart, and it can be documented that his conversion from being a romantic, dualistic, and Augustinian-minded monk in the fifties to being a prophetic Christian in the sixties occurred while he was studying Zen and Meister Eckhart. Hindu scholar Ananda Coomaraswamy compares Eckhart to Vedantist traditions. Quaker mystic Rufus Jones acknowledges a debt to Eckhart as well he should, for Quaker founder George Fox is in many ways Eckhartian-influenced. (M. Fox, 1980, pp. 1–2)

MATTHEW FOX AND THE FOURFOLD PATH

Matthew Fox has defined and articulated four paths in the theology of Eckhart.[2] These four paths form a spiritual journey. "[The journey] is *not* a journey up a ladder but a spiral of expanding consciousness that has no limits" (Fox, 1980, p. 9). The four paths can be described in various ways, including the traditional Latin names:

1. The experience of God in creation (*Via Positiva*)
2. The experience of God by letting go and letting be (*Via Negativa*)

3. The experience of God in breakthrough and giving birth to self and God (*Via Creativa*); and

4. The experience of God by way of compassion and social justice (*Via Transformativa*) (Fox, 1980, p. 10; Fox, 1981, pp. 215 ff; Fox, 1983, passim).

All paths intersect and intertwine with one another. They are interdependent (Fox, 1981, p. 245). Out of this fourfold journey emerges a tapestry of myth, metaphor, assumptions, emphases, and themes, each of which suggests and gives shape to the contemplative paradigm.

The four paths are also linked to the contemplative experience discussed earlier in that they can be viewed as offering various ways into the presence or ways of being fully present, concepts used by both psychiatrist Gerald May and Episcopal priest Tilden Edwards[3] in presenting contemplative exercises or methods (Edwards, 1987, p. 2; G. May, 1989). Being immersed in the medieval (Christian) world, Eckhart, of course, uses the term *experiencing God*, rather than the secular, 20th-century term used by Gerald May, *the contemplative experience*. It is assumed, for our purposes here, that both Eckhart and May are pointing to the same experience but use different terms to name it. Thus, Eckhart's four paths might be described as the means of entering into the contemplative experience

1. through an appreciation of the material world (Appreciation);
2. by letting go and letting be (Detachment);
3. through creative breakthroughs (Creativity); and
4. by means of social justice and compassion (Compassion).

THE CONTEMPLATIVE EXPERIENCE: RELIGIOUS OR SECULAR?

It may be helpful at this point to distinguish the contemplative experience from the religious or nonreligious context from which it arises. As described by May (1987) contemplation is a "direct, immediate, open-eyed encounter with life as-it-is. . . . It is a specific psychological state characterized by alert and open qualities of awareness" (p. 28).[4]

There is nothing particularly religious about this description. In fact, many contemplative exercises such as paying attention to one's breath, visualization, the repetition of a word or phrase (a mantra, for example) are used by both religious and nonreligious people. A so-called secular person may intend that the repetition of a mantra will induce a state of relaxation and promote cardiovascular health (see, for example, Benson, 1975), while a Christian monk may intend to be present to God and consider the exercise a form of prayer (see, for example, Edwards, 1987, pp. 40–43; and Keating, 1986). Edwards (1987) offers a definition of contemplative experience that is grounded in a Christian context but is pointing to the same reality to which Gerald May points:

> By contemplative I mean attention to our direct, loving, receptive, trusting presence for God. This attention includes the desire to be present through and beyond our images, thoughts and feelings. . . . It is our deepest human home and calling; all other homes and callings derive their authenticity from it. (p. 2)

In attempting to distinguish between religious and secular contemplative experience, one might observe individuals gingerly participating in a meditation class for the first time and their asking how the activity is alike or different from Zen or transcendental meditation or prayer or the relaxation exercises they learned at the health club. One response to this inquiry is to ask, "What is your intent?" Some participants might respond, "To lower my stress level." Meister Eckhart (and his Christian medieval colleagues) would likely answer, "To be open to God's presence." For Eckhart then, the same exercise is religious. Thus, for Eckhart, the four paths—appreciation, letting go/letting be, creativity, and compassion/social justice—might be considered spiritual or religious exercises in that these four paths lead into an experience of God, whereas in 20th-century secular terms, the four paths lead into the contemplative experience described previously by May.

The experience of Eckhart—and May—and their contemplative colleagues is available to any human being at any time in history, although some individuals or some cultures may pay far less attention to that particular aspect of human experience than Meister Eckhart did. For Eckhart and his fellow contemplatives, such as St. Teresa of Avila, St. John of the Cross, or Thomas Merton, life is focused on the contemplative experience or, in their terms, on being present to God. Their focus on this experience, this particular aspect of life, shapes their worldview, their assumptions about human beings and the universe, that is, it shapes their operating paradigm, and, accordingly, their ways of thinking, perceiving, valuing, inquiring, and acting.

The writings of Meister Eckhart and his colleagues, then, link the metaphor of the contemplative experience described earlier with the values, assumptions, and worldview of the contemplatives.[5] This contemplative approach to life focuses on that ordinary (but often neglected or unrecognized) reality named the contemplative experience (rather than another ordinary reality such as aggression and violence as the Yanomamo do). Eckhart's life was focused on experiencing God, that is, on the contemplative experience, and his understanding of life was informed by his contemplative experience. He described the experience, told stories about it, preached sermons about it, explored its implications, and helped others to journey on the fourfold path of the contemplative experience. An examination of the four paths or four themes will now serve as an introduction to these contemplative values, assumptions, and worldview.

NOTES

1. "One mark of Meister Eckhart's stature as a major thinker in the history of Western theology and spirituality is that there can never be any 'final' interpretation of Eckhart" (Colledge & McGinn, 1981, p. 25).

2. Fox's *four-path* framework will be used as a primary outline for the contemplative paradigm. This four-path framework is applied by Fox to a variety of authors in *Original Blessing* (1983). Fox particularly attributes the fourfold path to Eckhart (Fox, 1980, 1981, and 1982). Such attribution, however, does not necessarily represent the scholarly consensus. Whether the fourfold path can properly be attributed to Eckhart or whether it is Fox's unique and helpful contribution is an issue beyond the scope of this book. Though the four-path framework may at times be referred to as Eckhart's for the sake of convenience and brevity, the framework is more accurately and completely described as Fox's fourfold path that he asserts is derived from Eckhart's writings.

3. Tilden Edwards and Gerald May are both members of the executive staff of the Shalem Institute for Spiritual Formation, Inc., 5430 Grosvenor Lane, Bethesda, MD 20814; 301-897-7334; fax: 301-897-3719; e-mail: shalem@compuserve.com.

4. This is not to imply that May never uses explicitly religious (Christian) language when discussing the contemplative experience or that there are no other dimensions to the experience than the psychological dimension.

5. The observation in chapter 10 that "a contemplative state can be used for good or ill" signals a shift from examining the contemplative experience as a metaphor for the contemplative paradigm to the articulation of the contemplative paradigm itself. A metaphor is never identical to the reality to which it points. A fundamental assumption of the Western contemplatives is that whatever powers one enjoys are to be used for good rather than ill.

11

The Fourfold Path:
Appreciation

This first of the four paths considers how human beings enter into the contemplative experience through an appreciation of the material, created world. It is a journey into the center by the pathway of creation. It is a pathway of gratitude, sensuality, beauty, joy, awe, wonder, and passion.

As on each of the paths, here Eckhart includes a variety of interconnected themes that disclose his approach to life. Because 14th-century Eckhart does not present his worldview primarily in propositional form, as a 20th-century systematic theologian might, but rather in sermons based on Biblical texts and in Biblical commentaries, an investigation of Eckhart's understanding of reality includes an examination of some of his foundational (and Biblical) myths and stories that are explicated in his commentaries and sermons. That is, just as it would be more difficult to comprehend the violent Yanomamo culture without understanding their fundamental organizing myths or stories, Eckhart's basic mythology provides a context for some of his understandings and assumptions.

UNDERLYING MYTHOLOGY

It is not surprising that the Biblical creation myths are the starting point for an exploration of this path. According to the creation myth of

Genesis 1:1–2:3, there is an intimate relationship between the Creator and the created order inasmuch as God created the universe by means of his own creative energy (Hebrew: *Dabhar*) or *Word*. That is, God's own self is invested in this undertaking.

> In the beginning when God created the heavens and the earth, the earth was a formless void and darkness covered the face of the deep, while a wind from God swept over the face of the waters. Then God said, "Let there be light": and there was light. And God saw that the light was good; and God separated the light from the darkness. . . . And God said, "Let there be a dome in the midst of the waters, and let it separate the waters from the waters." So God made the dome and separated the waters that were under the dome from the waters that were above the dome. And it was so. God called the dome Sky. . . . And God said, "Let the waters under the sky be gathered together into one place, and let the dry land appear." And it was so. God called the dry land Earth, and the waters that were gathered together he called Seas. And God saw that it was good. (Gen. 1:1–10, New Revised Standard Version)

The story continues with this same pattern applied to the creation of vegetation, stars, sun, moon, birds, fish, and other animals, each being brought into existence by the Creator saying, "Let there be . . ." followed by the confirmation, "And so it was." Each new aspect of creation is affirmed with the phrase, "And God saw that it was good."

A second foundational myth, which for Eckhart is closely linked with the Genesis story, is the Incarnation, that is, the birth of Jesus, or the divine becoming human. Although the Christmas story of Luke 2:1–20 that inspires the typical manger scene with Mary and Joseph, animals, shepherds, and angels, may be more familiar, the story of the Incarnation at the beginning of the Gospel of John may be more helpful in understanding Eckhart's theology with respect to the Genesis story. In this story John uses the term *Word* (Greek: *logos*) repeatedly. In a manner similar to the Hebrew term *Dabhar*, used in the Genesis story and also translated as *Word*, *logos* means more than speech: here *logos* is *God in action*, creating and redeeming (New Revised Standard Version, p. NT-125). In addition, *Word of God* here refers to Jesus, that is, the *Son of God*, that is, God incarnate as a human being. The story here also makes reference to Jesus' function as the redeemer (or as Fox prefers, Jesus as the one who reminds us of our origins in a universe pronounced good and of our likeness to God) and to later events in Jesus' life, including his rejection, as well as the concept of the preexistent (before creation) logos (Fox, 1981, p. 218).

> In the beginning was the Word, and the Word was with God, and the Word was God. . . . All things came into being through him, and without him not

one thing came into being. What was come into being in him was life, and the life was the light of all people. The light shines in the darkness, and the darkness did not overcome it. . . .

He was in the world, and the world came into being through him. He came to what was his own, and his own people did not accept him. But to all who received him, who believed in his name, he gave power to become children of God. . . .

And the Word became flesh and lived among us, and we have seen his glory as of the father's only son, full of grace and truth. . . . No one has ever seen God. It is God the only Son, who is close to the Father's heart, who has made him known. (John 1:1–18, New Revised Standard Version)

A later section in the Gospel of John clarifies and amplifies the divine motive in the Incarnation: "For God so loved the world that he gave his only Son" (John 3:16, New Revised Standard Version). The contemplative viewpoint, accordingly, recognizes a love relationship between the creator and the creation, especially the human creation.

A third foundational myth, part of the creation story outlined earlier, concerns the origin of humanity. After all other elements of the universe were created (in ascending order of importance), human beings were created.

Then God said, "Let us make humankind in our image, according to our likeness. . . .

So God created humankind in his image. . . .

And it was so.

God saw everything that he had made, and indeed, it was very good. (Gen. 1:26–31, New Revised Standard Version)

This story forms the basis for the reverence given to fellow human beings and the intimate relationship between God and humanity, explained later, that is, God created human beings in his own image, and he then pronounced his creation very good.

In the chronologically earlier and wonderfully anthropomorphic creation story of Genesis 2:4b–25, God "formed man from the dust of the ground, and breathed into his nostrils the breath of life; and man became a living being" (Gen. 2:7, New Revised Standard Version). Eckhart draws upon this version of the creation myth to emphasize humanity's earthiness, that is, its close relationship to and kinship with the rest of creation as well as the sanctity of the bodiliness of our material nature. Matthew Fox (1983) explains how Eckhart links this earthy story with the concept of humility:

Meister Eckhart . . . points out that the word "humility" comes from the word humus or earth. . . . [T]o be humble means to be in touch with the earth, in touch with one's own earthiness, and to celebrate the blessing that our earthiness, our sensuality, and our passions are. (p. 59)

These three foundational myths give rise to primary understandings that support the various themes in Eckhart's worldview, discussed in detail later:

1. Creation is a gracious gift, the result of the Creator's own creative energy.
2. The creative energy, that is, the Word, remains with the Creator as well as going forth from him.[1]
   a. Accordingly, the Creator is present in all creation, rendering that creation sacred.
   b. The Creator is not separated from the creation.
   c. Furthermore, because it is the result of the Word going forth from the Creator, creation reveals and continues to reveal the Creator.
   d. Creation is an ongoing activity.
3. The creation is good, inspires reverence, and can be appreciated and enjoyed.
4. Human beings are created in the image of God and are accorded divine dignity.
5. God loves the creation, especially human beings.

Matthew Fox (1980) explains the importance of these creation-related concepts to Eckhart's theology in commenting on one of Eckhart's sermons dealing with the Word (in all senses to which reference has been made here) based on Jeremiah 1:9.[2]

All of Meister Eckhart's theology can be understood as an exegesis of or development of the biblical concept of Dabhar or Word. This is the Word with which Genesis begins the Scriptures—it is the dynamic, active word that, when spoken, creates. God said, "Let there be light" and there was light, we are told. God's Word gets things done. Thus Eckhart can say that the Father or Creator is a speaking action—who truly creates and does not merely cogitate about truth or about creating. So full of mystery and power is this creative Word who is God that we humans are left dumb and speechless by the beauty of creation. Creation is almost too holy for us, surely too holy for mere human words. "The entire created order is sacred," says Eckhart. Like all truthful and authentic words, this Word of God both left God and remained within God: God's exit is his entrance, we are told. . . .

And yet God has spoken a divine word in creation itself. There is revelation in creation and natural things—the existence of a stone reveals God—and all creatures may indeed echo God. Creatures are an echo of the divine, they are a communication of the divine. . . .

All creation is good and gift-giving. It is itself a blessing from God. Creatures—all of them—are a divine blessing and a word from God. It is in their activities and in expressing their fullest potential that creatures echo God most loudly. . . .

Eckhart has said that all creatures are words of God and elsewhere he explains that "the purpose of a word is to reveal" (Quint, 1963, p. 421). Thus again, all creation itself is forever going on. It is a process we can experience daily. (Fox, 1980, pp. 60–61)

The various themes that arise from these foundational myths interweave to form the *via positiva*. This first of four paths of Meister Eckhart's contemplative theology will now be examined in detail as a series of themes.

CREATION IS A GRACIOUS GIFT

According to Meister Eckhart, we first experience God in creation. "For Eckhart, creation is itself a grace. It is an experience of the Creator who is profoundly present in creation" (Fox, 1981, p. 220).

The first path that we are to travel in our deepening journey . . . is the pathway of creation. For Eckhart, creation is a revelation of God, a home for God and a temple for God. It is a grace, an overflow of the goodness and beauty that God is. For Eckhart, "being is God," and our spiritual depth depends on our ability to grasp this truth. For while all beings are equal and are words and revelations of God, humans have a unique capacity, due to their having been created in the image and likeness of God, to relate to all of being and to return to their primordial origins, which are in God. The journey of return and renewal is a return to the truth of creation: namely, that creatures, like fish in an ocean, swim in an ocean of divine grace. Our spiritual journey is waking up to the divine sea in which we swim. The return is not a narcissistic return but a refreshing and energizing one which is meant to renew us to ourselves, carry on the holy work of creation and birthing (Path Three below) and even of the new creation which will be known as compassion (Path Four below). For one reason we should return to creation is to learn what human history has done to destroy its goodness and to detract from its divinity.

Creation for Eckhart is a blessing. (Fox, 1980, p. 55)

In the contemplative approach to life, the created, material world is neither a burden to be managed nor a possession to be exploited, but a gift to be enjoyed. Furthermore, just as a gift reveals something of the giver, the creation—mountains, seas, skies, food, drink, relationships—reveals the generosity and majesty of the one who brought it into being. An exploration of the wonders of the created universe, a tasting of the world around us, can be seen as a grateful response to the generosity of the gift-giver.

THE PRESENCE OF THE CREATOR IN ALL OF CREATION RENDERS IT SACRED

Although Eckhart was condemned by the Inquisition for being a *pantheist*, that is, for allegedly asserting that "everything that is, is God," thereby denying and destroying God's transcendence, Eckhart is, in fact, a *panentheist*, asserting instead that "God is *in* all things. The more he is in things, the more he is outside things; the more he is within, the more he is without" (Clark & Skinner, 1958, p. 58, emphasis added). Panentheism is the perspective that the divine is present in all things, one effect of which is the possibility (or even anticipation) of experiencing the sacred in whatever one encounters (Fox, 1981, p. 218).

> [Eckhart] rejects all subject-object images for God's and humankind's relationship and instead insists on how all is in God and God is in all things. "God created all things in such a way that they are not outside himself, as ignorant people falsely imagine. Everything that God creates or does he does or creates in himself." (pp. 217–218).

Anthropologists have highlighted the reverence with which certain so-called primitive cultures approach the natural world. Although the worldview supporting this reverence differs from the worldview of the contemplative, the experience of various indigenous cultures may offer some insight into the effect of one's operating paradigm (often presented in the form of myth, rite, and symbol) on how one interacts with nature or material things. A recent photographic essay in the *National Geographic* on the Koryak people of Russia's Kamchatka provides an example of the effect of the sacralization of creation (in this case, animals) on how one conducts one's everyday affairs.

> "Forgive us, reindeer," the Koryak of northern Kamchatka say as they chase their animals with lariats, pull them from the herd, and dispatch them with a spear. . . . [T]he Koryak . . . remain spiritually bound to the animals that assure their survival in this life and beyond. Only the spirits of the deer, they believe, can deliver human souls to "the other side." Thus an animal must die for a departed human. In giving water to the dead deer [accompanying photograph shows woman pouring water into the dead deer's mouth], the utmost respect is paid for its sacrifice.
>
> Honoring their dead kin, the Koryak cook and eat every scrap of meat from the first day's harvest of sacrificial reindeer. On the second day, ritual acts—like the daubing of deer blood on children's faces—continue as the regular harvest begins. (Hodgson, 1994, pp. 62–67)

For the contemplative, the world is not divided into the sacred and the not-sacred. Every encounter with the physical universe has the potential for an experience of the holy, the transcendent. The creation is dripping with the sacred presence.

THE CREATOR IS NOT SEPARATED FROM CREATION

The significance of Eckhart's panentheism is that he rejects the dualism between God and the creation. "Still respecting the transcendence of God, he grasps as a primary starting point the fact of all being in God and God in all" (Fox, 1981, p. 218). This basic approach to life or this worldview of Eckhart, the contemplative, is in contrast to the Enlightenment view that the Creator is separate and detached from the creation, that is, the metaphor of God as a watchmaker who winds up the universe and then sits back and watches it go.

> In the infinite and multi-populated universe conceived by seventeenth-century scientists and philosophers the conception of a universe constructed by atoms which move forever in accordance with a few God-given laws changed many men's image of the Deity Himself. In the clockwork universe God frequently appeared to be only the clockmaker, the Being who had shaped the atomic parts, established the laws of their motion, set them to work, and then left them to run themselves. Deism, an elaborated version of this view, was an important ingredient in late seventeenth- and eighteenth-century thought. As it advanced, the belief in miracles declined, for miracles were a suspension of mechanical law and a direct intervention by God and his angels in terrestrial affairs. By the end of the eighteenth century, an increasing number of men, scientists and nonscientists alike, saw no need to posit the existence of God. (Kuhn, 1957, pp. 262–263)

For Eckhart and his fellow contemplatives, the universe is alive and dynamic. Creation is a continuing process—a process in which the creation is involved.

CREATION REVEALS THE CREATOR

Every creature is a revelation. For Eckhart, all of creation and existence reveal the divine because they are of God. Drawing on the images of God creating the universe by means of spoken word,[3] Eckhart affirms in one of his sermons,

> All creatures are words of God. My mouth expresses and reveals God but the existence of a stone does the same and people often recognize more from actions than from words. . . . All creatures may echo God in all their activities. It is, of course, just a small bit which they can reveal. (Fox, 1980, p. 55)

Twentieth-century contemplative monk Thomas Merton reflects on God's glory as revealed in ordinary creatures, each in its own way:

[E]ach particular being, in its individuality, its concrete nature and entity, with all its own characteristics and its private qualities and its own inviolable identity, gives glory to God by being precisely what He wants it to be here and now, in the circumstances ordained for it by His love and His infinite Art.

The forms and individual characters of living and growing things, of inanimate beings, of animals and flowers and all nature, constitute their holiness in the sight of God. . . .

The special clumsy beauty of this particular colt on this April day in this field under these clouds is a holiness consecrated to God by His own creative wisdom and it declares the glory of God.

The pale flowers of the dogwood outside this window are saints. The little yellow flowers that nobody notices on the edge of that road are saints looking up into the face of God.

This leaf has its own texture and its own pattern of veins and its own holy shape, and the bass and the trout hiding in the deep pools of the river are canonized by their beauty and their strength.

The lakes hidden among the hills are saints, and the sea too is a saint who praises God without interruption in her majestic dance.

The great, gashed, half-naked mountain is another of God's saints. There is no other like him. He is alone in his own character; nothing else in the world ever did or ever will imitate God in quite the same way. That is his sanctity. (Merton, 1961, pp. 30–31)

Thus, in the contemplative paradigm, there is value in being present to the created world, of becoming acquainted with it on intimate terms. In much the same way that a lover of fine paintings will sit and listen to what a work of art has to say, the contemplative can watch and listen to what the material world has to reveal—whether through natural phenomena or the aspects of creation that are the work of human hands.

THE CREATION IS GOOD AND HOLY

"All that is is holy for Eckhart—star and caterpillars, stones and flowers, you and me. . . . Eckhart's spirituality . . . makes demands on our everyday awareness of the holy all about us" (Fox, 1981, p. 221).

Thomas Merton, in a chapter entitled "Everything That Is, Is Holy," develops this theme and debunks what he sees as popular misconceptions about the contemplative's relationship to things.

There is no evil in anything created by God, nor can anything of His become an obstacle to our union with Him. The obstacle is in our "self," that is to say in the tenacious need to maintain our separate, external egoistic will. It is when we refer all things to this outward and false "self" that we alienate ourselves from reality and from God. It is then the false self that is our god, and we love everything for the sake of this self. We use all things for the worship of this idol which is our imaginary self. In doing so we pervert and corrupt things, or rather we turn our relationship to them into a corrupt and sinful relationship. We do not thereby make them evil, but we use them to increase our attachment to our illusory self.

Those who try to escape from this situation by treating the good things of God as if they were evils are only confirming themselves in a terrible illusion. They are like Adam blaming Eve and Eve blaming the serpent in Eden. "Woman tempted me. Wine has tempted me. Food has tempted me. Woman is pernicious, wine is poison, food is death. I must hate and revile them. By hating them I will please God . . ." These are the thoughts and attitudes of a baby, of a savage and of an idolater who seeks by magic incantations and spells to protect his egotistic self and placate the insatiable little god in his own heart. To take such an idol for God is the worst kind of self-deception. It turns a man into a fanatic, no longer capable of sustained contact with the truth, no longer capable of genuine love.

In trying to believe in their ego as something "holy" these fanatics look upon everything else as unholy.

It is not true that the saints and the great contemplatives never loved created things, and had no understanding or appreciation of the world, with its sights and sounds and the people living in it. They loved everything and everyone.

Do you think that their love of God was compatible with a hatred for things that reflected Him and spoke of Him on every side?

You will say that they were supposed to be absorbed in God and they had no eyes to see anything but Him. Do you think they walked around with faces like stones and did not listen to the voices of men speaking to them or understand the joys and sorrows of those who were around them?

It was because the saints were absorbed in God that they were truly capable of seeing and appreciating created things and it was because they loved Him alone that they alone loved everybody.

Some men seem to think that a saint cannot possibly take a natural interest in anything created. . . .

A saint is capable of loving created things and enjoying the use of them and dealing with them in a perfectly simple, natural manner.

The saint knows that the world and everything made by God is good, while those who are not saints either think that created things are unholy, or else they don't bother about the question one way or another because they are only interested in themselves.

The eyes of the saint make all beauty holy and the hands of the saint consecrate everything they touch to the glory of God. (Merton, 1961, pp. 21–25)

Eckhart rejects the body-soul dualism and recognizes the unity of body and soul and the goodness of both. The body and the senses are a blessing and are to be appreciated.

Eckhart says that the soul travels into all parts of the body, and thus establishes a unity. . . . We are not divided, body against soul, but are one entity. . . . Not only are body and soul one for Eckhart, but they form an intimate unity. . . . We have seen . . . how noble and divine the soul of the human person is, but the body too is noble. All things corporal are noble, he declares. After all, they all share the grace of existence. Eckhart conceives of the relationship of soul and body as a relation of friends, not of objects at war. He says, "The soul loves the body" (Quint, vol. II, p. 747). This attitude of mutual interdependence between soul and body is . . . very much unlike Platonic ideas about conflict that the Augustinian tradition presumes. (Fox, 1980, p. 122)

Also, for Eckhart, the various senses "are vehicles for good persons who see, feel, taste, hear to their profit whether the objects of such senses be good or bad" (Fox, 1980, p. 123). It is possible to experience the holy through the sensual enjoyment of life.

[Senses] are the "ins" and "outs" through which the soul goes out into the world, and through these ins and outs the world, in turn, goes to the soul. . . . I am certain that whatever good people see will improve them. If they see bad things, they will thank God for guarding them from such things and ask God to convert people in whom there is evil. If they see goodness, however, they will long to have it accomplished in themselves. (Quint, 1963, p. 296)

ORDINARY EXPERIENCES INVITE REVERENCE AND DISCLOSE THE AWE

This panentheistic approach to life shapes how one will relate to the mundane, the material, the ordinary. Each encounter with the creation, whether a magnificent sunset or an insignificant sparrow or a fellow human being, retains the potential for manifesting life's deepest significance. This approach invites one to receive ordinary experiences with reverence and to approach the ordinary as one would approach holy ground.

Eckhart uses the story of Jacob's ladder to illustrate Jacob's dawning awareness of God's presence. Jacob dreams of a ladder reaching up into heaven. God stands over Jacob and announces that God will give Jacob and his descendants the land on which he is sleeping. God promises to keep Jacob safe and never desert him. Jacob awakes and says, "'Surely the Lord is in this place—and I did not know it!' And he was afraid, and said, 'How awesome is this place! This is none other than the house of God, and this is the gate of heaven'" (Genesis 28:16–17, New Revised Standard Version). Eckhart states:

I am as certain as I am that I am a man that nothing is so "near" to me as God. God is nearer to me than myself. My being depends on the fact that

God is "near" to me and present for me. He is also near and present for a stone or piece of wood, but they *know* nothing about this fact. If a piece of wood knew about God and perceived how "near" he is to it, as the highest angel perceives this fact, then the piece of wood would be just as happy as the highest angel. And for this reason people are happier than a stone or piece of wood because they are aware of God and *know* how "near" God is. And I am all the happier to the extent that I am aware of this fact. I am all the less happy to the extent that I am unaware of it. I am not happy because God is within me or "near" me or because I possess him, but rather because I am *aware* of how "near" God is and because I *know* about God. In the Psalms the prophet says, "You should not be unknowing like a mule or horse." The patriarch Jacob makes another statement: "Truly God is in this place, and I never knew it!" ...

When I reflect on the "kingdom of God," I am often left mute by its greatness. For the "kingdom of God" is God himself with all his wealth. . . . Whoever *knows* and is aware *how near* the kingdom of God is can say with Jacob: "God is in this place, and I never knew it!" ...

God is equally near to all creatures. The wise man says in Ecclesiasticus: God has his net, his hunter's ploy, spread out over all creatures. . . . Thus all people can find him in everything, so long as they can penetrate this net filled with creatures and keep God in mind and recognize God in everything. Thus we find a teacher saying that the person who knows God most truly is the one who can find him equally in all things. (Fox, 1980, pp. 137–138; see also Quint, ed., 1958–1976, vol. III, #68)

Fifteenth-century mystic Nicholas of Cusa echoes the theme of the divine within the ordinary:

Divinity
is the unfolding and enfolding of
everything that is.
Divinity
is in all things in such a way
that all things are in divinity. (Yockey, 1987, p. 29)

CREATION SLOWLY UNFOLDS AND REVEALS ITS WONDERS

Another aspect of Eckhart's contemplative approach to creation is that the contemplative receives life first as a gift, innocently and with gratitude, waiting patiently for the wonder of life to unfold and reveal itself, much as a rosebud comes eventually into full bloom. There is a receptive listening to the undercurrents of life that surge below surface concerns. This is an attitude of reverence to all of life. It is an honoring of the ordinary. Adopting a contemplative stance, one can take pleasure in the mundane moment and be open to the deep sense of joy and wonder that can well up in the midst of ordinary experiences. It is possible to stop, look, and listen—and celebrate for no particular reason. Life is good as it is—not perhaps as one would like it to be or think it should be. This theme is closely related to themes in the *via negativa* concerning the need for silent listening and letting go of control.

LIFE CAN BE EMBRACED, ENJOYED, AND SAVORED FOR ITS OWN SAKE

Because creation is a gracious gift, life can be embraced as it comes to human beings and enjoyed and savored on its own terms. The contemplative can receive life as it is.

> And, as Eckhart points out, "all honey-sweetness comes from God." The source of all authentic pleasure is God. Anyone who has taken time to savor the blessings of life knows that they are profoundly, deliciously, deeply sweet. And naturally so. (Fox, 1983, p. 52)

Sights and sounds are absorbed first without abstraction or judgment. They are experienced on their own terms without any intervention or effort. Dorothy Sölle reflects on the possible responses on seeing a flower. The first is a simple appreciation, "ah!" The next three responses recognize the flower's beauty but move beyond a simple appreciation. It is beautiful, and I want it—but I will just let it as it is. It is beautiful, I want it, and I cannot let it be—so I will take it with me. It is beautiful—so I will sell it. The final response is the disinterested exhalation, "So?" (Sölle, 1979, vol. 36, #10).

The first response is the simple appreciation with no need to judge the experience, abstract it, or even give it a name. Neither is there any need to use or sell or otherwise develop the beauty one encounters. Flowers, people, and experiences are appreciated for what they are, without concern for their utility or for how one thinks they ought to be, or how one would like them to be. There is no need to pick the flower, sell it, or find a use for it—but neither is the flower to be ignored or dismissed. There is a quality of simple presence to what one encounters.

> In that first flash of meeting there is always an "Ah!"—a quality of simple presence. It comes and goes so fast that we usually miss it altogether. That flash of presence is likely to reveal itself when we are not primed to get or fear something. Thus we are more likely to allow it breathing room when we are on vacation than in the middle of work. In that "looser" time we are slowed down a bit. We let life be a little longer before we do something to it. Sitting peacefully on the porch in the evening we find ourselves just present "in" the sunset, or in the play of children, or in our friend's hummed tune. (Edwards, 1977, p. 140)

Tilden Edwards expands upon this concept of simple presence in a later work in which he introduces contemplative exercises using icons and distinguishes among innocent seeing, split seeing, and participative seeing.

Innocent seeing is the wide open, uncritical, drinking in of what is before us. "When we open our eyes to look, just as when we open our ears to hear, there is an instant before we separate from what we see in order to interpret it with our minds. We are just present *in* what we see, with an open innocence" (Edwards, 1987, p. 44). It is the unpretentious, ignorant, unselfconscious gaze of a child.

Split seeing takes over when we objectify what we see, when we separate ourselves from the object. We are conscious of ourselves. "The innocent flash fades as our minds step outside the unity in order to see through the mind's interpretive power. . . . Desires rise in concert with this sense of separateness: to reach out and possess in word or fact what we no longer are part of, or to protect what now feels vulnerably separate" (Edwards, 1987, pp. 44–45). Our logical-rational training allows us to relate to the world analytically. Scientific and industrial advances are grounded in our ability to analyze and manipulate the natural world. However,

> [t]he bitter fruit is the tendency of this way of seeing to imperially define itself as the only valid way of seeing. . . . [T]his way of seeing has almost totally eclipsed the participative, contemplative way of seeing (and thus, knowing) that was widely affirmed in the Church prior to the sixteenth century (with some exceptions since then in the realm of the arts and continuing contemplative traditions). (Edwards, 1987, p. 45)

Participative seeing is different from either innocent seeing or split seeing and is the threshold of contemplative awareness. One is innocently present but with the addition of "an intentional quality of energetic awareness" (p. 45).

> Such participative seeing qualifies our understanding of analytical insight. . . . It is possible to see analytically without finally separating from either the situation or God. However, our confused, willful egos easily bury this reality and we then find this spiritual eye blinded, leaving our sight controlled by our grasping, protecting, split-off little-self consciousness. (p. 45)

For the contemplative, there is an alternative to analyzing, judging, or abstracting an experience, although these responses are also available to the contemplative. An ordinary encounter, a mundane experience—or an extraordinary experience or encounter—can be received on its own terms, without having to be explained. Eckhart comments,

"[T]he only way to live is like a rose which lives without a why" (Fox, 1982, p. 30).

CREATED IN THE IMAGE OF GOD, HUMAN BEINGS ARE HELD IN REVERENCE

For Eckhart, although God is present in all that exists, human beings are particularly held in reverence. According to the Genesis creation myth, human beings are created "in the image of God" (Genesis 1:27) and the likeness of the Creator. In one of his sermons Eckhart develops this creation theme:

> Then God said: "Let us make one like us." To create is an easy thing; one does it when and how one will. But what I make I make myself and with myself and in myself, and I impress my image into it fully (J. Clark, p. 182).
> When God made man, he wrought an equal work in the soul, his active and eternal work. The work was great and it was nothing other than the soul, and the soul was God's work. (Fox, 1981, p. 223)

There is a special relationship between the Creator and humankind that is beyond the relationship between God and the rest of creation. Eckhart, in his sermon entitled "The Greatness of the Human Person," explicates the relationship between the soul and God.

> Now the prophet is astonished over two things. First he marvels over God's activities with the stars, the moon and the sun. But second, he marvels at something concerning the soul—namely that God has done so many great things with it and on its behalf and still continues to do them, for God does what he wants for the soul's sake. He does countless great things for the soul's sake and is fully occupied with it and this because of the greatness in which the soul is made. . . . Note that the concern is how great the soul is. I form a letter according to the image of that letter in me, in my soul, but not according to my soul itself. It is very much the same with God. God made everything according to the image that he had of all things, but not according to himself. He made some things in a very special way according to what flows from himself—like goodness, wisdom, and whatever qualities we attribute to God. But the soul is what God made, not only according to the image which is in him or even according to what flows from himself and what we humans can express of him. The soul is what is truly made in God's own image, in the image of all that he is according to his nature, according to his Being, and according to his outflowing, yet remaining within works, and according to the ground where he remains himself, where he gives birth to his only begotten Son and from which the Holy Spirit blossoms. It is according to this outflowing, yet remaining within works, that God has made the soul. (Fox, 1980, pp. 102–103; see also Quint, 1958–1976, vol. I, #24)

In the same sermon, Meister Eckhart deals directly with human nature[4] and its relation to the divine, using the story of the Incarnation.

> The masters say that human nature has nothing to do with time and is completely unmovable and much more inward and present to a person than the person is to himself or herself. And this is why God took on human nature and united it with his Person. Thus the human nature became God, for God assumed the pure human nature and not a human person. So if you want to be this same Christ and God, empty yourself of everything which the eternal Word did not assume. The eternal Word did not assume a human being, so empty yourself of everything which is purely personal and peculiarly you and assume human nature purely, then you will be the same in the eternal Word as human nature is in him. *For your human nature and that of the divine Word are no different—it's one and the same.* What it is in Christ, it is in you. (Fox, 1980, p. 104; emphasis added)

Colledge and McGinn (1981), in explaining this aspect of Eckhart's theology, that is, that the eternal Word took upon himself human nature rather than a human person, point to the ethical implications for relating to other human beings.

> [I]n taking up a human nature rather than a human person, the Word has provided the grounds for our obligation to love all persons equally and without distinction. We must love human nature in them, not what is distinct, that is, human personality. (p. 46)

According to Fox, Eckhart's focus with regard to the Genesis creation myth is the divine image in which human beings were created rather than the fall of humanity dramatized in the expulsion of Adam and Eve from Eden. This approach to the origins of human beings is reflected in the concept of human nature for Eckhart.

> It is not original sin that occupies Eckhart's interest in the creation story but the divine in the very nature of every human being. "How nobly humanity is constituted by nature" he exclaims, for "the seed of God is in us. If it was cultivated by a good, wise, and industrious laborer, it would thrive all the more and would grow up to God, whose seed it is, and the fruit would be like the divine seed. The seed of a pear tree grows into a pear tree, a hazel seed into a hazel tree, a seed of God into God" (Clark & Skinner, pp. 149, 151). The nobility of humans, indeed their divinity, is potential only. It is a seed. It needs work, as Eckhart says, "good, wise, industrious labor" in order to come to fruition. The work is not so much one of being freed from an original sin as it is a return to our divine origins. . . . The fall for Eckhart . . . is a fall into superficiality or, in his words, a fall into the "outer" rather than the "inner" person. The fall then is *our* fall and not an inherited one only. It is up to us to fall out of the superficial and outer person and into the deep, full, and divine one. The superficial or

outer person is vulnerable to "what is wicked, evil, and devilish" while the rooted or inner person is "the field in which God has sowed his image and his likeness . . . the seed of divine nature (Clark & Skinner, p. 150).

We see then that Eckhart's optimism toward human nature is not based on a naive repression of the human potential for the demonic, nor on a denial of sin. Rather it is . . . an emphasis on the goodness of creation as described in the first chapters of Genesis. (Fox, 1981, pp. 223–224)

Thus, Eckhart does not adhere to a naive, Pollyanna–inspired view of human nature. He faces the reality of evil and destruction and understands such occurrences as particularly tragic inasmuch as they are a denial of and rebellion from the original, divine nature of human beings. (The via negativa, later, addresses the paradox of evil within a good creation, particularly as manifested in humanity.)

For the contemplative, the Incarnation also is a radical affirmation of humanity, that is, God took upon himself flesh and blood and became a real human being. It is also a radical affirmation of God's steadfast love for humanity. In a somewhat earthy illustration in one of his German sermons Eckhart dramatizes not only how the Incarnation is a sign of God's love for humanity, but also that humanity, although created in God's image, is not perfect.

The greatest good that God ever performed for man was that he became man. I ought to tell a story that is very apposite here. There were a rich husband and a wife. Then the wife suffered a misfortune through which she lost an eye, and she was much distressed by this. Then her husband came to her and said: "Madam, why are you so distressed? You should not distress yourself so, because you have lost your eye." Then she said: "Sir, I am not distressing myself about the fact that I have lost my eye; what distresses me is that it seems to me that you will love me less because of it." Then he said: "Madam, I do love you." Not long after that he gouged out one of his own eyes and came to his wife and said: "Madam, to make you believe that I love you, I have made myself like you; now I too have only one eye." This stands for man, who could scarcely believe that God loved him so much, until God gouged out one of his own eyes and took upon himself human nature. (Colledge & McGinn, 1981, p. 193)

This story leads into the final theme of the via positiva, the love between God and humankind.

GOD AND HUMAN BEINGS ARE IN A PASSIONATE LOVE RELATIONSHIP

This final theme has been interwoven throughout the earlier discussion and will be implicit in the explication of the remaining three paths. According to Eckhart, God is in love with humanity and eternally seeks to be united with the ones he has created. Both the Creation and the Incarnation are acts of love. Human beings, in turn, have a seed of God's love that is planted within them that causes them continually to long for God and seek to return to God, to be reunited.

Drawing upon the metaphor of a seed that is planted by God, Eckhart begins with the creation of human beings in the image of God.

> God has sowed his image and his likeness, and . . . he sows the good seed, the roots of all wisdom, all knowledge, all virtues, all goodness—the seed of the divine nature. The seed of divine nature is the Son of God, the Word of God. (Quint, 1963, p. 41; Fox, 1980, p. 118)

This seed must mature and grow. This seed planted by God cannot be ignored. It has an eternal persistence and a homing instinct for God.

> God himself has sown this seed, and inserted it and borne it. Thus while this seed may be crowded, hidden away, and never cultivated, it will still never be obliterated. It glows and shines, gives off light, burns, and is unceasingly inclined toward God. (Quint, 1963, p. 141; Fox, 1980, p. 118)

Eckhart states that this seed is the Word of God. "It cannot be covered up, silenced, or forgotten for long. . . . Seeds grow and need to grow. So do we; so does the divine seed within us" (Fox, 1980, p. 118).

The only limit to the growth of this seed is God. "The ambition of the soul to expand into its divine dimensions is a starting point for spiritual growth. Our discontent ought to be recognized. . . . The soul will not rest content with anything smaller than God" (Fox, 1980, pp. 118–119). Human beings have an eternal longing for God. "[W]e are admonished not to flee from dissatisfaction but to recognize it as the starting point for a divine adventure" (p. 119). Using the image of a vortex, Eckhart dramatizes how the soul is drawn to its divine origins.

> [The human spirit] does not allow itself to be satisfied with that light (which is come down from heaven). It storms the firmament, and scales the heavens until it reaches the spirit that drives the heavens. As a result of heaven's revolution, everything in the world flourishes and bursts into leaf. The spirit, however, is never satisfied; it presses on ever further into the vortex (or whirlpool) and primary source in which the spirit has its origins. (Quint, 1963, p. 291; Fox, 1980, p. 120)

This theme of an eternal longing for God, a passionate desire to be reunited with the One who loves human beings, to return home, is a recurring theme in contemplative literature. The poetry of St. John of the Cross, the 16th-century Carmelite Spanish mystic, is rich in imagery of the love affair between the soul and God. In *The Spiritual Canticle:*

Songs Between the Soul and the Bridegroom, John captures the longing of the soul for God.

1. Where have You hidden,
Beloved, and left me moaning?
You fled like the stag
After wounding me;
I went out calling You, and You were gone.

2. Shepherds, you that go
Up through the sheepfolds to the hill,
If by chance you see
Him I love most,
Tell Him that I sicken, suffer and die.

3. Seeking my Love
I will head for the mountains and for watersides,
I will not gather flowers,
Nor fear wild beasts;
I will go beyond strong men and frontiers.

4. O woods and thickets
Planted by the hand of my Beloved!
O green meadow,
Coated, bright, with flowers,
Tell me, has He passed by you? (Kavanaugh & Rodriguez, 1979, p. 410)

In John's poetry there is often a bittersweet and even painful character to the longing for union with God. The imagery John uses in *The Living Flame of Love* exhibits a wild passion in the relationship between God and human beings.

STANZAS WHICH THE SOUL RECITES

In the intimate union with God, its beloved Bridegroom

1. O living flame of love
That tenderly wounds my soul
In its deepest center! Since
Now You are not oppressive,
Now Consummate! if it be Your will:
Tear through the veil of this sweet encounter!

2. O sweet cautery,
O delightful wound!
O gentle hand! O delicate touch

That tastes of eternal life
And pays every debt!
In killing You changed death to life.

3. O lamps of fire!
In whose splendors
The deep caverns of feeling,
Once obscure and blind,
Now give forth, so rarely, so exquisitely,
Both warmth and light to their Beloved.

4. How gently and lovingly
You wake in my heart,
Where in secret You dwell alone;
And in Your sweet breathing,
Filled with good and glory,
How tenderly You swell my heart with love. (Kavanaugh & Rodriguez, 1979, pp. 578–579)

This theme of God's love for his creation and the unquenchable desire of the human creature for reunion with God is also found in the writings of Julian of Norwich, a fourteenth- to fifteenth-century English mystic. Her work offers a wealth of examples, of which the following is only one:

In our making he first knitted us and joined us to himself. By this joining we are kept as clean and as noble as we were created to be. By virtue of the same precious joining, we love our maker and become like him, praise and thank him, and endlessly rejoice in him. (Del Mastro, 1977, p. 187)

Gerald May, too, speaks of this attraction to God, this longing to love God in return, and identifies it as the deepest desire of our hearts.[5] Introducing his discussion on addiction and freedom, May (1988) draws upon Meister Eckhart:

God creates us out of love, or perhaps, as the fourteenth-century German mystic Meister Eckhart is supposed to have said, out of the laughter of the Trinity, which is the same thing. . . . I am certain that [this love] draws us toward itself by means of our own deepest desires . . . that this love wants us to have free will. We are intended to make free choices. Psychologically, we are not completely determined by our conditioning; we are not puppets or automatons. Spiritually, our freedom allows us to choose as we wish for or against God, life, and love. The love that creates us may be haunting, but it is not enslaving; it is eternally present, yet endlessly open.

    It seems to me that free will is given to us for a purpose: so that we may choose freely, without coercion or manipulation, to love God in return, and to love one another in a similarly perfect way. *This is the deepest desire of our hearts.* In other words, our creation is by love, in love, and for love. It is both our birthright and our authentic destiny to participate fully in this creative loving, and freedom of will is essential for this participation to occur. (p. 13, emphasis added)

The via positiva has, indeed, a positive character. It is a way of love, appreciation, gratitude, reverence, awe, and wonder—all in the context of ordinary human life rather than being limited to special experiences available only to a few. The sacred bleeds through the mundane and the routine. For the contemplative, there is no such thing as an insignificant time or place or person. Each moment, each encounter with the created world, each human relationship, has the possibility for revelation of the divine—if a person is awake to it. The via positiva grounds the contemplative in the universe in a positive and significant way.

NOTES

1. This concept is an allusion to the Incarnation. Eckhart explains this reference in a sermon, which is explained in more detail later:

> God is a Word which speaks itself. Wherever God is, there he speaks this Word; wherever he is not, there he does not speak. God is spoken and unspoken. The Father is a speaking action and the Son is an active speech. What is in me goes out from me; if I am only thinking it, then my word reveals it and yet remains inside me. It is in this way that the Father speaks the unspoken Son and yet the Son remains in the Father. I have often said that God's exit is his entrance (Fox, 1980, p. 57). See also "Misit dominus manu suam et tetiget os meum et dixit mihi . . . Ecce constitui te super gentes et regna" (Quint, 1958–1976, vol. II, #53).

2. "Misit dominus manu suam et tetiget os meum et dixit mihi . . . Ecce constitui te super gentes et regna" ["The Lord has stretched his hand out and has touched my mouth and has spoken to me . . . See, today I appoint you over nations and over kingdoms."] [Jer. 1:10] (Quint, 1958–1976, vol. II, #53).

3. See, for example, Genesis 1:3–1:24. Here God says, "Let there be . . .," and that aspect of the creation comes into being solely by the power of God's word.

4. Admittedly, Eckhart may not be using this concept in the same manner as 20th-century writers.

5. May, of course, is not the first to describe this longing in such a manner.

12

The Fourfold Path: Detachment

As indicated previously, each of the four paths of the contemplative journey is a way of experiencing God. The first path, the via positiva, the way of appreciation, focuses on the material creation, including the vast wealth of sensory input of sights, sounds, smells, words, images, ideas, and imagination. This is the way of experiencing God (or entering into the contemplative experience) through sunsets, Beethoven, crackling dish-detergent bubbles, icons, a freshly cut watermelon, incense, dance, chant, a child's smile, stories, good sex, or a starlit night. This way includes a deep appreciation for what is, an enjoyment of the wonders of life, gratitude for the gift of life. It is a celebration of creation—and of the Creator.

The via negativa, or the second path, is also a way of experiencing God or entering into the contemplative experience, but in a startlingly different way. It is an encounter with God in the absence of images, ideas, imagination, or sensory input. It involves an entering into the dark, the emptiness, the silence and a letting go of concepts, symbols, understandings, and images.

Eckhart says that the way to God is not a burden but a blessing. "The path is beautiful and pleasant and joyful and familiar." And so, from our experience in Path One with the blessing that creation is as it flows out but remains within the Creator, that is the case. . . . However, Eckhart is not naive about the brokenness of the way we perceive creation and interact with it. "Every angel is with his whole joy and his whole bliss inside me and God himself with his whole bliss. Yet I do not perceive this."

In Path Two, then, Eckhart deals with how we heal our broken ways of seeing and loving the world. "We love everything according to our own goodness," he declares. If we could heal our own goodness we could begin to heal the things we love. In the first path, that of creation, we have traveled the *via positiva* toward the cataphatic God or the God of light, of being, of life, of creation. In this path we travel the *via negativa* toward an apophatic God, the unnamable, hidden, dark God of nothingness. Neither way to God is a way of fear, however. For this path too is a path that is "beautiful and pleasant and joyful and familiar." (Fox, 1980, p. 166)

It may be helpful at this point, as the discussion shifts from the via positiva (Path One) to the via negativa (Path Two), to examine the oft-made distinction between two major branches of contemplative or mystical tradition, the *apophatic* tradition (associated more with Path Two) and the *kataphatic* (or *cataphatic*) tradition (more associated with Path One).

The Catholic tradition is marked, moreover, by two different approaches to the mystical life. First, there is the via negativa, the apophatic way, which stresses that because God is the ever-greater God, so radically different from any creature, God is best known by negation, elimination, forgetting, unknowing, without images and symbols, and in darkness. God is "not this, not that." All images, thoughts, symbols, etc. must be eliminated, because, as St. John of the Cross points out, "all the being of creatures compared with the infinite being of God is nothing. . . . Nothing which could possibly be imagined or comprehended in this life can be a proximate means of union with God" (Kavanaugh & Rodriguez, 1973, pp. 79, 127).

Secondly, there is the *via affirmativa*, the kataphatic way, which underscores finding God in all things. It emphasizes a definite similarity between God and creatures, that God can be reached by creatures, images and symbols, because He has manifested Himself in creation and salvation history. The incarnational dimension of Christianity, too, forces the mystic to take seriously God's self-revelation in history and in symbols. (Egan, 1978, p. 403)

Egan (1978) later explains that *apophatic* and *kataphatic* are not discrete categories but that "each way contains certain elements of the other way" (p. 422). Nevertheless, these two paths described in the theology of Meister Eckhart represent polar opposites in the contemplative tradition.

In interpreting Eckhart, Fox (1981) raises the question of why a second path is needed at all if God can be experienced through any and all of creation.

> The first reason why creation is not the only experience of God is that creation is limited while God is not. Creation is not big enough, one might say, for Eckhart's spiritual expectations. . . . God is so much vaster than creatures. . . . The point of a needle is larger in relation to the entire sky than is the whole universe in relation to God, he points out. (p. 225)

Fox also explores the relationship of these two paths.

> When the Via Negativa is ignored, the prophetic voice is invariably silenced. Life becomes superficial, easily manipulated, and ultimately as boring as it is violent. And, above all, cheap. For while the Via Positiva teaches us the cosmic *breadth* of living, of our holy relationship to stars and atoms, to royal persons and to blessed bodiliness, the Via Negativa opens us up to our divine *depths*. When one has suffered deep pain and allowed pain to be pain, one can visit the Grand Canyon and learn that it has nothing on the human person who is even deeper and more powerfully carved over millions of years by the flowing tides of pain. . . .
>
> There is no Via Negativa without a Via Positiva. How can one let go of what one has not fallen in love with? The depth of nothingness is directly related to the experience of everythingness. The void is the convex of the concave surface of the cosmos. We learn we are cosmic beings not only in our joy and ecstasy but also in our pain and sorrow. (Fox, 1983, p. 130)

The via negativa is a way of silence, emptiness, detachment, and negation. It involves letting go and letting be.[1] This way of the contemplative includes detaching oneself from all that may give comfort, familiarity, and security—ideas, relationships, work, and material things. Whereas a contemplative exercise within the themes of the via positiva might involve visualization, icons, readings, and ideas—the creation of images—the contemplative exercises found on the via negativa would include, for example, insight meditation, or the letting go of whatever thoughts enter one's mind. Perhaps the experience of sitting motionless—and perhaps lost and disoriented— in a pitch-black underground cavern listening to the silence is the metaphor for the via negativa in the same manner that watching a sunset from a mountaintop might be the metaphor for the via positiva. The via negativa, like the via positiva, brings one to the point of awe and wonder, but rather than the awe and wonder of a beautiful sunset or a Beethoven symphony, the via negativa involves entering into the awe and wonder of emptiness, darkness, surrender, and silence. It is the awesomeness, that is, the fear and fascination, of mysterious unknowing. The via negativa beckons the contemplative to enter the unknown, unfamiliar territory.

Again, as in the first path, Meister Eckhart's theology can be expressed in a number of interconnected themes. Furthermore, whereas the via positiva is deeply rooted in the creation and incarnation myths, the via negativa, in large part arises from the crucifixion/resurrection myth—or more generally the concept of life arising from death—a freely given death.[2] The Gospels are replete with images of death being necessary for life, of the need to let go or leave behind or take up one's cross, of being born again after entering the womb a second time, of drowning the old self in Baptism—all of which point in the direction of the via negativa.[3] In a typically paradoxical series of sayings concerning detachment from relationships and from one's own life, for example, Jesus tells his followers,

> Whoever loves father or mother more than me is not worthy of me; and whoever loves son or daughter more than me is not worthy of me; and whoever does not take up the cross and follow me is not worthy of me. Those who find their life will lose it, and those who lose their life for my sake will find it. (Mt. 10:37–39, New Revised Standard Version)

In a number of his sermons and commentaries, discussed later, Eckhart develops the concepts of letting go and letting be and explores what it means to surrender, to let go of one's will and knowledge, to be detached from accomplishments and possessions, to wait patiently and to listen to the silence.

RADICAL DETACHMENT ALLOWS APPRECIATION OF CREATION

Though he explicates the wonders of creation in Path One, in Path Two Eckhart directly confronts the issue of why our everyday experience does not always seem so wonder-filled and begins to set forth a rationale for the via negativa.

> Creation is good—divinely good—but are we? "If we had divine love, God and all the works that God ever performed would delight us" (Quint, ed., vol. III, p. 513). Creatures are good but so often they do not give rest to the soul. Why not? Because we do not see with the divine goodness. . . . The problem is the way we relate to creation. "You yourself are the very thing which hinders you. For you are related to things in a perverted way." (Clark & Skinner, 1958, p. 75; Fox, 1980, p. 170)

Eckhart uses the concept of hating from a saying in the Gospel of Luke (paralleling the Matthean saying cited previously) to create a tension with the via positiva, which emphasizes love of creation. "Whoever comes to me and does not hate father and mother, wife and children, brothers and sisters, yes, and even life itself, cannot be my disciple. Whoever does not carry the cross and follow me cannot be my disciple" (Luke 14:26–27, New Revised Standard Version). Fox (1980) explains:

> Eckhart comments immediately on this passage that it means that a person empty himself of his ego, keeping nothing back for himself. But the tension still remains between the via positiva and the via negativa and Eckhart makes no effort to relieve the tension. Rather he invites us to explore the tension in greater depth. For, on the one hand, God is love whom all creatures seek to love. (p. 171)

This tension between the via negativa and the via positiva is manifested in other themes. For example, with regard to the divine presence in creation, Eckhart also says that "everything which is created, in itself is nothing" (Benz & Koch, 1938–1975, vol. II, p. 354; Fox, 1981, p. 225). "All creatures are a mere nothing. I do not say that they are something very slight or something, but that they are a mere nothing" (J. Clark, 1957, p. 80; Fox, 1981, pp. 225–226). As Fox explains further, Eckhart is not creating a dualism but emphasizing that creatures get their existence, their isness, from God. Without God, they are nothing (Fox, 1981, p. 226). Eckhart uses an analogy of color and a colored object to hold the tension, "The color of the wall depends on the wall, and so the existence of creatures depends on the love of God. Separate the color from the wall and it would cease to be. So all creation would cease to exist if separated from the love that God is" (Blakney, 1941, p. 244; Fox, 1981, p. 226). Whereas the via positiva emphasizes that the divine is manifest in all creatures, the via negativa points to the fact that without this divine presence, creation is nothing. The significance of all created things is their embodiment and revelation of the divine presence. They have no intrinsic value or purpose in themselves—their beauty, awe, and wonder is in their pointing to the Creator. When human beings take these created things as valuable and lovable in themselves, without regard to their divine source, Eckhart says, human beings are grasping after and clinging to an empty husk. With such attachment, created things lead human beings away from the source of all creation and the origin of all life and meaning. Whereas the via positiva points to an exploration of the fullness of life, the via negativa leads to an exploration of the emptiness and nothingness of life; in the via positiva there is an invitation to immerse oneself in the creation, whereas the via negativa invites one to let go and let be.

This detachment or letting go and letting be will be considered in the next three themes in terms of detachment from knowledge, from the will, and from possessions.

DETACHMENT FROM WILL AND DESIRE INVITES A SURRENDER

This theme further considers the attitudes or perspectives of poverty, detachment, letting-go, emptying, and surrender. Eckhart uses these terms to describe how human beings may be truly happy. In a sermon dealing with poverty,[4] Eckhart begins with one of the beatitudes from the Sermon on the Mount in the Gospel of Matthew, "Blessed are the poor in spirit, for theirs is the kingdom of heaven" (Mt. 5:3, New Revised Standard Version).

> Now there exist two kinds of poverty: an *external* poverty. . . . Of this poverty I do not want to speak any further. For there is still another kind of poverty, an *inner* poverty, by which our Lord's word is to be understood when he says: "Blessed are the poor in spirit." (Fox, 1980, p. 213)

Eckhart then continues his sermon with a clever comment regarding the need for a poverty of knowing—in order to understand—a concept to which he later alludes: "Now I beg you to be just so poor[5] as to understand this speech. For I tell you by the eternal truth, if you are not equal to this truth of which we now want to speak, then you cannot understand me" (Fox, 1980, p. 213). The sermon then sets forth three characteristics of a poor person:

1. One who wills nothing
2. One who knows nothing
3. One who has nothing

Eckhart begins with a discussion of poverty of will, distancing himself from what he considers to be incorrect interpretations of this concept:

> First, we say that one is a poor person who wills nothing. What this means, many people do not correctly understand. These are the people who in penitential exercise and external practices, of which they make a great deal, cling to their selfish I. The Lord have pity upon such people who know so little of the divine truth! Such people are called holy on account of external appearance, but inwardly they are asses, for they do not grasp the real meaning of divine truth. Indeed, these individuals too say that one is a poor person who wills nothing. However, they interpret this to mean that one should so live as to never fulfill one's own will in any way, but rather strive to fulfill the ever–beloved will of God. These people are right in their way, for their intention is good and for that we want to praise them.

> May God in his mercy grant them the kingdom of heaven. But in all divine truth, I say that these people are not poor people, nor do they resemble poor people. They are highly considered only in the eyes of those who know no better. I, however, say that they are asses who understand nothing of divine truth. . . .
>
> These days, if someone asks me what a poor person is who wills nothing, I answer and say: So long as a person who has his own wish in him to fulfill even the ever-beloved will of God, if that is still a matter of his will, then this person does not yet possess the poverty of which we want to speak. Indeed, this person then still has a will with which he or she wants to satisfy God's will, and that is not the right poverty. For a human being to possess true poverty, he or she must be free of his or her created will as they were when they did not yet exist. Thus I say to you in the name of divine truth, as long as you have the will, even the will to fulfill God's will, and as long as you have the desire for eternity and for God, to this very extent you are not properly poor, for the only one who is a poor person is one who wills nothing and desires nothing. (Fox, 1980, p. 214)

Thus, Eckhart defines a poverty of will in radical terms of not desiring anything, even to do God's will.

The other side of this radical detachment or poverty is radical obedience or the surrender of the will to the Creator. As in the discussion of poverty of knowing and poverty with respect to acquired things, poverty of will results in freedom. If one does not need to have one's own way, that is, if one is detached from one's own will, if a person does not have to have his or her own way, it is possible to turn on a dime and take a totally new direction. That person is completely available. On the other hand, if continuing in the current direction is what is required, a detached person cannot be tempted to stray from the necessary course and can be persistent and unshakable because there is nothing that a person so desires or wills that he or she can be deterred, that is, there is nothing that can tempt.

Gerald May expands on the concept of letting go or surrendering one's will in commenting on this poem by Dag Hammarskjöld:

> I don't know Who—or what—put the question, I don't know when it was put. I don't even remember answering. But at some moment I did answer *Yes* to Someone—or Something—and from that hour I was certain that existence is meaningful and that, therefore, my life, in self-surrender, had a goal.
>
> From that moment I have known what it means "not to look back," and "to take no thought for the morrow." (Hammarskjöld, p. 205)

May (1983) shares some of his own experience as a medical professional in discussing the need to take control of one's life, the need to be master of one's own destiny in contrast with the possibility of self-surrender.

All my life I have longed to say yes, to give myself completely, to some Ultimate Someone or Something. . . .

Society, to say nothing of medical and psychiatric training, had taught me to say no rather than yes, to try to determine my own destiny rather than give myself, to seek mastery rather than surrender. For a long time, I tried to believe that I could learn enough and strengthen my will enough to take complete charge of my own life, but it never quite seemed to work. . . .

I am convinced that there is something in each of us that resonates with the great words of Dag Hammarskjold that opened this chapter. There is something in our hearts that calls for a reconciliation of the individual, autonomous qualities of will with the unifying and loving qualities of spirit. But such a reconciliation is difficult. We cannot go around saying yes and surrendering to everyone and everything that comes our way. Our willingness to give ourselves cannot occur at such a superficial level. It must address the very essence of who we are, and the foundations of life itself.

Surrender does not come easily. It has long been treated as a noxious concept in our society. We are taught never to give up, never to allow ourselves to be determined by anyone or anything other than our own self-will. We have been so well taught to say no that when we do say yes we are liable to feel spineless and unassertive. Our confusion is deepened by the fact that too often we really *are* spineless and unassertive. Too often we *do* go along with the currents of social whim or the desires of other people instead of standing up for what we sense is right within us. Such surrender to other people, institutions or causes is, in my opinion, the opposite of true spiritual surrender. The destructiveness of such distortions is likely to make us fear any kind of surrender, spiritual or otherwise.

. . . Surely we do not want to be passive doormats for the world to walk upon; but the world is so immense . . . and so mysterious . . . and so wonderful . . . that we cannot quite find comfort in seeing ourselves as its masters either.

And then there are those brief, ecstatic moments when something approximating spiritual surrender does come upon us. There are rare times when we can surrender to a loved one, whispering, "Yes, my darling, yes." Occasionally while swimming in the ocean we are able to give ourselves to the waves and just float upon them, letting their strength bear us up. Or now and then while we are walking, a breeze may creep up behind us and boost us along a little and we might—just briefly—entertain the fantasy of being picked up and carried on its currents.

But such things are only momentary glimpses of what it means to really say yes; only little hints of what the great surrender or real willingness might be like. They never last long, and inevitably we must pull ourselves back to "reality," back to a world in which we carry our destinies on our own shoulders, where we carve our marks upon the world with our own muscles, where we must forge some semblance of meaning and purpose through the efforts of our personal willpower. We have been taught very well that meaning and purpose can be achieved only through the exercise of personal mastery and self-determination. Yet there is Hammarskjold—

and something in our hearts—haunting us with a call to self-surrender. (G. May, 1983, pp. 1–5)

Thus, the surrender of will or detachment from desire outlined by Eckhart on the via negativa is not an absence of will or desire born of boredom or weakness, but a letting go or a dying to what an individual wants. Eckhart describes a radical detachment that results in a radical freedom. The next theme, concerning detachment from knowledge, also describes a certain freedom that comes from an attitude of not knowing.

DETACHMENT FROM KNOWLEDGE INVITES AN ATTITUDE OF NOT KNOWING

For the contemplative, a discussion of knowledge begins with the divinity. God is ultimately mystery and cannot be known. However, it is necessary for human beings to name God, to create images or representations of God, and to use intellectual constructs about God. In general, human beings think, communicate with others, form relationships, and generally conduct their lives by means of words, ideas, metaphor, images, stories, and the like. These intermediaries are never the full reality of their referents: They are necessary, but not complete. For the contemplative, the various names of God—Jahweh; Creator; Lord God of Power and Might; God of Abraham, Isaac, and Jacob; Father; His Majesty; Holy One of Israel; Lord; Holy Spirit—cannot contain God. He—or she—spills out over any intellectual container. Analogously, the same is true when the contemplative encounters the mystery that life ultimately is. Our rational and logical structures of knowledge, although necessary, cannot contain our experience or express life in its fullness.

The 20th-century monk Thomas Merton in a chapter entitled "What Is Contemplation" weaves together aspects of the via positiva and the via negativa in explaining how contemplation is beyond knowing and involves a death and a letting go of knowledge:

Contemplation is the highest expression of man's intellectual and spiritual life. It is that life itself, fully awake, fully active, fully aware that it is alive. It is spiritual wonder. It is spontaneous awe at the sacredness of life, of being. It is gratitude for life, for awareness and for being. It is a vivid realization of the fact that life and being in us proceed from an invisible, transcendent and infinitely abundant Source. Contemplation is, above all, awareness of the reality of that Source. It *knows* the Source, obscurely, inexplicably, but with certitude that goes beyond reason and beyond simple faith. For contemplation is a kind of spiritual vision to which both reason and faith aspire, by their very nature, because without it they must always remain incomplete. Yet contemplation is not vision because it sees "without seeing" and knows "without knowing." It is a more profound depth of a faith, a knowledge too deep to be grasped in images, in words or even in clear concepts. It can be suggested by word, by symbols, but in the very moment of trying to indicate what it knows, the contemplative mind takes back what it has said, and denies what it has affirmed. For in contemplation we know by "unknowing." Or better, we know *beyond* all knowing or "unknowing."

Poetry, music and art have something in common with the contemplative experience. But contemplation is beyond aesthetic intuition, beyond art, beyond poetry. Indeed, it is beyond philosophy, beyond speculative theology. It presumes, transcends, and fulfills them all, and yet at the same time it seems, in a certain way, to supersede and deny them all. Contemplation is always beyond our own knowledge, beyond our own light, beyond systems, beyond explanations, beyond discourse, beyond dialogue, beyond our own self. To enter into the realm of contemplation one must in a certain sense die: but this death is in fact the entrance into a higher life. It is a death for the sake of life, which leaves behind all that we can know or treasure as life, as thought, as experience, as joy, as being.

And so contemplation seems to supersede and to discard every other form of intuition and experience—whether in art, in philosophy, in theology, in liturgy or in ordinary levels of love and of belief. This rejection is of course only apparent. Contemplation is and must be compatible with all these things, for it is their highest fulfillment. But in the actual experience of contemplation all other experiences are momentarily lost. They "die" to be born again on a higher level of life.

In other words, then, contemplation reaches out to the knowledge and even the experience of the transcendent and inexpressible God. It knows God by seeming to touch Him. Or rather it knows Him as if it had been invisibly touched by Him. ... Touched by Him Who has no hands, but who is pure Reality and the source of all that is real! Hence contemplation is a sudden gift of awareness, an awakening to the Real within all that is real. A vivid awareness of infinite Being at the roots of our own limited being. An awareness of our contingent reality as received, as a present from God, as a free gift of love. This is the existential contact of which we speak when we use the metaphor of being "touched by God." (Merton, 1961, pp. 1–3)

Considering the second aspect of being poor, that is, of knowing nothing, Eckhart, in his sermon on the beatitude "Blessed are the poor in spirit," develops the theme of standing empty:

Second, a poor person is one who knows nothing. We have said on other occasions that a person should live a life neither for himself, nor for the truth, nor for God. But now we say it differently and want to go further and say: Whoever achieves this poverty must so live that they not even know themselves to live, either for oneself or for truth or for God. One must be free of all knowledge that he or she does not know or recognize or perceive that God lives in him or her; even more, one should be free of all knowledge that lives in him or her. For, when people stood in God's eternal being, nothing else lived in them. What lived there was themselves. Hence we say that people should be as free of their own knowledge as when they were not yet, letting God accomplish what God wills. People should stand empty. (Fox, 1980, p. 215)

Whereas the first path emphasized knowing creation in the most intimate ways and reveling in its concreteness and sensuality, the second path begins with an appreciation of the limits of our knowing. There is a certain humility with regard to knowledge that attends this approach to life: One cannot claim to possess the truth or have a monopoly on how it can be presented or apprehended. This approach implies a willingness to listen, to receive the insights of others, and to know that the truth will never be grasped in its completeness and depth. Meister Eckhart's contemplative theology begins the second path here by facing the ineffability, the transcendence, and the mystery of God.

The most radical limit of all to creation is our understanding of creation. . . .

For Eckhart, the nothingness of creatures should not be ignored, forgotten, repressed or covered-up. It should be explored. The adventure of exploring nothingness will itself yield a profound, a truly eschatological revelation: That there, in the depth of our desert as dependent beings, God not only lives but gives birth constantly to God. That, beyond God who is namable as Creator lies the Godhead who is unnameable Trinity and who is "a negation of all names" (Quint, vol. I, p. 253).

. . . We need to enter a desert where God is not defined for us. A God beyond God might then be listened to whose name is ineffable. "The highest and loftiest thing that man can renounce is to renounce God for the sake of God" (J. Clark, p. 225). The unnamed Deity is not subject to our naming. In the depth of us lives the true God, but even our seeking needs to cease for us to find God there. "Truly, 'Thou art a hidden God,' in the ground of the soul where God's ground and the soul's are one ground. The more one seeks Thee, the less one can find Thee. You should seek him in such a way as never to find him. If you do not seek him, you will find him" (J. Clark, p. 245). We are urged to cease our craving—not because objects are evil but because the very process or dynamics of craving blocks out still greater possibilities. "For as long as the craving for more and more is in you, God can never dwell or work in you. These things must always go out if God is to enter in" (J. Clark, p. 219). Cease greed we are told, for greater gifts await you. "This above all, then, be ready at all times for the gifts of God and always for new ones." (Blakney, 1941, p. 32; Fox, 1981, pp. 227–229)

Within Eckhart's theology there is a recognition of necessary ambiguity, of letting go of our firm but imperfect grasp on knowledge. The contemplative honors the cloudy, hidden, vague, paradoxical, shadowy nature of life. We never quite have the eyes to see nor the ears to hear the full depth and richness of life, to which Jesus often alluded in the telling of his ubiquitous and paradoxical parables in the Greek Scriptures (see, for example, Mark 4:1–12, 23, New Revised Standard Version). It is as if the contemplative recognizes the limits of propositional statements in communicating the realities of life and resorts to narrative forms such as parable, story, and myth.

Contemporary author Jacques Pasquier in his 1977 article, "Experience and Conversion," considers this poverty of knowing, or detachment from what we know to be true (as well as the surrender of will discussed earlier), drawing on the concepts of conversion and idols to dramatize the need to let go of images if we are to enjoy freedom.

> At the centre of conversion is the destruction of our own image of God, in order to allow God to be God for us: a God who not only is other than what we are, but is also other than what we want him to be. It is in the acceptance lived at the daily level of our experience that "My ways are not your ways" (Isaiah 55:9), that a person begins the long process of conversion. (Pasquier, 1977, p. 115)

Pasquier (1977) explains that any representation or image—especially our images of God—can be used as a "security blanket," reducing reality to a static vision. "Our whole life needs to be submitted to this constant critical attitude which is not only the destruction of our own images but an openness to the reality, to the truth" (p. 115).

Faith—or the contemplative stance, one might also say—is defined as the readiness, the openness to the destruction of each and every one of our cherished images, including our image of God, to allow God to be the ultimate reality rather than our pinched and static rendition.

> The history of Israel, like the history of the Church, can be understood as a continual process of destroying one idol after the other, in order that his people might grow in the knowledge and experience of who God is. At the centre of conversion is the experience that no tabernacle can ever be built, no image of God can ever be possessed; but that God is always working at the limit, the edges, stretching us beyond the today and leading us to learn how to trust and how to love, opening us to a constantly new reality, a new truth.
>
> The passage from one image to another (unfortunately we always need an image—be it of ourselves or of God) and the constant call to leave behind the present image is the process of death and rebirth [of which Jesus is speaking when he tells Nicodemus that he must be "born again"]. In death, life is not taken away; it is radically transformed. In our experience of powerlessness, of being stripped of our masks, we come to realize that new life is given, a new call, a new reality. (Pasquier, 1977, p. 115)

Eckhart himself introduced this theme more than 500 years earlier when he announced, "I pray God to rid me of God" (Fox, 1981, p. 217). "To experience the true Godhead . . . it is necessary to be rid of all—including our names for God" (Fox, 1980, pp. 221–222).

Although Pasquier focuses his discussion on one's image of God, his approach is not limited to this particular topic. Any representations and images—of society, of management, of ourselves, of the world around us—operate as security blankets and can block with a static vision. It may be said that when individuals die to their images and representations, when they give them up or empty themselves of the images and representations, the individual's knowledge structure is radically transformed and given back anew. Perhaps this metaphor could be stretched to say that one experiences a death and rebirth of knowledge and understanding when one experiences a paradigm shift. The via negativa recognizes the *aha!* experience of suddenly seeing something in a radically different way when we loosen our mental grip on our initial understanding of what we are seeing.

For the contemplative, the insistence on, or clinging to, ideas or images or understandings limits freedom or availability for the truth. Human beings can be attached to intellectual concepts and make idols of them just as wealth or fame can become idols. The via negativa provides a process of emptying or, in 20th-century contemporary terms, of unlearning. The via negativa allows one to approach a new experience with a childlike innocence, deliberate ignorance, an open mind, and allow the experience to reveal itself, to provide its own explanation. The way of emptiness, darkness, and silence could be said to provide room for new theories, new worldviews, new intellectual constructs of all kinds. In this sense it can be said that poverty or detachment provides freedom.

In the midst of a discussion of this innocent ignorance of the via negativa, it must be emphasized that Eckhart is not anti-intellectual:

> [Eckhart] was most likely the finest intellect with the best education of any philosopher or theologian of his century. . . . [F]rom knowledge we must come to a state of ignorance. In other words, we need to have something to let go of, before we dare let go! The via negativa presumes an intellectual life, a thinking and a vital consciousness that already relates deeply to creation. It presumes Path One. . . . [Eckhart] is talking about our coming to a transformed knowledge, and one does this by experiencing a transformed ignorance, that is, a willful ignorance that comes after knowledge and does not precede it. (Fox, 1980, pp. 261–262)

No discussion of the contemplative approach to forgetting and letting go of knowledge would be complete without mention of the anonymous, 14th-century classic of Christian mystical experience, *The Cloud of Unknowing* (which the editor has cross-referenced with the works of St. John of the Cross who, the editor argues, was closely influenced by *The Cloud*) (Johnston, 1973, pp. 30–31). In the following excerpt, the author describes the way of contemplation, in the midst of which he weaves together many of the themes of the via negativa:

> This is what you are to do: lift your heart up to the Lord, with a gentle stirring of love desiring him for his own sake and not for his gifts. Center all your attention and desire on him and let this be the sole concern of your mind and heart. Do all in your power to forget everything else, keeping your thoughts and desires free from involvement with any of God's creatures or their affairs whether in general or in particular. Perhaps this will seem like an irresponsible attitude, but I tell you, let them all be; pay no attention to them.
>
> What I am describing here is the contemplative work of the spirit. It's this which gives God the greatest delight. For when you fix your love on him, forgetting all else, the saints and angels rejoice and hasten to assist you in every way. . . . Yet for all this, when God's grace arouses you to enthusiasm, it becomes the lightest sort of work there is and one most willingly done. Without his grace, however, it is very difficult and almost, I should say, quite beyond you.
>
> And so diligently persevere until you feel joy in it. For in the beginning it is usual to feel nothing but a kind of darkness about your mind, as it were, a cloud of unknowing. You will seem to know nothing except a naked intent toward God in the depths of your being. Try as you might, this darkness and this cloud will remain between you and your God.[6] You will feel frustrated, for your mind will be unable to grasp him, and your heart will not relish the delight of his love. But learn to be at home in this darkness and this cloud. Return to it as often as you can, letting your spirit cry out to him whom you love. For if, in this life, you hope to feel and see God as he is in himself it must be within this darkness and this cloud.[7] (pp. 48–49)

This approach of letting go of thoughts and remaining in the darkness or cloud is further developed and echoed in a later work by the same anonymous author, *The Book of Privy Counseling*:

> When you go apart to be alone for prayer, put from your mind everything you have been doing or plan to do. Reject all thoughts, be they good or evil. Do not pray with words unless you are really drawn to this; or if you do pray with words, pay no attention to whether they are many or few. Do not weigh them or their meaning. . . . See that nothing remains in your conscious mind save a naked intent stretching out toward God. Leave it stripped of every particular idea *about* God (what he is like in himself or in his works) and keep only the simple awareness *that he is as he is.* . . . This awareness, stripped of ideas and deliberately bound and anchored in faith,

shall leave your thought and affection in emptiness except for a naked thought or blind feeling of your own being. . . .

Let that quiet darkness be your whole mind and like a mirror to you. For I want your thought of self to be as naked and as simple as your thought of God, so that you may be spiritually united to him without any fragmentation and scattering of your mind. (Johnston, 1973, pp. 149–150)

St. John of the Cross's *Dark Night of the Soul* also echoes the theme of detaching from knowledge, desire, and even the usual pleasure in *the things of God*. Although a brief quotation from the *Dark Night* does not do justice to this masterpiece of 16th-century mystical writing, the following sample provides a glimpse into John's understanding of the *dark night*, which, contrary to popular usage, is not just a time of feeling depressed over everything going wrong, but a stage of the spiritual journey that is beyond the usual delights of the beginnings of the contemplative way, a "passive experience in which the soul dies to itself and begins to live a life of love with God" (Welch, 1990, p. 90). The dark night is a time of detaching, letting go, and letting be.

The first [sign] is whether, when a soul finds no pleasure or consolation in the things of God, it also fails to find it in any thing created; for, as God sets the soul in this dark night to the end that He may quench and purge its sensual desire, He allows it not to find attraction or sweetness in anything whatsoever. (Peers, 1959, p. 64)

Contemporary Carmelite priest John Welch (1990) interprets the *dark night* in a manner that seems to highlight the difference between the via positiva and the via negativa.

This night happens to those people whom John calls "beginners." Beginners are those who are converted to God and practice meditation; through the night they will be led into contemplation which is the prayer of proficients. The goal is the state of the perfect who are in union with God.

God nurtures the beginner "like a loving mother who warms her child with the heat of her bosom, nurses it with good milk and tender food, and carries and caresses it in her arms." God gives the beginner enthusiasm and satisfaction.

The beginner, then, experiences a false sense of security: "The soul finds its joy, therefore, in spending lengthy periods at prayer, perhaps even entire nights; its penances are pleasures; its fasts, happiness; and the sacraments and spiritual conversations are its consolations."

The problem, as John analyzes it, is that the beginner relies upon, and actually is motivated by, this satisfaction and consolation. Although feeling strong, the beginner is actually in a feeble condition. It is this condition that is changed in the experience of the night. "But as the child grows older, the mother withholds her caresses and hides her tender love; she rubs bitter aloes on her sweet breast and sets the child down from her arms, letting it walk on its own feet so that it may put aside the habits of childhood and grow accustomed to greater and more important things." (p. 90)

Thus, the via negativa is a bewildering, confusing way of letting go of what has given security, satisfaction, understanding, and direction. It is a radical detachment from knowledge as well as from desire. In the next section Eckhart's understanding of detachment from possessions, in the broadest sense—that is, material goods, accomplishments, status or anything else to which we apply the concept of ownership—is considered.

DETACHMENT FROM MATERIAL POSSESSIONS INVITES THE FREEDOM OF POVERTY

The third point in Eckhart's sermon on poverty of spirit focuses on material possessions—and actions—in relation to poverty and again uses the concept of being empty—so that God has a place in which to act.

[O]ne is a poor person who has nothing. Many people have said that perfection consists in people possessing none of the material things of the earth. And indeed, that is certainly true in one sense: when one holds to it intentionally. But this is not the sense that I mean.

I have said before that one is a poor person who does not even will to fulfill God's will, that is, who so lives that he or she is empty both of his own will and of God's will, just as they were when they were not yet. About this poverty we say that it is the highest poverty. Second, we have said one is a poor person who himself understands nothing of God's activity in him or her. When one stands as free of understanding and knowing [as God stands void of all things], then that is the purest poverty. But the third kind of poverty of which we are now going to speak is the most difficult: that people have nothing.

Now give me your undivided attention. I have often said, and great masters say this too: People must be so empty of all things and all works, whether inward or outward, that they can become a proper home for God, wherein God may operate. But now we say it differently. If people stand free of all things, of all creatures, of God and of themselves, but if it still happens that God can find a place for acting in them, then we say: So long as that is so, these persons are not poor in the strictest poverty. For God does not desire that people reserve a place for him to work in. Rather true poverty of spirit consists of keeping oneself so free of God and of all of one's works that if God wants to act in the soul, God himself becomes the place wherein he wants to act—and this God likes to do. For when God finds a person as poor as this, God operates his own work and a person sustains God in him and God is himself the place of his operation, since God is an agent who acts within himself. Here, in this poverty, people attain the eternal being that they once were, now are, and will eternally remain. (Fox, 1980, pp. 216–217)

Matthew Fox (1980) comments on Eckhart's sermon and sets forth some key ideas on detachment in Eckhart's theology:

1. Humanity originates in the eternal abyss or emptiness of divine being. "God stands empty of all things. . . . God is free of all things, and therefore he is all things."
2. We, too, should become so Godlike that we touch these states of nothingness: These states are of God and we are God's image.
3. "We too should stand empty and should will nothing, desire nothing, and have nothing."
4. It is only when we and God are one that the human person can have full joy (Fox, 1980, p. 219).

Fox (1980) explains that, according to Eckhart, the kataphatic path of the via positiva is not enough, that Eckhart seeks to experience our precreaturely state in a mystical return to the womb, to the time of humanity's preexistence, before we flowed out from God (pp. 219–220). The via negativa provides poverty as a way to unity. But it is a poverty that is beyond the concept of not having a lot of things.

> Detachment from things does not mean setting up a contradiction between "things" and "God" as if God were another "thing" and as if His creatures were His rivals. We do not detach ourselves from things in order to attach ourselves to God, but rather we become detached *from ourselves* in order to see and use all things in and for God. (Merton, 1961, p. 21)

Merton emphasizes that possessions or things, of themselves, are not the issue. Again, as with detachment from, or poverty of, knowledge and understanding, human beings need things and possessions in order to interact with the world. But they do not, of themselves, lead to unity with God or the radical and vulnerable openness to the divine that is the heart of the contemplative way, or, as Fox explains, being in touch with nothingness.

> His answer is in terms of poverty. . . . But Eckhart has a very definite understanding of what he means by poverty. It is an inner poverty and a radical poverty. A poverty so radical and so in touch with our ground where Godhead and we are one, that such a poor person wills nothing, knows nothing, and has nothing. This kind of blessedness and poverty is in touch with nothingness. (Fox, 1980, p. 220)

How does one become a truly blessed and happy person through this poverty? Fox (1980) explains Eckhart's use of the terms *letting go* and *letting be*.

> But how does this happen? Not by a lot of ascetic practices, not by penitences and external practices which cling to the selfish *I*. Rather it happens by our learning to let go. Eckhart invented the words for letting go and letting be. The two words are *Abgeschiedenheit* and *Gelassenheit* respectively and while some people translate the former as "detachment," that word has borne too heavy a burden from dualistic and ascetic spiritualists since Eckhart's day to do justice to his meaning. Letting go is what Eckhart means. . . . The letting go is the act by which we enter into nothingness. . . . Letting go allows us to touch nothingness. . . . It is this radical letting go of willing, of knowing, and of having that allows God to enter. . . . The person who has learned to let go is one without objects in his or her life, even life itself is no longer an object. There is true living without why or wherefore. . . .
>
> Furthermore, there are no limits to this kind of poverty, no depths, one might say, to the vortex that is our spirit and our potential for letting go or, if you will, God is the limit. (p. 221)

Fox (1981) discusses Eckhart's use of the term *letting be*, that is, Gelassenheit, in weaving together the first and second paths, the via positiva and the via negativa, particularly with respect to detachment from things:

> Consequent on letting go, there occurs a deepening experience of reverence for all things—God, self, others, creation. It is a process of letting be (*Gelassenheit*).
>
> The biggest gift that awaits us is the realization of God. "There where the creature ends, God begins to be. God does not ask anything of you other than that you go out of yourself according to your mode as creature and that you let God be God in you." Here lies the crux of the journey: letting God be God (and not just our preconceived ideas of God) in us. It is for this reason that we abandon even the names we have given to God. "I pray God that he may quit me of God." And we abandon suppositions about Jesus Christ. "It is good that I leave you" Eckhart quotes Jesus saying to the disciples, and Eckhart comments. "Let images go therefore and unite yourselves to the being without form."
>
> One who is truly "poor in spirit" is one who has made this journey of letting go. Such a person has learned that "becoming poor in spirit is letting God be God" and possesses an inward poverty wherein one's quests of wanting, knowing, and having are stilled. . . . *The attitude of letting go is clearly the opposite of control, clinging to, grabbing, hoarding.* The radical openness that Eckhart advises is a readiness to experience realized eschatology. It is eternal life before death; ecstasy before death; life before death; God now. It is a letting God happen within and among us. It is also an

emptying, which is an image that Eckhart employs often. "If a cask is to contain wine, one must necessarily pour out the water; the cask must be bare and empty. Therefore, if you would receive divine joy and God, it is necessary for you to pour out the creatures. . . . Everything that is to receive and to be receptive must and should be empty." Eckhart instructs us in a profoundly antimaterialistic spirituality when he tells us to let go of all objects.

What should never be lost sight of in comprehending Eckhart's nothing-ness and letting-go-pathway is how it belongs altogether *within* his appre-ciation of the grace-fullness of creation. One does not let go of objects because objects are bad or inferior but because, as one learns from loving God in creation, our way of knowing requires an emptiness for every fullness, a void for every ecstasy, a desert for every lush meadow. (pp. 229–230, emphasis added)

St. Ignatius Loyola, a 16th-century Spaniard and founder of the Society of Jesus (the Jesuits), who is generally identified with the kataphatic tradition, presents the concept of detachment from a slightly different perspective in a key prefatory statement, "First Principle and Foundation," to his classic *Spiritual Exercises*. The translator uses the term *indifference* (*detached* can also be used)[8] to communicate the stance of not insisting on or even desiring health, wealth, honor, or long life–or sickness, poverty, dishonor, or a short life—but of accepting or using these conditions to the extent they enable one to achieve the purpose for which he or she is created, expressed in the words of Ignatius's era, that is, to praise, reverence, and serve God.

> Man is created to praise, reverence, and serve God.
> The other things on the face of the earth are created for man to help him in attaining the end for which he is created.
> Hence, man is to make use of them in as far as they help him in the attainment of his end, and he must rid himself of them in as far as they prove a hindrance to him.
> Therefore, we must make ourselves *indifferent* to all created things, as far as we are allowed free choice and are not under any prohibition. Consequently, as far as we are concerned, we should not prefer health to sickness, riches to poverty, honor to dishonor, a long life to a short life. The same holds for all other things.
> Our one desire and choice should be what is more conducive to the end for which we are created. (Puhl, 1951, p. 12, emphasis added)

Any human being enjoys certain specific conditions at particular times, for example, a state of health, a degree of wealth, a stature in the community, a place in a family, and the like. For the contemplative, these conditions are worn with the nonchalance of a suit of clothes. If it is a hot summer day, a person would wear shorts and a T-shirt;

if it is raining, a raincoat. If the temperature drops, a person might add gloves, parka, and muffler—because that is what is necessary or required under the circumstances. A contemplative wears—or uses—what is necessary for the situation. When it is necessary, one can wear a business suit or blue jeans and fatigue jacket; live in a homeless shelter or an elegant high-rise apartment. A contemplative is indifferent to either style of life, using what is needed and letting go of the rest. For St. Ignatius, to insist on, or even desire, a long life, good health, or honor (or a short life, poor health, and dishonor), when it is not needed, is to compromise one's freedom and is as ridiculous as dragging along heavy boots and a parka in 100 degree heat. This indifference extends to nonmaterial possessions such as jobs, roles, status, self-understandings, ideas, theories, opinions, values, goals, and plans. Human beings certainly need jobs, roles, status, self-understandings, ideas, theories, and so forth, to participate in life, but with an attitude of detachment, the contemplative holds all of these items lightly, never grasping or clinging. This indifference or detachment is one perspective on the traditional religious vow of poverty.

Such an attitude of detachment in a contemporary organizational setting might be illustrated by an intern's experience during a brief assignment in a nonprofit organization. (It is, of course, not possible to discern an individual's attitude with certainty from external actions, but the example may suggest what indifference might look like.) There had been a recent change in leadership in the organization. The previous director, as would be expected, had occupied the largest, two-window, office with built-in bookshelves. The associate director had the smaller, one-window, office, also with built-in bookshelves. Three other staff persons of lesser status shared a large but windowless office—with no bookshelves.

After both the director and associate director left the organization within months of each other, the interim director (formerly an occupant of the windowless office) moved into the largest, two-window, office—but shared it with another staff person. The third occupant of the windowless office now had the entire (windowless) space to himself. When the intern arrived, he was assigned the one-window office with the built-in bookshelves, giving him the best accommodations of any of the staff.

Because the interim director had been a high-ranking military officer with years of Pentagon experience, this unusual office assignment could not have been the result of his failure to understand the significance of office assignments. The director eventually explained that in order for the internship to provide the proper training experiences, the organization's membership needed to see the intern as a person with authority. The intern needed the impressive office to gain that authority.

The director did not. This may be an illustration of personal detachment and indifference with regard to office space—at least on the part of the interim director.

Indifference, as used by St. Ignatius, is not synonymous with apathy, complacency, or quietude. On the contrary, if the situation requires a particular status, degree of wealth, role, and the like, the contemplative will labor assiduously to acquire it. The reverse of this radical detachment might be seen, then, as radical engagement or, to use traditional terms, radical obedience.

After considering the various forms of detachment, that is, from will, knowledge, and possessions, attention is turned to one effect of such detachment, the pain of letting go.

THE PAIN OF LETTING GO MUST ALSO BE LET GO

Not surprisingly, the detachment from what one wants, knows, or possesses is not comfortable, and the contemplative acknowledges, rather than denies, the pain of letting go. It is not surprising then that terms such as death and crucifixion are used to describe the letting go. Another level of detachment, the letting go of the pain itself, and allowing the new to emerge, is also an important element of the contemplative paradigm.

This pain of loss, of course, is not limited to contemplatives. The process of losing one's basic understandings or beliefs about life and one's place in the universe is applicable to Eckhart's discussion of letting go of knowledge, possessions, or whatever one holds dear. The pain that follows the loss or destruction of basic understandings about life is described and illustrated by social worker Beverly Flanigan in her book, *Forgiving the Unforgivable: Overcoming the Bitter Legacy of Intimate Wounds*. Flanigan (1992) chronicles not only the process of betrayal and loss, but also, sometimes, of forgiveness or letting go, that occurs when people in close relationship—lovers, spouses, parents, children, friends—experience abuse, abandonment, or betrayal. Flanigan's work is helpful in understanding Eckhart's discussion of detachment or letting go and letting be by examining in detail the process by which the basic understandings that give human beings a sure footing—understandings about justice, control over one's life, fundamental roles—are destroyed, grieved, and let go. Flanigan's examples of betrayal and injury that destroy these basic understandings include a woman who discovers that her best friend of many years is having an affair with her husband, parents who abandon a teenage child, and a trusted business partner who embezzles a business into bankruptcy. Flanigan identifies the shattering of the injured person's belief structure as a primary source of the pain one endures in the midst of such an unforgivable injury. It is the sudden loss of mundane expectations that throws a person into confusion, alienation, and despair. Flanigan (1992) explains that the harm caused by these unforgivable injuries extends to the injured person's core beliefs—the control one has over his own life, whether anyone can be trusted, whether the world is a safe place (p. 52). The injurer permanently alters and destroys a person's beliefs about himself or herself, other people, and the world.

Although not all crumbling of structures of knowledge or destruction of what one always thought was true involve personal betrayal and wounding as did the anecdotes of the unforgivable provided by Flanigan's subjects, letting go of one's beliefs or understandings (and relationships) is painful and often involves a sense of loss with the accompanying grieving. There is a note of disappointment or even disorientation evident in the phrase "But I always thought that . . ." that accompanies the loss of expectations.

Flanigan (1992) offers an example of an injury with the accompanying loss of beliefs or assumptions by the various parties involved. A girl named Deborah was awakened one night by her mother's cries during a violent attack by the husband one night. As she watched from the top of the steps, Deborah saw a scene she never forgot. Her mother's eye was ripped out of the eye socket and was hanging down her face. Deborah knocked her father unconscious with a milk bottle (pp. 91–92). Deborah and her brothers were sent to separate foster homes and lost touch with each other.

Typical beliefs that fail after such an experience, according to Flanigan, include beliefs about personal values, personal control, trusting, justice, the family's motives. Beliefs that fail especially for children are the beliefs that parents are together forever, that the world is safe, that mothers are stable, and that fathers are loyal and truthful (Flanigan, 1992, pp. 94–95). These beliefs and understandings fail, at least in part, because they are no longer true, because they no longer conform to reality or present reasonable possibilities for the future. The failure or loss of these beliefs often makes room for other understandings that will help the person make new decisions and take new directions. These losses, in a sense, provide a certain freedom that was not present or recognized before.

In describing the forgiveness or recovery phase for person's who have suffered the unforgivable, Flanigan (1992) delineates a series of miniconversions that injured persons undergo as they give up long-held beliefs and understandings and allow a new knowledge structure to take hold. Telling the story of the Joneses whose son was shot and killed by Martin, a boy the family had befriended, Flanigan articulates the demise of many of their cherished beliefs. There were many outward changes, including this middle-aged couple's eventual adoption of a baby, but there were also inner shifts. The couple eventually were able to forgive Martin, but, in the process, substituted almost all their core beliefs with new ones. "They gave up the church. They no longer believed in the concept of fairness. And they no longer equated their good deeds with rewards to follow. Everything they had believed had changed. They were different people" (p. 160).

In describing the possible aftermath of having one's understandings shattered, this social worker makes interesting use of the concept of conversion, a theme that will be taken up in more detail on the fourth path of Meister Eckhart's theology, the *via transformativa*. Flanigan describes forgiving an unforgivable injury as a conversion process. The one who forgives must come to terms with the fact that his core beliefs have given way and will be replaced by new ones. There is a series of miniconversions that the forgiver must undergo. He becomes a new person with a perspective on life that has radically shifted.

> In a paradoxical way, unforgivable injuries present you with one of life's opportunities to change fundamentally. The experience of being wounded may force you against your will to alter your dreams, myths, and expectations of life; but where else can you experience a confrontation so rare? To really be able to transform one's essential beliefs is a chance of a lifetime. To do it well is an art. (Flanigan, 1992, p. 161)

Flanigan observes that our core ideas about life—crime, poverty, fairness, God, religion, luck, rich people, and so on—are formed early in life and do not easily change. They form the foundation of lifelong maps of one's world. Perceptions are filtered and synthesized through these fundamental understandings until the data fits our map of the world.

> Someone who considers all believers in UFOs . . . to be eccentric dreamers probably concludes that the alien he sees standing next to a spaceship in his backyard is the next-door neighbor kid dressed in a space suit. This fits his belief. A true believer in alien visitors, [however], might think a distant Frisbee obscured in the sunlight is a flying saucer. . . . People see what they believe. Over time, they become stuck in their beliefs about life and each other. Everything fits nicely together in a comfortable but unchanging package. (Flanigan, 1992, p. 161)

Although it is extremely painful to have one's core beliefs pulled out from their roots and destroyed, there is an opportunity in the midst of the destruction and pain.

> It is like a moment when a disbeliever confronts an alien from outer space and *knows* it is an alien from outer space; he has been given a chance to restructure his very basic beliefs about life itself. . . . The unharmed never have to face such serious challenges to their assumptions. Forgivers do;

and through the process of forgiving, they find and create new answers
that, in a way, make them new people. . . . [I]t is one of life's ways of giving
people a second chance. To be wounded, in this strange way, is to be given
a gift. (Flanigan, 1992, p. 161)

Although Flanigan's subject is "overcoming the bitter legacy of
intimate wounds," her insights into conversion and the shattering of
important beliefs and understandings can be extended to the
contemplative's perspective that the experience of life in the fullest
involves a letting go and letting be of knowledge and understanding—and perhaps will, desire, and accomplishments or possessions
as well. Although the contemplative knows that human beings need
knowledge, understanding, beliefs, even paradigms, as well as
dreams, desires, relationships, and possessions, to function in life, the
contemplative also knows that his or her existence is not dependent
on or tied to any particular knowledge, understanding, belief, paradigm, dream, desire, relationship, or possession, that these all can be
held lightly and released when it is necessary. Although not every
letting go is as painful as those experienced by the subjects of
Flanigan's book, it is not necessary to deny the pain that is involved
when it is time to let go of one's own understandings, dreams,
relationships, or possessions. Who does not experience some measure
of grief upon seeing a child graduate from college and move into a
new relationship as an adult? Many will ache at the thought of having
to trade in a favorite car when the odometer finally tops 100,000
miles. There was significant discomfort when Copernicus's colleagues
were confronted with the picture of the earth revolving around the
sun. For the contemplative, this letting go and detaching is an often
admittedly painful but necessary move in the dance of life. It is the
pain before the joy of the new life that Flanigan describes. It is the
dying before the resurrection to which Eckhart and many others
allude.

A significant theme for Eckhart on the via negativa is not only the
pain that one encounters in this letting go, but the necessity of letting go
of the pain itself. In discussing the need to let go of our own wills, Eckhart notes that we can become attached to suffering and need to let go of
that as well. Fox (1980) explains Eckhart's approach to happiness, evil,
and suffering:

But if God wishes our happiness and we wish our happiness, why are we
not happier? Why is there so much suffering and so much pain? Eckhart
would reply that it is because we have not let go of our wills radically
enough. "The restlessness of all our storms comes entirely from self-will,
whether we notice it or not." Eckhart urges us, within the context of

discussing our need to let go of will, to let go of suffering as well. Too often we cling to our suffering and become attached to it. . . .

It is suffering with attachment which is "hard for you to bear," but suffering "for the love of God . . . does not hurt and is not hard to bear" (See Fox, 1980, p. 273 ff.). Eckhart tells the story of a man who had one hundred marks and lost forty. When he concentrates only on the last forty, he

> remains in despair and grief. How could he be comforted and free from sorrow if he turns to his loss and his pain and pictures it to himself and himself in it, and looks at it, and it looks at him again and talks to him. He speaks to his loss and the loss talks to him again, and they see each other face to face.

This is no way to let go of suffering, Eckhart is cautioning. Pain compulsively clung to is pain that is doubled. "Turn your back" on the lost forty marks, Eckhart advises, and concentrate [on the remaining sixty]. . . . We suffer to the extent that we are shallow in our letting go of things and to the extent that we cling to things instead of experiencing their transparency. (pp. 233–234)

Fox (1983) further explicates the necessary embrace and release of pain and presents the possibility of the pain becoming a source of energy:

> Jesus had the same insight: love your enemies. Pain is our enemy, but that is no excuse to run from embracing it, kissing it long enough so that we might truly let go of it. . . . Every rose has its thorns. The Japanese poet Kenji Miyazawa left us a powerful image of dealing with pain when he said that we must embrace pain and burn it as a fuel for our journey. The image that comes to mind on hearing this advice is the following: we pick up our pain as we would a bundle of sticks for a fireplace; we necessarily embrace these sticks as we move across the room to the fireplace; then we thrust them into the fire, getting rid of them, letting go of them; finally we are warmed and delighted by their sacrificial gift to us in the form of fire and heat and warmth and energy. (pp. 142–143)

An essential presupposition to letting go of our own will, enduring the resulting pain, and giving ourselves to God's ways and God's will, according to Eckhart, is that God's will is trustworthy. Furthermore, as stated earlier, the creation is good, and although evil is present, it does not triumph.

> One reason why letting go of will and sinking into the freedom that is God's will is a way to be trusted is that the goodness of the Creator is to be trusted. Evil is not as radical to creation as goodness is. . . .
> Evil does not have the last word. (Fox, 1980, p. 232)

Pain, of course, also has the potential to break the artificial boundaries between human beings and bring home the contemplative reality that all human beings are related to every other human being.

> [T]o relieve another's pain or to celebrate another's joy is to relieve one's own pain and to celebrate one's own joy. Here the unnatural boundaries between inner and outer, personal and social, I and you, truly melt. (Fox, 1983, pp. 152–153)

Thus, the contemplative way involves a disposition of openness, trust, and vulnerability in the encounter with the unknown. It involves the ultimate risk, the risk of death, or the letting go and giving up of whatever is most important, however that may be for the individual. This way is not safe or secure, except for the safety and security that come from knowing that no knowledge, relationship, accomplishment, or possession ever granted safety or security. In the midst of the loss that is inevitably involved, there is no denial of the reality of pain and loss; instead, the contemplative is free to embrace this pain and then let it go.

The next section considers the contemplative approach to the future, that is, the patient waiting for history to unfold and reveal itself.

LETTING GO AND LETTING BE INVOLVE PATIENT WAITING FOR THE UNFOLDING OF LIFE

The letting go of, or detachment from, both knowledge and the will on the via negativa implies also a letting go of control, a hands–off approach to the future. For the contemplative, the future cannot be orchestrated or manipulated, although one need not be passive or inactive. Carl Jung applied Eckhart's concept of action through nonaction to psychological processes, although it is applicable elsewhere:

> The art of letting things happen, action through non-action, letting go of oneself, as taught by Meister Eckhart, became for me the key to opening the door to the way. We must be able to let things happen in the psyche. For us, this actually is an art of which few people know anything. Consciousness is forever interfering, helping, correcting, and negating, and never leaving the simple growth of the psychic processes in peace. (Jung, 1962, p. 93)

Patience may be one of the key qualities of the contemplative paradigm. This is the patience that waits for the catalytic moment, somewhat like a snake that watches and waits until the moment arrives to strike with swiftness and accuracy. This is an active, alive, conscious watching and waiting. Twentieth-century German philosopher Josef

Pieper captures this and several themes, from both the via positiva and the via negativa, in a discussion of leisure. Pieper (1993) first clarifies his use of the term *leisure*, distinguishing it from idleness or merely time off. Idleness is the absence of leisure. "Leisure is only possible when people are at one with themselves, when they acquiesce in their own being, whereas the essence of *acedia* [lassitude, dejection—sloth] is the refusal to acquiesce in one's own being" (p. 8). For Pieper, leisure is first of all an attitude of mind and not dependent on external factors.

In further explicating his concept of leisure, Pieper states that leisure is a contemplative attitude and uses terms closely associated with the contemplative paradigm such as silence, receptiveness, mysteriousness of the universe, openness, loose reins, intuition, trust, affirmation and celebration, letting things happen. "Leisure is a form of silence, of that silence which is the prerequisite of the apprehension of reality; only the silent hear and those who do not remain silent do not hear" (Pieper, 1993, pp. 9–10).

The deep happiness that accompanies leisure is rooted in an appreciation and acknowledgment of "the mysteriousness of the universe and the recognition of our incapacity to understand it, that comes with a deep confidence, so that we are content to let things take their course" (Pieper, 1993, pp. 9–10). Leisure is an attitude, an approach to life that has less to do with grabbing all you can, but of being open, having a loose grip. It is the letting go of falling asleep.

> Sleeplessness and the incapacity for leisure are really related to one another in a special sense, and a person at leisure is not unlike a person asleep. . . . When we really let our minds rest contemplatively on a rose in bud, on a child at play, on a divine mystery, we are rested and quickened as though by a dreamless sleep. . . . And in the same way God's great, imperishable intuitions visit a person in moments of leisure. It is in these silent and receptive moments that our souls are sometimes visited by an awareness of what holds the world together—only for a moment perhaps, and the lightening vision of our intuition has to be recaptured and rediscovered in hard work. (Pieper, 1993, p. 10)

Leisure has an attitude of contemplative celebration. To be at leisure, one needs to be at one with herself, at one with the world. It is not simply a nonactivity. There is more to it than peace and quiet. "Something of this is conveyed in Holderlin's fragment *Leisure*, where he compares himself to a loving elm standing in a peaceful meadow, while the delight of life plays about him, embracing him like a vine" (Pieper, 1993, p. 10).

Although Path Two, the via negativa, (and Pieper's reflection) is infused with themes and concepts that give fullness to letting go and letting be—silence, emptying, surrender, poverty, darkness, imagelessness, detachment—this path contains the seeds for Path Three, the *via creativa*. For, according to Eckhart and his interpreter, Matthew Fox, this emptying and letting go create a space for unity, creativity, fruitfulness, and joy.

> Such is the trust and confidence that is born of a true path of letting go and letting be. . . . Indeed, integral to true letting go is letting go of lack of trust, lack of confidence, and lack of self-love. . . . Only this kind of letting go will allow God and God's love to happen. It alone bears fruit. There will be no fruit without it.
>
> Eckhart plays with the concept of the fruits of the spirit in this sermon on bearing fruit. The fruits of the spirit he enunciates are joy, youthfulness or eternity, and simplicity. . . . This joy overcomes suffering—the joy of the person would be so great that all the suffering and all the poverty would be too little. For Eckhart, then, the via negativa culminates in joy. . . .
>
> Another fruit of this union and this release of the divine spark in us is freedom and the simplicity and spontaneity that freedom brings. We become as free and transparent as God is. We become free of all names and bare of all forms, totally free and void, just as God is void and free in himself. . . . The truth of the unity of God and creation, the full panentheistic truth, become ours to behold in a direct way. . . . So totally one and simple is this castle, and so elevated above all modes and powers is this unique way and power that a power or a mode can never gaze into it—not even God himself.
>
> In this castle or divine spark, which has now been allowed air and space to burn, God glows and burns with all his wealth and all his bliss. . . . [E]ven suffering would become totally a joy and a pleasure. And we learn to give our sufferings to God to bear for us. We can, finally, even let go of our sufferings. (Fox, 1980, pp. 288–289)

Fox, in the preceding excerpt, is commenting on a sermon by Eckhart[9] in which he uses the metaphor "a virgin who is also a wife," a metaphor that provides the link between the via negativa and the via creativa.

> The word *virgin* means a person who is free of all false images, and who is detached as if he or she did not yet exist. . . .
>
> Now pay attention and examine what I say carefully! If this person were always a virgin, no fruit would come from him or her. If this person is to become fruitful, then it is necessary for him or her to become a *wife*. . . . It is good for a person to receive God into himself or herself, and in this receptivity he or she is a virgin. But it is better for God to become fruitful within the person. This is because becoming fruitful as a result of the gift is the only gratitude for the gift. . . .
>
> Many good gifts are received in virginity, but they are not born back to God in wifely fruitfulness with thankful praise. These gifts spoil and come to nothing, so that the person will never become more blissful or better as

a result. Therefore, that person's virginity is of no use, for he or she does not become through it a wife in full fertility. (Fox, 1980, pp. 273–274)

Thus, Eckhart shifts his listeners from the second to the third path and invites them to consider experiencing God through creativity and birthing.

NOTES

1. *Abgeschiedenheit* and *Gelassenheit* (Fox, 1981, p. 224).

2. World mythology is replete with death-followed-by-life myths such as the phoenix arising from the ashes or the new life of spring following the dead of winter. The death/life imagery of the Greek scriptures (New Testament) contains an important element of willingness in the dying. That death/life myth is not one of a valiant battle to the death followed by a vengeful return from the grave. It is a conscious and willing giving up or letting go of life.

3. As with any narrative, the Gospels and their various parables, sayings, and stories are rich with meaning. Exploring a particular level of interpretation or perspective does not negate or deny others.

4. See generally, "Beati pauperes spiritu, quia ipsorum est regnum coelorum" ["Blessed are the poor in spirit, for theirs is the kingdom of heaven."] (Quint, 1958–1976, vol. II, #52).

5. Colledge and McGinn (1981), at p. 199 translate this phrase, "I beg you to be *disposed* to what I say" (emphasis added). Placing oneself at the disposal of another is perhaps an additional way of speaking of poverty, detachment, or indifference, as used by a variety of authors in discussing the via negativa.

6. St. John of the Cross, *Ascent of Mt. Carmel*, book 2, chapter 9, 4; *The Dark Night of the Soul*, book 2, chapter 11, 1. (See especially, Peers, 1959, p. 132, "For this present kind is an enkindling of spiritual love in the soul, which in the midst of these dark confines . . . to have a certain realization and foretaste of God, although it understands nothing definitely, for, as we say, the understanding is in darkness.")

7. St. John of the Cross, *Ascent of Mt. Carmel*, book 2, chapter 24, 4.

8. See Puhl, 1951, p. 168. The term *inordinate attachments* is used a number of times in the *Spiritual Exercises*. See, for example, Puhl, pp. 71, 72, and 75.

9. "Intravit Jesus in quoddam castellum et mulier quaedam, Martha nomine, excepit illum in domum suam," (based on Luke 10:38, "In the course of their journey he came to a castle, and a woman named Martha welcomed him into her house.") (Quint, 1958–1976, vol. I, #2).

13

The Fourfold Path: Creativity

The third segment of the fourfold path, creativity, focuses on giving birth, being creative, bearing fruit, enjoying the blessings of the new birth. The second part of the fourfold path, the way of detachment, invited a letting go of everything—fear, death, distrust, even a letting go of letting go. This detachment, this loosening of the grip of control, is essential for creativity and birthing. "When we learn to let go even of letting go, then we learn how birth comes about" (Fox, 1980, pp. 291).

> Eckhart envisions a threefold birth that takes place when we have journeyed the *via positiva* of creation and the *via negativa* of letting go. These births are the following: the birth of ourselves in a breakthrough in consciousness, the birth of God in us, and the birth of ourselves as sons and daughters of God. The theology of the divinization of humanity is overwhelmingly in evidence throughout all of . . . Path Three. For Eckhart is concerned with the breakthrough that divinity has made and can make in human history, human consciousness. Indeed, he will insist that "the essence of God is birthing" and that therefore those who give birth are participating in a divine activity. (p. 291)

For Eckhart, the way of creativity, fertility, generativity, is linked to the first two paths, appreciation and detachment.

For with birth there is blessing, but without birth there can be no blessing. In the birth, Eckhart declares, "you will discover all blessing." But "neglect the birth and you neglect all blessing." A creation or blessing spirituality, then, culminates in giving birth to still more blessing. The formula behind such a spirituality appears to be as follows:

via positiva (creation) + *via negativa* (letting go) > *via creativa*

Eckhart's is a spirituality of the *via creativa*: how all are birthers and creators, as God is birther and Creator. He admits a dialectic and tension between the *via positiva* and *via creativa*. Interestingly enough, this tension between living and creating is, according to psychiatrist and artist Otto Rank, *the* single most basic struggle in the soul of any artist. Eckhart's therapy for healing such a struggle would appear to be Path Two: letting go and letting be. To create, the artist needs to let go radically of creating. The *via negativa*, then, becomes a bridge that heals and links Paths One and Three and thereby encourages rather than discourages further birth and creativity. The first of the births that occur is that of the individual: an awakening, a rebirth, a birth of oneself. For this awakening Eckhart invented a word. He called it "breakthrough" [*Durchbruch*]. (Fox, 1980, pp. 291–292)

Eckhart and his contemplative colleagues map the contours of the third path, the experience of God through creativity.

TO BE FULLY HUMAN IS TO BE CREATIVE

Once again, as on the first two paths, Eckhart's theology on the third path, the *via creativa*, is rooted in primal myths. The Incarnation and the Genesis myths serve as starting points for the via creativa also. In a sermon from the midnight Christmas liturgy, Eckhart affirms the necessity of our giving birth to the divine in our time:

We celebrate here in temporality with a view to the *eternal* birth, which God the Father has accomplished and accomplishes in eternity, so that this same birth has now been accomplished *in time* within human nature. What does it avail me if this birth takes place unceasingly and yet does not take place within myself? (Fox, 1980, p. 293, emphasis in original)

"[T]he birthing we all do is nothing less than the birthing of God's word, God's Dabhar, God's Son" (Fox, 1983, p. 176). Fox looks back to the Hebrew creation stories and the concept of *Dabhar* or creative energy to introduce the via creativa:

In letting both pleasure and pain happen, both light and darkness, both naming and unnaming, both cosmos and void, we allow a third thing to be born: and that third thing is the very power of birth itself. It is Dabhar erupting out of humanity's imagination. It is the image of God, the image of the Creator, coming alive and expressing its divine depths and divine fruitfulness. It is our creativity which is the full meaning of humanity's being an "image of God." (Fox, 1983, p. 175)

According to Eckhart, human beings experience God, not only through the created world or by letting go, but also by being cocreators and by giving birth. The creative action is, from the beginning, a participatory activity. The created ones reflect the wonder of the creator. For Eckhart, when we create, we praise God.

We are the sons and daughters of the Father! But to be children of the Father who is pure generation means that we too are to generate, we too are to be birthers who are divinely fruitful. This is our praise of God, namely our creativity.

What praises God? That which is like him. Thus, everything in the soul which is like God praises God. Whatever is at all unlike God does not praise God. In the same way, a statue praises the artists who has imprinted on it all the art that he has in his mind, thus making it so very like his conception. The similarity of the work of art to the artist's conception praises the master without words (J. Clark, 1957, p. 164). (Fox, 1980, pp. 404–405)

Inasmuch as we are created in the image of God, we also are intended to be creative, to be artists, to continue the onward flow of creativity.

Elsewhere Eckhart explains that the Father and the Son are related as the artist to his or her art. Art stays with the artist like the Word stays with the Father. It flows out yet remains within. Eckhart links in an explicit way his theology of creativity with his theology of the Word.

From the start, once he has become an artist and as long as he is an artist capable of creative work, art remains with the artist. This is the meaning of "The Word was in the beginning with God," that is, the art with the artist, coeval with him, as the Son is with the Father in God (Clark & Skinner, p. 249).

God's Word is God's work. . . . Since we too are God's children, it follows that we too are God's works of art. But also, being heirs of God come of age, we too are artists, for "humankind lives by art and reason, that is to say, practically." (Benz & Koch, vol. III, p. 10) We are heirs of God, heirs of creativity. (Fox, 1980, pp. 404–405)

An essential part of our inheritance as "children of the heavenly Father" is to be creative, fruitful human beings, and reflect the divine creativity.

IN *LETTING GO*, HUMAN BEINGS ENCOUNTER CREATIVITY

The mere fact of letting go—of preordained forms, ideas, methods—fosters creativity. The ability to risk increases the range of possibilities for any human being. Gerald May (1987), from a contemporary perspective, lists several effects of contemplation, including increased clarity and breadth of awareness, an increased confidence in intuitive abilities, and increased knowledge of the nature and substance of thoughts, sensations, emotions, memories, images, and other mental functions (p. 29). When we sink deeply into our truest nature as contemplative beings, we hit flowing springs of creativity.

The contemplative tradition includes numerous images of water—water in the desert, a cup filled to overflowing, the succulence of growing plants, and other metaphors of flowing abundance. St. Teresa of Avila, the 16th-century fellow Carmelite and companion of St. John of the Cross, was both a contemplative and a gifted administrator, leading a reform movement and establishing numerous religious houses. She uses the image of a garden to describe the journey of contemplative prayer:

> Beginners must realize that in order to give delight to the Lord they are starting to cultivate a garden on very barren soil, full of abominable weeds. His Majesty [God] pulls up the weeds and plants good seed. . . . Now let us keep in mind that all this is already done by the time the soul is determined to practice prayer and has begun to make use of it. And with the help of God we must strive like good gardeners to get those plants to grow and take pains to water them so that they don't wither but come to bud and flower and give forth a most pleasant fragrance to provide refreshment for this Lord of ours. Then He will often come to take delight in this garden and find His joy among these virtues. (Kavanaugh & Rodriguez, 1987, vol. 1, p. 113)

St. Teresa continues and describes how the garden is watered, beginning with water drawn from a well (which she explains is the first of the four degrees of prayer), and then with water obtained by means of a water wheel. The third means is water flowing from a river or stream, and the fourth is water pouring down as rain.

> But let us see now how it must be watered so that we may understand what we have to do, the labor this will cost us, whether the labor is greater than the gain, and for how long it must last. It seems to me the garden can be watered in four ways. You may draw water from a well (which for us is a lot of work). Or you may get it by means of a water wheel and aqueducts in such a way that it is obtained by turning the crank of the water wheel. . . . Or it may flow from a river or stream. (The garden is

watered much better by this means because the ground is more fully soaked, and there is no need to water so frequently—and much less work for the gardener.) Or the water may be provided by a great deal of rain. (For the Lord waters the garden without any work on our part—and this way is incomparably better than all the others mentioned.) (Kavanaugh & Rodriguez, 1987, vol. 1, p. 113)

St. Teresa later explains that "discursive work of the intellect" is what is meant by the hard work of fetching water from the well (p. 115). However, the other forms of prayer, for which the metaphors of aqueduct, river, and rain are used, might be described as requiring "comparatively little effort on the part of our reasoning or imagination," that is, what has been referred to as contemplative prayer (Green, 1979, p. 43).

St. Teresa recognizes the wellspring of energy that can be tapped deep within, as one drops into the moist emptiness. There is, on the via creativa, an appreciation of the breakthrough, refreshment, and creativity of laughter and play. Although humor and laughter could just as easily be found in the via negativa, because of the letting go implicit in humor, it may also properly be placed in the via creativa. Tilden Edwards (1990) describes a typical scene, from the perspective of a contemplative, in the midst of exhausting work, when humor breaks through. After much serious work, laughing, joking, and storytelling break through, and the earnestness of the group activity dissolves.

> We realize how much of God and life is beyond our comprehension and control; we're in touch with the absurdities and paradoxes of life that don't make sense to our little minds. The reins of our minds suddenly feel looser. Instead of angrily or fearfully rejecting the limits we see, we're free to accept everything just as it is for the moment. (p. 1)

Edwards reflects on the laughter and notices the freedom from controlled mental processes that it induces, the loosening emotion. Using metaphors such as explosion in both mind and body, shaking of the chain of one connected thought or feeling after the other, play, and mental flexibility.

> Our pretenses are lightly deflated, leaving us with less to defend and fear. We experience a certain perspective and expansiveness, as when tightly held-in waters flow over their banks and spread over a broad plain. We become free for God and for appreciation of God's creation in a special way. (Edwards, 1990, p. 1)

Although humor can be used to destroy creativity and escape from necessary tasks, it can also be an invitation to trust.

> You don't have to know everything and do everything just right on your
> own; indeed, you cannot. . . . Right now, just relax a little and give me a
> chance to play with you."
>   . . . When our unconditionally loved nature really sinks into our trust,
> we're not only freer to laugh but also freer to be useful to the world's
> well–being, as an inspired reverberation of that love we know, rather than
> as a way of trying to win it. (Edwards, 1990, p. 1)

Edwards is able to articulate not only how laughter, as a way in to God
or the contemplative experience, fosters creativity, but also how the
open appreciation of the via positiva is linked to both the letting go in
the via negativa and the spontaneous, celebrative action of the via
creativa.

Contemporary spiritual writer Adrian van Kaam (1974), in discussing
gentleness and playfulness as a means of entering into the divine
presence, weaves together the themes of creativity, letting go, and being
at one or at peace.

> Gentle playfulness is lived in those rare moments when I feel at one with
> the Divine Presence, finely attuned to His inspiration, released from divi-
> sive concerns. I feel gracious, with the soft, flowing grace of a dancer,
> joyous with the lightheartedness of a child. Such moments grant me a
> glimpse of eternity, a rehearsal of the playful life to come. For a breathtak-
> ing moment, I see the divine playfulness lighting up the world of daily
> appearances. No longer blinded by arrogant sophistication, make believe
> poses, empty words, I respond to grace with graciousness, blissfully at one
> with the Eternal Presence that fills the universe. (p. 177)

The breakloose of laughter is also the breakloose of energy and creativity on the third path.

THE CONTEMPLATIVE LIFE UNITES BEING AND ACTION

Action is an integral part of the contemplative approach to life. Fox
(1980), in an explication of one of Eckhart's sermons,[1] discusses the
necessity of action for the contemplative:

> When we are in God and the divine image that is in our soul is allowed to
> become what it is, then we share the qualities of the Persons of God. . . .
> We become the Trinity in action, ushering power, wisdom, and goodness
> into human history. Indeed, it is absolutely essential to Eckhart's theology
> that this Trinitarian union bear fruit in action. . . . Why must action be so
> integral a part of our union with the Divinity? Divinity is not just being, it
> is being diffusing itself, it is power, wisdom, and goodness pouring forth
> on the world. There action and being are one. And so, where the soul is,

there is only being and action. This is where God is—where action and being are one. Eckhart is calling for a revitalized form of action, one that truly flows from our being; but he insists that being without action is not true divine being. . . . Action is the key to Eckhart's mysticism—so long as it is action that flows from our being. This distinguishes his mysticism from many species of quietistic spiritualities that have held sway in the West since his day. Indeed, Eckhart takes it for granted that action is part of being in God. . . . The issue is not to stop acting, but to make sure our actions, like our being, are in God. Our union with God means that we become God's tools—God is our overseer—as we do God's work. . . . Union reaches its fullness when things are accomplished "divinely in God." The soul now functions in the divine power just like that power. The union and rest with the Trinity are not introverted or narcissistic but outward-oriented. (pp. 394–395)

The importance of Fox's comments on Eckhart's theology is twofold. First, the contemplative life does not mean only silence and internal stillness. The contemplative life, from Eckhart's perspective, is also a life of action. This perspective is important in understanding Path Four, the *via transformativa*, the way of compassion and the celebration of justice. The deep well of energy that can be tapped in the contemplative experience, coupled with the radical detachment outlined in the via negativa, generates the potential for powerful and even relentless action. Second, the action born of the contemplative experience is deliberate, unfrenzied, perhaps even focused. This action is somewhat akin to a batter awaiting the right pitch. A good batter waits patiently, absorbing intuitively a multiplicity of data. An impatient, frenzied, distracted batter will not do well. However, when the right pitch, the right moment arrives, the batter moves quickly and unambiguously. Nothing can stop him. He may swing and miss, but failure is not a deterrent for the contemplative batter (because he is detached from both success and failure), only an additional opportunity to be open to the reality that he is confronting.

The history of the contemplatives is replete with stories of unambiguous, energetic, even heroic, action. St. Teresa of Avila is known not only for her writings on prayer and the interior life but also for her work as a reformer of the Carmelite order. The founding, in Avila, Spain, in 1562, of St. Joseph, the first convent of the reformed (Discalced) Carmelites, provides an example of action informed and energized by contemplative experience. The building chosen to house the new convent site was small and poorly maintained and the circumstances difficult.

The euphoria [that she experienced upon the first day of operation of the convent] gave place almost at once to a mood of doubt and self-reproach. . . . Would not her nuns be wretched leading such a poverty-stricken, hand-to-mouth existence, and quickly run short of food? . . . Perhaps she had been altogether too ambitious in launching the new venture, when she was already a professed nun herself and ought to have been content with the common lot. The Devil, in short, might have put the whole idea into her head and beguiled her into believing it was inspired from on high. . . . Then suddenly the clouds cleared. A ray of light penetrated her soul, and she began to recognize her fears as put there by the Devil and to recall God's promises and her resolve to serve him, come what may. . . . Teresa vowed that she would do everything in her power to obtain the consent of her superiors for a transfer to the new house and there live a life of penance and strict enclosure.

"The moment I did this," she tells us, "the Devil turned tail and left me calm and happy; and thus I remained, as I have done ever since." (Clissold, 1979, pp. 94–95)

Teresa's determination and calm resolve remained throughout some challenging and even violent circumstances. Within a few months of the founding of St. Joseph, the convent came under physical attack.

An angry group gathered outside the convent shouting abuse. Then the Corregidor appeared in person and called on the nuns to leave. Otherwise, he threatened, he would order the doors to be forced. . . . Both sides prepared for battle. Some of the Council's men hammered on the doors, but the nuns reinforced them with wooden beams and the locks held. (Clissold, 1979, p. 96)

This was one of many challenges St. Teresa faced in the midst of her reform efforts. She exemplifies the activist contemplative, one whose powerful and persistent actions arise from a deeply rooted sense of peace or rightness.

CREATIVITY INVOLVES ACTION THAT IS DISCIPLINED AND AT PEACE

Creativity does not mean unfocused frenzy. Good art requires discipline along with inspiration. Jazz musicians engaged in a jam session, for example, are said to play with disciplined abandon. Tapping the well-spring of creativity demands that difficult choices be made. When a free decision is finally made, the contemplative can move forward with unambiguous passion, waiting patiently for the future to unfold and reveal the next image, idea, or course of action.

There is a kind of disciplined creative action that Eckhart describes as repose and that contemporary spiritual writer Adrian van Kaam describes as gentle. Eckhart discusses the concept of repose in his sermon, "In all things I sought rest."[2]

[T]he soul seeks repose in all its powers and motions, whether people know this or not. . . . I have also said that people can never feel joy or pleasure in any creature if God's likeness is not within it. . . . But nothing resembles God in all creatures so much as repose.

. . . God neither heeds nor needs vigils, fasting, prayer and all forms of mortification in contrast to repose. God needs nothing more than for us to offer him a quiet heart. (Fox, 1980, p. 381)

Adrian van Kaam (1994), describes an approach to life, work, and creativity that is the opposite of willful or frenzied and that is in accord with Eckhart's concept of repose, naming it the gentle lifestyle. Van Kaam begins his discussion of the gentle life: "Spiritual life may be most simply defined as the art and discipline of presence to the Sacred" (p. 9). Gentleness is one of the attitudes that van Kaam identifies as facilitating that presence (p. 10). Gentleness, in van Kaam's terms, is an alternative to goal-oriented utilitarianism. Gentleness may best be defined by van Kaam's own anecdote about writing a paper:

I spent part of last summer writing a paper. My decisiveness to get the thing over and done with made me feel tense and strained. Before going any further, I began to tell myself, "This time try to do your work with ease of mind." So I tried. I began to muse in a leisurely way about my topic. I read thoughtfully material related to it. Only then did I feel ready to write out a few paragraphs of pages. When the work became too much, I would stroll in a nearby park, look at the flowers, follow the antics of playful ducks in the pond. I tried not to let myself become upset, strained or willful. Neither did I try to obtain the results of my study instantly. I was sure my topic would speak to me in its own good time if I would keep myself quietly open for hints, sudden associations, flashes of insight. My faithful readings and reflections would sooner or later show me the main aspects of the question I was dealing with.

So I trusted. I also kept my inner freedom to occasionally close my books, halt my typing, and leave my notes to enjoy the radiance of the sun in the garden or the pleasant breeze along the lanes and meadows in the park. My new way worked. Slowly I would feel the ideas rise, the right words come. A gentle perseverance in my attention to the topic and its expression proved sufficient for the paper to be written. (pp. 24–25)

Van Kaam further clarifies his definition of the gentle lifestyle by noting the shift between the two modes of operation as he wrote the paper:

At first I approached my task with the anxious drive to get the work over with. Now I had given myself over to the calming effect of a gentle life style. I could almost feel the tautness leaving my head, the tenseness draining from my muscles. No longer was the will to force things present in me. I did not command my topic to make itself clear at once. I was content to be nothing more than I could be at the moment, content to make as much headway as I was humanly able to. There was no compulsion to be more efficient, more clever, or faster than I reasonably could be in a relaxed manner. Gone was the eagerness to hurry up the process of production. The spirit of gentility had invaded my work. (p. 25)

This gentle approach toward life (which seems in accord with what Gerald May and others have described as the contemplative approach), in van Kaam's experience, had a significant effect on the task at hand:

On other occasions my feelings were quite the opposite. At such times I wanted desperately to gain time. I came to my writing with a vehemence that shut out anything my topic itself could give me when patiently waited upon. The work had to be done as fast as possible, I felt, and the topic itself was not going to play a part in its production. I did not give the topic much chance to show itself to me. I ran through books and articles without really allowing them to affect me. The topic spoke, but I could not hear its message because I did not approach it gently as a reflective person should. My readings contained hints and suggestions, but I as a gentle and recep-tive listener was not there to receive them. Many pages were pregnant in meaning but not for me. Instead I gathered surface information as fast as I could. No time was given to let it sink in, to make it part of myself, to recreate it in my own manner. (van Kaam, 1994, pp. 25–26)

Van Kaam reflects on the treatment of time, contrasting the *gentle* way with the rushed manner, which he also experienced:

For the process of thought and its precise expression, time is of the essence. Gentility allows time to run its course. My concern was to gain time. I typed my information out like a reporter on the city desk. While I was hurrying on, I was neither concerned with the kind of people who would read my paper, nor with the people around me and their needs.

By contrast, gentility opens me to what people, events, and things may disclose to me or reasonably want of me. I allow these persons and things to change and affect me when such change is called for. Gentleness is an attitude of letting be, combined with a patient waiting and abiding with myself or with the person, task or problem God calls me to be involved in. This attitude leads to peace and contentment. (p. 26)

Van Kaam explains further the difference between contemplative gentleness and willfulness and how gentleness can be manifested in everyday activity:

I can be busily engaged in a demanding task like writing a paper, organ-izing a business deal, fighting for a cause, and yet be gentle inwardly. One condition is to keep in tune with the real me and my real life situation and not become a prisoner of my projects or of the outcome of my task. It is unrealistic to strive after something I cannot reach without overextending myself. . . . Even when I achieve such goals, frustration may still result. I may have so depleted myself in vehement strife that I cannot enjoy my success. It may seem meager in comparison to all I had to go through to make this achievement come true. For too long a time I may have used my life as merely a tool for achievement in the eyes of others. In spite of momentary success, I suffer the frustration of a vehement or willful life.

In contrast, the gentle attitude leaves room for what is more than mere usefulness. When I am willful instead of gentle, I program my life. Things are not allowed to appear to me as they are. The willful man squeezes every experience in a tight little box tied up with unbreakable string. His mind becomes a store house of these little air tight compartments. He does not allow any new situations to touch the content of his store. What he has done is to forfeit his ability to abide with things as if for the first time. He moves through life as a programmed computer, lacking any sense of wonder.

A vehement or willful person cannot "let go" in prayer, love or play. The most relaxing activity becomes just another form of work for him. He brings to love or play the same demands for accomplishment that deaden his daily life. Soon his spirit dies too. (pp. 26–27)

This image of the lifestyle of gentleness has implications for personal freedom, as described by van Kaam (1994):

The gentle person is more free. He can take himself and the world as they are because he feels free to be himself and to let all things be with the same gentility. There is a friendly accord between him and his life situation. He does not feel that he has to push himself forward or hold himself back. At home with himself he approaches every task and event in gentle self-possession. If he cannot feel at ease with what he is doing, he can put it aside for another time when he can more readily give his all. If the situation demands that he go on with the work at hand—in spite of his reluctance—he gently does what cannot be delayed. He does not allow himself to become upset by the less than perfect outcome due to the inauspiciousness of the moment. He takes things in stride. Being a gentle man he never forces people or situations. Neither would he tolerate anyone who forces himself or others, were he able to ward off such imposition. All people, events, and things, no matter how insignificant, draw his respect, for they all emerge from the same mystery. (pp. 27–28)

There is also the matter of the ego in the contemplative life in general and in the via creativa in particular. Van Kaam discusses the gentle lifestyle and the ego in relation to availability for God or staying attuned to God's presence, which has been described as the essence of contemplation (G. May, 1991, pp. 191 ff.).

In living the gentle life style, I may discover something else. It becomes easier for me to pray, to meditate, to stay attuned to God's presence. Gentility stills and quiets the greediness and aggressiveness of the ego. A silenced ego allows me to center myself in my divine ground. While it is helpful to have a strong ego, it is harmful to center my life in that ego alone. Greediness and arrogance might then absorb all my life. . . .

Any true gentility, human or divine, mellows the ego, not by weakening its strength but by diminishing its arrogance, its false exclusiveness, its pretense of ultimate. Any diminishment of the ego's arrogance makes me more available to the Divine. (van Kaam, 1994, pp. 28–29)

Matthew Fox (1983), in reflecting on Eckhart, emphasizes that art, though needing discipline, is hindered by judgmental thinking:

Says Eckhart, "Whatever I want to express in its truest meaning must emerge from within me and pass through an inner form. It cannot come from outside to the inside, but must emerge from within." What emerges from within is art. Art is born within us. Art is not the same as stream-of-consciousness spontaneity. "It passes through an inner form," as Eckhart observes. Perhaps that form is dancing or clay or paints or a musical instrument or a dramatic technique. Art as meditation is not meditation without form . . . .

The single largest obstacle in teaching adults to meditate by means of art is getting them to let go of judgmental attitudes toward their self-expression. . . . "You can't sing," or "You don't dance well," or, "You can't draw at all." Of course it should be emphasized that art as meditation presumes, as all creation spirituality does, trust. A trust that out of silence, waiting, openness, emptiness one can and will give birth to images. (pp. 192–193)

CONTEMPLATIVE ACTION REQUIRES DISCERNMENT

The concept of being at peace or in repose is of great importance in the contemplative tradition. It is at the heart of the discernment process. Although discernment is a concept considered by a wide variety of contemplative writers, St. Ignatius Loyola and those who follow in his footsteps have written extensively and systematically on this subject. For example, *The Spiritual Exercises of St. Ignatius* includes 22 separate "Rules for Discernment of Spirits" (Puhl, 1951, pp. 141–150), which have been the subject of numerous books and articles (for example, Toner, 1982; Green, 1984). Discernment is a process of reflection in a particular situation, particularly in ambiguous, gray situations where one must choose between black and black or white and white. Discernment is appropriate for the life situations in which rules or certainty do not apply. Thomas Green, S.J., a contemporary Jesuit priest and interpreter of Ignatius, begins his discussion of Ignatian discernment with the dictionary definition of the verb discern, that is, to perceive by sight or some other sense or by intellect and to distinguish mentally, recognize as distinct or different, discriminate.

> Thus, the ordinary usage of "discern" involves both perceiving and distinguishing or judging. In the case of spiritual discernment also, or "discernment of spirits" as it has been called traditionally, both perception and judgment are important. What is unique to and distinctive of this religious meaning of discernment is the *object* of our perceiving and judging. It is, surprisingly, our *feelings* that we distinguish and evaluate in spiritual discernment. For this reason it is essential to spiritual discernment that we be in touch with our feelings. . . . [I] have become convinced that the greatest obstacle to real discernment . . . is not the intangible nature of God, but . . . our own lack of self–knowledge—even our *unwillingness* to know ourselves as we truly are. Almost all of us wear masks, not only when facing others but even when looking in the mirror.
>
> These are the factors which make discernment a fairly rare art, and the idea of discernment difficult to grasp. . . . In essence discernment is an art, not a science; it is learned by doing, by trial and error. And it is a gift, not primarily the fruit of personal effort. (Green, 1984, p. 22, emphasis in original)

The importance of interior awareness in discernment does not rule out the use of rationality or of what Ignatius terms revelation. Ignatius's *Rules* set forth three sets of circumstances in which one is confronted with a decision. Only one is appropriate for discernment. There are, first, the rare times when one has an unshakable gut feeling (or revelation) that one course of action is correct. In these circumstances, there is nothing to discern. The decision is clear. One also often uses the natural powers of reason and observation and one's better judgment to sort out choices in a calm, rational analysis when circumstances make this possible. Discernment is not necessary in those circumstances either. St. Ignatius Loyola even offers some tools for this time of reasoning—tools that involve the imagination rather than just logic, but that still are not considered discernment (Green, 1984, pp. 86–87). For example, one can ask how one would advise a stranger who presented the same issue, or how one would respond looking back from the edge of the grave (Puhl, 1951, pp. 76–77).

Discernment is reserved, in Ignatian terms, for those times when neither gut reaction nor ordinary observation and reasoning are sufficient. Discernment is meant for the times of unclarity and uncertainty, when significant decisions are involved. When there is no obvious rational choice and no clear revelation, Ignatius suggests that one pay attention to the experience of desolation and consolation, the raw material of discernment (Green, 1984, p. 88). Consolation and desolation, as used by Ignatius, refer to internal movements of the heart or spirit. Much has been written in an attempt to clarify these two terms. A core concept of consolation is a sense of peace.

> Thus consolation can take many forms: It may involve strong emotion—being inflamed with love, shedding tears of love and praise—or it may be quiet and deep. The common denominator, I would say, is peace in the Lord; whether the soul be deeply and strongly moved, as in the emotional reunion of two lovers after a long separation, or quietly consoled, as might be the experience of a mother gazing on the sleeping form of her newborn child in the middle of the night and quietly marveling at the wonder of life which has come from her body—in either case, the strongly emotional or the quietly deep, the defining quality which makes it consolation is peace. (Green, 1984, pp. 97–98)

Other terms that have been associated with consolation include peace of mind, lightness of heart, quiet or inner rest, tranquillity, conviction, expansiveness, courage, harmony, zeal, joy, holy desires, simplicity of action, singleness of heart, patience, hopefulness, self-acceptance, simplicity and clarity of thought, and focused energies.[3]

Desolation, as used by St. Ignatius Loyola, is the opposite of consolation. In his "Rules for the Discernment of Spirits" in the *Spiritual Exercises*, Ignatius describes desolation:

> I call desolation what is entirely the opposite of what is described in the third rule, as darkness of soul, turmoil of spirit, inclination to what is low and earthly, restlessness rising from many disturbances and temptations which lead to want of faith, want of hope, want of love. The soul is wholly slothful, tepid, sad, and separated, as it were, from its Creator and Lord. (Puhl, 1951, p.142)

Green (1984) offers his own commentary on desolation:

> Thus desolation is the very opposite of consolation. And like consolation it can take various forms, from emotional turmoil of spirit to a deadening tepidity and sadness. The common note of all forms of desolation, I believe, is *loss of peace*. Whether the feelings be stormy or simply "blah," the absence of peace will mark desolation just as surely as the experience of peace marks consolation. (p. 99)

Other terms associated with desolation include a troubled mind, discontent, agitation, anxiety, fear, disruption, inertia, boredom, apathy, restlessness, disturbances, dejection, self-pity, involuted or convoluted reasoning, dissipation of energies, discouragement, and sadness.[4]

An important element of Ignatian spirituality, and of discernment, is developing an awareness of these internal movements within oneself and learning to use them as an internal compass to assist in discerning the right direction in which to move. A simple practice in discernment is to spend some time each day reflecting on when and where one experienced consolation or desolation and, over a longer period of time, note the patterns of consolation and desolation in one's life. An individual can then discern what brings a sense of peace and what brings a sense of unease, agitation, and the like, and presumably choose the direction that brings peace, joy, courage, harmony, and so forth. This discernment practice is, in essence, a form of contemplative decision-making for ambiguous and significant issues.

Contemporary Jesuit priest and interpreter of St. Ignatius, Jules J. Toner, S.J. (1982), notes the distinction between the discernment of spirits and the discernment of God's will, explaining that Ignatius, in writings other than the *Rules*, offers assistance in discernment of God's will, beyond the discernment of spirits.

> These directives of Ignatius for discerning God's will include his directions for discernment of spirits but also go beyond them. They show us how to use not only the movement of the spirits, but also such factors as the signs of the times, the lessons of our own and others' past experience, and reasonable projections of future consequences from alternative good courses of action, in order to judge which of these courses of action of options is likely to be "more conducive" to the glory of God. (pp. 12–13)

Toner also notes that discernment of spirits assumes a sound knowledge of moral precepts and that discernment is for "finding the better among alternatives not forbidden by any material moral precept" (p. 13). Discernment is between right and right rather than between right and wrong.

From his own noticing of his internal affective movements of the heart, St. Ignatius devised a number of rules for discernment, based on his personal experiences. Some of the rules are very practical and easy to apply—for example: "In time of desolation we should never make any change, but remain firm and constant in the resolution and decision which guided us the day before the desolation, or in the decision to which we adhered in the preceding consolation" (Puhl, pp. 142–143). Others are less straightforward and require more reflection and interpretation. (There are actually two sets of rules, depending where one is on the spiritual journey. Compare Puhl, 1951, pp. 141–146 and pp. 147–150.) However, there is an assumption of openness or detachment that underlies all the rules (Green, 1984, p. 95). There is also the implicit understanding that one will not apply these rules as an isolated individual, but will seek the objectivity and assistance of a guide, that is, someone with a gift for discernment, in part to avoid self-deception (Toner, 1982, pp. 5–6).

Discernment is grounded in detachment, recognizes ambiguity and uncertainty, and shows an appreciation for knowledge that is beyond the rational and logical.

NOTES

1. "Gott is die Liebe . . ." (Quint, 1958–1976, vol. III, #67). See also Fox, 1980, pp. 388 ff.

2. "In omnibus requiem quaesivi" (Sir. 24:11). See Quint, 1958–1976, vol. III, #60; and Fox, 1980, pp. 380 ff.

3. From unpublished notes provided by the Jesuit Center for Spiritual Growth, Wernersville, PA, 1979.

4. From unpublished notes provided by the Jesuit Center for Spiritual Growth, Wernersville, PA, 1979.

14

The Fourfold Path: Compassion

Eckhart's fourfold journey does not end in contemplation, but in compassion. The fourth path, experiencing God through compassion, brings together all the other paths. The first path, creation as a gift, a blessing, something to be appreciated, is linked to the fourth path.

> Indeed, compassion is the first of all blessings, for creation itself is bathed in compassion . . . and compassion is the last blessing, the blessing that we, the new creators, are to give to others. Compassion thus constitutes the ultimate blessing we receive and give. (Fox, 1980, p. 415)

The second and third paths, detachment and creativity, also lead to compassion. Compassion marks our return to the world to re-create society. This is possible because we have learned freedom from letting go (Path Two) and ecstasy from our breakthrough and birthing (Part Three): "People who have let go of themselves are so pure that the world cannot harm them. . . . People who love justice will be admitted to justice. They will be seized by justice, and will be one with justice." When we encounter God we encounter justice and compassion. . . . Compassion is the culmination of our rebirth and breakthrough and also our birthing, for the ultimate act of grace and beauty is compassion. Compassion, then, is the fruit of our spiritual journey of faith. . . . In compassion the creative Word that launched creation continues to renew all things through our creative work.

... The fullest artistic contributions to society are contributions of compassion, especially toward the poor and outcast. Since compassion means justice as well as cosmic awareness, in compassion, social justice and mysticism come together, and because compassion is a divine attribute, our meaning as sons and daughters of God, that is to say our divinity, is discovered.... Compassion reveals our divinity to ourselves and to others. ... In compassion we and our works become divine and God becomes a human once again. We return home to our divine—and compassionate—origin. All beauty in heaven and on earth is united in compassion, for "compassion eventually leads to glory." (Fox, 1980, pp. 415–416)

Once again, the themes of this path interweave with each other and those of the other three paths.

COMPASSION AND SOCIAL JUSTICE IS THE HIGHEST FORM OF CREATIVITY

Matthew Fox (1990) emphasizes that for the contemplative, creativity and compassion are strongly linked:

There can be no compassion without creativity. Whether we are talking about making work or living situations more compassionate, about making economic systems or the relationship of first and third world people more compassionate, whether we are facing the issues of food and famine, energy or nuclear proliferation, unemployment or overemployment, boredom or alcoholism, creativity lies at the heart. (pp. 104–105)

Eckhart states in his sermon on Luke 6:36 ff.,[1] "Be compassionate" (Fox, 1980, p. 418). In explaining this imperative, Eckhart states several bases for being compassionate, the third of which is that "compassion directs a person to relationships with his fellow human beings" (p. 421). Fox further explicates Eckhart's approach to compassion:

All these deeds of relief and healing of the pain of others is what constitutes the works of compassion for Isaiah (Is. 58:3–11). For it is not enough that one listen to the Word, Eckhart declares. One must develop communicability or the ability to give further whatever is received. In this way the word received becomes a creative word or work. . . . Our creativity culminates in creatively compassionate deeds. . . .

First, regarding the Incarnation, Eckhart teaches that Jesus became one of us because he lacked the human condition that would allow God to suffer what people suffer and thus to know what true human compassion is about. . . . We are sons of the Compassionate One, like he is. Because Jesus taught us what compassion means, he also taught us what salvation means. It means to be compassionate, which means to enter into the fullness of the blessing that all creation is and to work to pass creation on as a blessing. . . . The works of creation are the focus for our compassion—all of them, animals and earth, water and air, plants and music, children and adults. . . . Our works are to be simple and sincere—like God's are—works that do not look for rewards. Works without a why. Compassion is about works, but not about reward for our works. (pp. 432–433)

Thomas Merton (1961) echoes Eckhart's view of compassion, but in a contemporary voice, and destroys the notion that contemplation is privatistic:

One of the paradoxes of the mystical life is this: that *a man cannot enter the deepest center of himself and pass through that center into God, unless he is able to pass entirely out of himself and empty himself and give himself to other people in the purity of a selfless love.*

And so one of the worst illusions in the life of contemplation would be to try to find God by barricading yourself inside your own soul, shutting out all external reality by sheer concentration and will-power, cutting yourself off from the world and other men by stuffing yourself inside your own mind and closing the door like a turtle.

Unfortunately most of the men who try this sort of thing never succeed. For self-hypnotism is the exact opposite of contemplation. We enter into possession of God when he invades all our faculties with His light and His infinite fire. We do not "possess" Him until He takes full possession of us. But this business of doping your mind and isolating yourself from everything that lives, merely deadens you. How can fire take possession of what is frozen? (p. 64, emphasis in original)

For Eckhart, the fourth path, the via transformativa, is directly linked to the via creativa. The fourth way into the Divine Presence, or the contemplative experience, is through compassion and social justice.

ALL HUMAN BEINGS ARE EQUAL AND INTERDEPENDENT

In commenting on Eckhart's sermon "On the Lord's Prayer,"[2] Fox (1980) explains the origins of the contemplative view that human beings are equal and interdependent:

If all creatures are offsprings of God . . . then all creatures are interdependent. All are brothers and sisters with one, common, Parent. This Parent is our Creator and we swim together in the ocean that is being and that is God's love. . . . But insofar as humans are uniquely born as images and sons of this Father, and uniquely reborn as children of God, to that extent all humans are brothers and sisters. . . . We share the same earth, the same origin, the same destiny, the same divine Parent. (p. 504)

In this same sermon, Eckhart emphasizes that the Lord's Prayer is phrased in corporate rather than individual terms, emphasizing the interdependent nature of human beings with each other and also with the rest of the created universe.

> It should be noted that in the first three petitions, whenever the things of God are spoken of, they are spoken of in the singular—"your name," "your kingdom," "your will"—but in the other four petitions the plural form is used: "our bread," "our trespasses," "do not lead us," "deliver us." (Fox, 1980, p. 502)

Fox (1980) comments on this approach:

> One reason [that we do not love each other as brothers] is that we do not think enough in these terms of shared brotherhood and sisterhood. We too often think my instead of our. And yet this prayer—the only one Jesus left behind—does not have a single my in it. It is all about, indeed it entirely presumes a we—not me—consciousness. . . . But prayers of an our consciousness demand love, a consciousness that goes beyond my own needs to others' needs. It requires compassion and a getting beyond the puny I. . . .
> When we learn to respond to life and to God and to our inner selves with an our instead of a me consciousness, we learn some powerful and significant lessons about sharing the goods of the earth. Drawing on Saint Chrysostom's criticism of the me mentality that riches so often spawn, Eckhart warns:
>
> > Bread is given to us so that not only we might eat but that we recognize others in need, lest anyone say "my bread" is given me instead of understanding that it is ours, given to me, to others through me and to me through others.
>
> Here we have a beautiful summation of what the law of interdependence, the basis of what compassion is all about: an awareness of how energy flows to others through me—thus the divine importance of a gift consciousness and a capacity to receive the gifts of others. (Fox, 1980, pp. 504–505)

The understanding that human beings are equal and interdependent underlies the via transformativa and its focus on compassion and justice.

THE GIFTS OF LIFE ARE AVAILABLE TO ALL

Eckhart's view of the equality and interdependence of all human beings leads directly to a discussion of how the contemplative views the variety of gifts that life offers. These gifts, of course, include not only the items to which our usual concept of ownership is applied—land, money, material possessions—but also the less tangible gifts such as ideas, relationships, access, and participation. Thomas Merton (1961) focuses on these intangible gifts in his reflection on the use of talents:

> God does not give us graces or talents for ourselves alone. We are members one of another and everything that is given to one member is given for the whole body. I do not wash my feet to make them more beautiful than my face. (p. 56)

Continuing his reflection on Eckhart's sermon, "On the Lord's Prayer," Fox (1980) also expands the concept of gifts:

> Furthermore, the gifts themselves—the bread—are not mine but ours. The same holds for all things which are necessary for sustaining this present life—whether land or water, air or food, oil or rain, sunshine or laughter. All things . . . are given to us with others and because of others and given to others in us. (p. 505)

Eckhart is not proposing an attitude of collective ownership but of no ownership or possession at all, echoing the concept of detachment or poverty set forth in the via negativa. Instead, all goods, ideas, land or water, air or food, are on loan. Fox, commenting further on Eckhart's sermon, develops this point.

> All good things are from God—we saw this in Path One—and being from God, we have a right to good things. The very least of the good things we have is from God. But the issue at hand is that they are from God, not from ourselves. They are gifts, not objects. That means that they have been lent us, not given to us. They are meant to be returned. They are not meant to be hoarded, grabbed, clung to, or worshipped. That is why the paths of letting go and letting be are presumed in this sermon on the sharing of the gifts of the earth. For the way discussed in Path Two is the antithesis of greed.
>
> Eckhart develops this theme of experiencing the gifts of life as a loan on several occasions, for it is so important a part of the letting go and letting be pathway. God never gave property to anyone—not even his Mother, Eckhart notes.

> God does not wish in any way that we should have so much of our own as could be held in our eyes. For all the gifts that he ever gave us, both gifts of nature and gifts of grace, he gave to no other end than that he wishes us to have nothing of our own. And as to personal property, he never gave anything either to his Mother or to any person, or to any creature in any way (Clark & Skinner, p. 103).

For Eckhart there is no such thing in the long run as personal—or corporate—ownership. If we are involved with important things—the necessities of living—then they are ours on loan. They are not our property to be possessed. God alone owns the graces and beauties of existence. From him they come; to him they return, via all God's creatures who are invited to share in them.

> The ownership should not be ours, but his alone. On the contrary, we should have all things as if they were lent to us, without any ownership, whether they are body and soul, sense, strength, external goods or honors, friends, relations, house, hall, everything in fact (Clark & Skinner, 1958, p. 103). (Fox, 1980, pp. 506–507)

Eckhart's approach to the use of the various gifts, particularly in an organizational setting, might be analogized to the basketball itself as it is passed from player to player in a game. No player owns the ball. When he has the ball, the player uses it to the fullest extent. But when it appears that another player is in a better position to score, the first player detaches himself from the ball and passes it to another. Depending on strategy and individual ability, certain players may have the ball in their possession for greater periods of the game than other players. The ball is there for the entire team to use. It is on loan. For the contemplative administrator, ideas, power, status, space, and roles might be seen in a similar manner. Each of these gifts is there to be used with detachment, but never permanently owned.

ORDINARY WORK AND ACTION CAN BE YET ANOTHER *WAY* INTO GOD'S PRESENCE

As articulated in detail in the via creativa, God is present and available in all things. For Eckhart, this implies also that action, including work, is yet another way into God's presence, another opportunity on the four paths. Eckhart's contemplative theology is this-world oriented, rather than being interested in visions and other special experiences not available to most people. For Eckhart, ordinary, mundane work and engagement in the everyday tasks that make up individual lives are the way into the divine presence. The accomplished contemplative is the one who is fully present and aware in the midst of his or her daily commute, meetings, paperwork, and lunch, rather than the one caught up in the ecstasies of prayer.

In his sermon on the Gospel story of Mary and Martha,[3] Eckhart offers an unusual perspective to underscore the sacredness of ordinary work. In the story, Mary and her sister Martha visit with Jesus in Martha's home. Mary sat at Jesus' feet and listened while Martha was distracted by many tasks. Martha complains to Jesus and asks whether he does not care that Mary has left her with all the work, telling him to have

Mary help her. Jesus responds, "Martha, Martha, you are worried and distracted by many things; there is need of only one thing. Mary has chosen the better part, which will not be taken away from her" (Lk. 10:41–42, New Revised Standard Version). Bernard McGinn comments on this sermon:

> [T]he soul that is one with God lives without a "why" in the sheer delight of its existence. This is the goal of human life, the height of Eckhart's mysticism.
>
> It should be clear by now that living without a why does not involve any form of radical separation from the world, or seeking after some form of special or privileged experience, even after ecstasy or rapture. Eckhart's position on the relation between action and contemplation is paradoxically put, but this should not surprise us by now. In the eighty-sixth of the vernacular sermons the Meister commented on the story of Mary and Martha from the tenth chapter of Luke's Gospel. Tradition had identified Martha, "busy about many things," with the active life, and Mary who sought the "one thing necessary" with the higher contemplative life, but Eckhart reverses this, at least in this text. As long as we find ourselves in this life, Martha's way is to be preferred to Mary, who is advised to get up and "learn life." Martha is the type of the soul who in the summit of the mind or depth of ground remains unchangeably united to God, but who continues to occupy herself with good works in the world that help her neighbor and also form her total being closer and closer to the divine image. Martha, then, is the soul that is both a virgin and a fruitful wife, free and detached, and yet by that very reason able to work "without a why. . . ." It is paralleled by another crucial point, the insistence that God can be found everywhere and in all works: "When people think that they are acquiring more of God in inwardness, in devotion, in sweetness and in various approaches than they do by the fireside or in the stable, you are acting just as if you took God and muffled his head up in a cloak and pushed him under a bench." (Colledge & McGinn, 1981, p. 60, 183)

In Fox's reflection on this same sermon, he begins to articulate Eckhart's theology of work as a spirituality. Again, action and contemplation are not separate for Eckhart. Indeed, acts of compassion are contemplation.

> When does our work become a spirituality? A holy work? A work integral to building and maintaining spirituality?
>
> First, when it arises from the depth of our being. . . . Eckhart develop[s] at some length his theology of work as a theology of the creative Word— that all true work is born from the depths of one's creativity. Indeed, that only creative work is authentic human work. . . . In the present sermon he lists three elements to what he calls the work of the mature person or three elements to what the economist E. F. Schumacher in our day calls "good work." First is a depth of being which was thoroughly trained to the most

external matters—in other words, Martha had the experience that practice brings in doing her work well. Indeed, she had such self-confidence in her own skills that she believed that no one else was so well suited for activity as herself. She had pride in her work and in her capacity to do her work well. Second, Martha, who is Eckhart's symbol of a mature person and a mature worker, possessed a wise prudence that knew how to achieve external acts to the highest degree that love demands. In other words, she could translate her goals of love and living without a why into her actions and her activity. She knew how to bring compassion about. And third, her work of serving Christ was born of the noble dignity of the person she was serving. The sign of Martha's maturity was the fact that her work did not hinder her relationship to God and vice versa. She knew this ultimate truth about the interdependence of work and spirituality: activity in time is just as noble as any linking of self and God. . . . Eckhart believes that contemplation is not better than, nor, in the mature person, even different from, work. . . . Compassion and the works born of compassion are themselves acts of contemplation. (Fox, 1980, pp. 488–489)

Work, as a justice-making activity, is one way of being fully present, of experiencing the contemplative dimension of life that is available to every human being. Work, as well a beautiful sunset, a moment of silence, or a Beethoven symphony, is for Eckhart, a means of experiencing God, or, in contemporary terms, a contemplative experience.

NOTES

1. "Be compassionate as your Father in heaven." (Fox, 1980, pp. 417 ff.). See also Quint, 1958–1976, vol. IV, #12.

2. "Super Oratione Dominica" (Benz & Koch, 1938–1975, vol. V, pp. 109 ff.; Fox, 1980, pp. 495 ff.).

3. "Intravit Jesus in quoddam castellum, et mulier quaedam, Martha nomine, excepit illum." (Quint, 1958–1976, vol. III, #86). See also "Jesus went into a certain city, and a certain woman named Martha received him" (Lk. 10:38; Fox, 1980, pp. 478 ff.).

15

The Contemplative Paradigm in a Contemporary Context

In the preceding chapters, the contemplative paradigm was articulated using the fourfold path identified by theologian Matthew Fox based on his study of the writings of medieval contemplative Meister Eckhart, that is, the via positiva, via negativa, via creativa, and via transformativa. Although the four-path is a helpful map of the contemplative approach to life as understood by Eckhart and his colleagues, other categories are more useful in defining and clarifying the contemplative paradigm for contemporary organizational leaders.

This chapter proposes first to articulate and summarize the values, assumptions, and worldview that comprise the contemplative paradigm in a manner that is more directly related to organizational life and, second, to tie certain strands of the contemplative paradigm to threads of emerging contemporary thought, suggesting the relevance and possibilities of some of the alternative assumptions of the contemplative paradigm.

The contemplative paradigm might be represented as a multidimensional array, each assumption or understanding having multiple relationships with other assumptions and understandings. Each perspective on this multidimensional array would highlight different relationships and reveal alternative categories. Much of this Rubik's-Cube complexity of interrelationships is necessarily lost when the multidimensional array is reduced to a two-dimensional map. Nevertheless, the following 4x4 outline (Figure 15.1) of the contemplative paradigm is an initial attempt to present this alternative view of life with its complexity and richness. The following is a description of life seen through contemplative eyes.

AWE AND MYSTERY

One of the basic assumptions of the contemplative paradigm is that life is suffused with awe and wonder, that existence is fundamentally mysterious. This aspect of the contemplative paradigm affects how the contemplative leader faces reality, particularly with regard to causality and knowledge.

Ambiguity and Uncertainty

At the core of life is unexplainable mystery. Ambiguity and uncertainty are characteristic of human experience. Certainly people can interact with the universe and gain information that can help them function, but, for the contemplative, there is no assumption that it all could be explained or pinned down if one just worked hard enough. The contemplative accepts this ambiguity, uncertainty, and paradox as normal and functions within these conditions without necessarily having first to resolve the ambiguity, uncertainty, and paradox.

Ruth Beyth-Marom and Shlomith Dekel, two contemporary scientists and educators at the University of Jerusalem, have explored decision making with the observation that uncertainties and ambiguity accompany nearly every action in individual and organizational life. The authors, in *An Elementary Approach to Thinking Under Uncertainty*, identify intuition and probability as tools to be used in everyday life in dealing with uncertainty.

> Nearly every step we take, whether as private citizens, as groups, or as a whole society, is the result of a decision made under uncertainty. . . .

Figure 15.1
The Basic Understandings and Assumptions
of the Contemplative Paradigm

I. Awe and Mystery	II. Openness and Detachment	III. Engagement and Responsiveness	IV. Human Significance
Ambiguity and Uncertainty	Innocent Ignorance	Willingness	Bodiliness
Causality and Indeterminacy	Loose Grip	Creativity	Love
Reverence and Wonder	Embracing Loss	Freedom	Meaningfulness
Intuition and Rationality	Trustworthy Existence	Discernment	Justice

Most people, however, don't try to eliminate all uncertainty. They live with it with the help of their *intuition*. Intuition is a kind of sensation or inner feeling that guides us and shows us how to act. It is a personal tool that we use without asking how it really functions. (Beyth-Marom & Dekel, 1985, p. xii)

The role of intuition in the contemplative paradigm is discussed in a separate section later, but the authors' observation about the pervasiveness of uncertainty in modern life is in accord with the contemplative paradigm.

Uncertainty has also been used extensively in another arena of modern life, the world of quantum mechanics. Although professional physicists comprise a relatively small segment of society, the concepts underlying quantum theory have invaded and influenced the vocabulary and mind-set of nonphysicists as well.[1] Though the cloud of unknowing is a favorite contemplative metaphor to communicate mystery and ambiguity, Heisenberg's uncertainty principle functions as a contemporary metaphor that is in accord with this contemplative perspective of fundamental mystery. If we know some things (for example, the position of a particle) with a high degree of certainty, we can know other things (for example, the momentum of the particle) with only a lesser degree of certainty. This uncertainty has nothing to do with the quality of the measuring instruments (Capra, 1984, p. 127).

[T]here can be no state in which the physical quantities, coordinate q and momentum p, both have a well-defined value. This situation, unknown in classical mechanics, is expressed by Heisenberg's famous uncertainty relations. We can measure a coordinate and a momentum, but the dispersions of the respective possible predictions as expressed by Δq, Δp are related by the Heisenberg inequality $\Delta q \, \Delta p \geq h$. We can make Δq [the uncertainty in the position or *coordinate*] as small as we want, but then Δp [the uncertainty in the momentum] goes to infinity, and vice versa. (Prigogine & Stengers, 1984, p. 223)

This entrenched view of reality in quantum mechanics has been compared to an attempt to catch a bunch of frogs with one hand. When we have a firm grasp of one aspect of reality (for example, the position of a particle), certainty with respect to another important aspect of reality (for example, the momentum) will suddenly elude our grasp.

In addition, probability is often used in modern physics to describe various concepts. In describing the import of Heisenberg's uncertainty principle, contemporary physicist Fritjof Capra (1984) explains, "This means that we can never predict with certainty where a subatomic particle will be at a certain time, or how an atomic process will occur"

(p. 119). This does not mean that physicists are ignorant of the physical reality about them.

> In quantum theory, we have come to recognize probability as a fundamental feature of the atomic reality which governs all processes, and even the existence of matter. Subatomic particles do not exist with certainty at definite places, but rather show "tendencies to exist," and atomic events do not occur with certainty at definite times and in definite ways, but rather show "tendencies to occur." (p. 120)

This presumption of ambiguity and uncertainty is not foreign to contemporary high school students. It was not long ago that chemistry students were presented with the (Rutherford-Bohr) model of the atom as a number of electrons whirling about a nucleus in precise orbits. This view has been superseded in the scientific community by the model of a nucleus surrounded by a cloud of electrons, the clouds of electrons taking various dumbbell, rosette, and other kinds of shapes, depending on the type of atom and energy level of the electrons (Capra, 1984, pp. 120–121). The concept of a cloud of electrons is that a particular electron has a high probability of being somewhere in that cloud and an extremely low probability of being somewhere else. This, again, is not to say that the scientist knows nothing about the electrons or their location. To the contrary, a modern physicist knows far more about the atom than did a physicist of 100 years ago. However, the contemporary scientist is comfortable with the uncertainty, the ambiguity that characterizes the knowledge about the atom. Neither the contemplative nor the modern physicist assumes that all can be known with certainty.

This uncertainty principle leads to a rethinking of the classical or dominant concepts of independence, causality, and objectivity in a manner also congruent with the contemplative paradigm (Prigogine & Stengers, 1984, pp. 222–224). Twentieth-century physicist Niels Bohr emphasized that the inability, in quantum mechanics, to speak absolutely of the location of an object implies a need to let go of the realism of classical physics. This observation also implies a fundamental interdependence and absence of an objective standpoint.

> For Bohr, Planck's constant[2] defines the interaction between a quantum system and the measurement device as nondecomposable. It is only to the quantum phenomenon as a whole, including the measurement interaction, that we can ascribe numerical values. All description thus implies a choice of the measurement device, a choice of the question asked. In this sense, the answer, the result of the measurement, does not give us access to a given reality. We have to decide which measurement we are going to perform and which question our experiments will ask the system. Thus

there is an irreducible multiplicity of representations for a system, each connected with a determined set of operators.

This implies a departure from the classical notion of objectivity, since in the classical view the only "objective" description is the complete description of *the system as it is*, independent of the choice of how it is observed.

. . . We can measure coordinates or momenta, but not both. No single theoretical language articulating the variables to which a well-defined value can be attributed can exhaust the physical content of a system. Various possible languages and points of view about the system may be complementary. They all deal with the same reality, but it is impossible to reduce them to a single description. The irreducible plurality of perspectives on the same reality expresses the impossibility of a divine point of view from which the whole of reality is visible.

The real lesson to be learned . . . consists in emphasizing the wealth of reality, which overflows any single language, any single logical structure. Each language expresses only part of reality. Music, for example, has not been exhausted by any of its realizations, by any style of composition, from Bach to Schönberg. (Prigogine & Stengers, 1984, pp. 224–225)

On a very basic level, as set forth in the discussion of the Heisenberg uncertainty principle, it can be observed that the variables q and p, location and momentum, although independent in classical mechanics, are interdependent in quantum mechanics. Quantum mechanics emphasizes the interconnectedness of entities and the relationships with other entities rather than the entities themselves—assuming, for the purpose of discussion, that there are such abstractions as entities.

Subatomic particles, then, are not "things" but are interconnections between "things," and these "things," in turn, are interconnections between other "things," and so on. In quantum theory you never end up with "things"; you always deal with interconnections.

This is how modern physics reveals the basic oneness of the universe. It shows that we cannot decompose the world into independently existing smallest units. . . . [N]ature does not show us any isolated basic building blocks, but rather appears as a complicated web of relations between the various parts of a unified whole. (Capra, 1982, pp. 80–81)

This interconnectedness to the whole is related, in quantum mechanics, to the role of probability. In classical mechanics, probability is used when some of the mechanical variables and factors are unknown, for example, throwing dice. If one knew all the relevant variables of each die, the surface upon which it is thrown, the force with which it is thrown, and so on, it would, in principle, be possible to predict the outcome. But because it is difficult to measure these local variables, that is, the details that reside within the objects involved, probability is used. Although there are local variables involved in atomic and subatomic physics, there are nonlocal connections that are instantaneous and cannot be predicted in a precise mathematical way. "Each event is influenced by the whole universe, and although we cannot describe the influence in detail, we recognize some order that can be expressed in terms of statistical laws" (Capra, 1982, pp. 81–82).

The hologram provides a metaphor for the interdependence of knowledge. A motivational poster asserts, "None of us is as smart as all of us." Knowledge is spread out among people and does not reside in its most complete form in any particular person. A hologram is created by light from two sources falling on a photographic plate. The swirls on the plate do not resemble the original object at all, but when the image is reconstituted (by means of a laser beam), a three-dimensional likeness is projected into space some distance from the plate. These eerie images have become less of a novelty. The characteristic of a hologram that is apropos here is that if the holographic plate is broken into pieces, the entire hologram can be projected from each piece, but the projection will not have the clarity of the image from the complete, unbroken plate (Ferguson, 1980, p. 179). The hologram is a helpful metaphor for corporate and participatory methods.

Accordingly, as discussed in more detail later, the worldview of the quantum physicist incorporates a different understanding of the concepts of causality and predictability than are included in the worldview of the classical physicist. In modern physics, conditions can be created in which the probability that a particular event will occur are greater, but there is no certainty that the event will occur or that the event is caused by the conditions that preceded it. This is also true for the contemplative and results in an attitude toward change that reduces one to neither master nor victim. A contemplative manager cannot make it happen but does have the capacity to change a situation so that a state of affairs is more likely to come about.

Another aspect of the contemplative's fundamental assumption of ambiguity and uncertainty is that any models or maps of reality are necessarily flawed and incomplete. All models are flawed representations of life and are wanting in some respect. Some models may account for more data or be more helpful in interactions with life, but any portrayal of life will have frayed edges—uncertainties, inaccuracies, and ambiguities. Any model is a human invention, a mask put on the mystery. We are human and need to have models or images, even if they cannot capture the mystery in its fullness. Much of the earlier discussion of Kuhn (1970), Boulding (1956), Morgan (1986), Harmon and Mayer (1986), and others, articulates this contemplative value or perspective as it is embedded in contemporary thought, and will not be repeated here. The limited and incomplete nature of maps and models, of course, does not imply that the contemplative administrator never attempts to use ideas, models, maps, or images, but that the contemplative acknowledges this manifestation of the flawed nature of life and does not need to wait for the perfect model or idea in order to move ahead in the midst of uncertainty and unclarity.

Paradox is sometimes used to represent the ambiguity, uncertainty, and mystery that is encountered, and stories are often vehicles for communicating paradox and complexity of meaning. The paradoxical nature of a model is not necessarily a weakness. Much of what Eckhart communicated of the contemplative life is paradoxical and not rule-oriented—for example, the story of Mary and Martha, the notion of the virgin wife, or the need to be both detached and engaged. Paradox is not unknown in contemporary scientific circles either. The seemingly incompatible notions of light as a wave and light as a particle are a paradox with which the scientific community is comfortable. Indeed, the wave/particle paradox is an accepted way of presenting the nature of light. A paradox may be a holding category, that is, a temporary means of dealing with something that is not yet fully understood. There is something uncomfortable, something unfinished about a paradox. A paradox embodies a tension that begs to be resolved. Paradox allows a tolerance for the seemingly ridiculous, nonsensical, impossible, or even mysterious.

A related aspect of the contemplative paradigm, as applied to organizational life, is the use of narrative, myth, and story to communicate some aspect of reality. Business consultant and futurist Peter Schwartz (1991), in developing his method of scenario-building, discusses the power of narrative and the role of storytelling in organizing knowledge:

It is a common belief that serious information should appear in tables, graphs, numbers, or at least sober scholarly language. But important questions about the future are usually too complex or imprecise for the conventional languages of business and science. Instead, we use the language of stories and myths. Stories have a psychological impact that graphs and equations lack. Stories are about meaning; they help explain *why* things could happen in a certain way. . . .

Stories are an old way of organizing knowledge, but their place in the world has been less visible since the rise of scientific philosophy during the Enlightenment. Theories about (for example) the way gases respond to heat and pressure were provable, always correct, and often simple. Even outside the sciences, the paradigm for truth was that it should be law-like, preferably reduced to the form of a solvable equation. However, since complexity has emerged as a driving force in the way the world works, the dominant belief in a deterministic and reliably quantifiable truth has begun to yield. There are now many ways of knowing. Our need for realism and proof is strong, but we can find and express that in this different way. . . .

Stories have many advantages. They open people to multiple perspectives, because they allow them to describe how different characters see in events the meaning of those events. Moreover, stories help people cope with complexity. . . .

Scenarios are stories that give meaning to events. (pp. 40–41)

Storytelling as a means by which managers interpret their world, that is, producing and accumulating knowledge, is explained and defended in a recent article by Ralph P. Hummel (1991) in *Public Administration Review*. In describing the value of storytelling as an alternative to the rational, objective, analytical approach of the traditional scientist, Hummel analyzes the needs of the contemporary manager and suggests an approach to knowledge that is not unlike the contemplative approach:

When managers are asked how they determine what is going on in their world, they refer to "intuition," "judgment," "flying by the seat of your pants." . . .

However, conversations with managers can show that they can critically think about their own thinking. They can judge the utility of basic assumptions of science and rationalistic inquiry for their work world. Managers can be engaged not only in counterposing their own assumptions against those of science and pure reason but to suggest valid alternatives to those forms of inquiry. . . . Like the original scientist's world, the manager's world seems to be a world founded on synthesis, not analysis.

But managers' needs also differ from those of paradigm-setting scientists. Managers question the need for all-pervasive objectivity; to them reality is constituted not by consensus of all imaginable detached observers but by the present community of those involved in a problem who must be brought along to constitute a solution. They question the relevance of the analytic scientific tenet that experiences pile up into an aggregate about which rules then can be formed; to the manager this still leaves the problem of judging whether a rule about by-gone experiences applies to a new situation at hand. They question the principle of the separation of reality and observer; that the observer is separate from what is observed, can usefully be detached from what is observed, and can leave the observed undisturbed. (pp. 32–33)

Hummel summarizes his observations on the value of storytelling for the manager, "In sum, managers first and foremost communicate through stories that constitute or construct their world. How could it be otherwise?" (p. 39) Indeed, the concept of story and narrative have recently received much attention in a variety of academic circles.

In recent years appeals to "narrative" and to "story" have been increasingly prominent in scholarly circles, to the delight of some, the consternation of others, and the bewilderment of many. Such appeals have caused delight in that narrative and story appear to provide a cure, if not a panacea, to a variety of Enlightenment illnesses: rationalism, monism, decisionism, objectivism, and other "isms." (Hauerwas & Jones, 1989, p. 1)

Myths and many other literary forms such as Sufi stories, Zen koans, and Christian parables—forms often favored by contemplative writers—do not have a single meaning or moral that can be reduced to a linear, propositional form, but leave room for various perspectives and complexities and are well suited for the contemplative worldview.

Causality and Indeterminacy

The ambiguous, uncertain, and mysterious view of reality just described has implications for how one considers causality and freedom. For the contemplative executive, the universe is a paradoxical mix of determinism and freedom. Life is predictable at a certain level, inasmuch as human beings are able to plan and order their lives and are not defenseless victims who could not follow a recipe or rely on a bus schedule. But life is also full of surprises, unexplained transformations, breakthroughs, new beginnings, as well as continuous, predictable, causal occurrences. Sudden turnabouts and unexpected shifts as well as routine and predictable patterns are part of human experience. There is a steady drumbeat to life, but there are also the wild interruptions and aberrations, the inexplicable changes, the turning points, the choices of road that make all the difference. There is even the unexplainable experience of synchronicity in which everything seems to fall in place or come together at the right time.

This paradoxical mix of determinism and freedom is related very directly to the contemplative's view of control, discussed in more detail later. The image of a surfer on a wave highlights the observation that the surfer participates actively in the surfing experience and is not merely a piece of flotsam to be tossed about. By shifting his weight and position, the surfer can maneuver about the wave. The surfer, however, is not master of the wave. The solid blue wall of water may suddenly become a white froth that is no longer capable of supporting the board, and the surfer wipes out. And, most certainly, the surfer does not control the wave. If waves were completely predictable and reliable, surfing would probably lose its appeal. The surfer participates in an amalgam of determinism and freedom that includes both the predictable and the unexpected.

A modern metaphor for this mix of determinism and freedom is cascading bifurcations, described by Nobel Prize–winning chemist Ilya Prigogine, with Isabelle Stengers, in *Order out of Chaos*. Prigogine describes how certain chemical reactions develop in a very predictable way until reaching a decision point or bifurcation point where the reaction can fall one way or another into one of two again-predictable patterns. The way the reaction falls at the bifurcation point is not predictable, but the progression after the bifurcation point is predictable (Prigogine & Stengers, 1984, pp. 160 ff.). Earlier in this book, the model of a rigid pendulum that has been given an initial push sufficient to bring it to a vertical position with zero velocity is used to illustrate this mix of determinism and chance. The "direction in which it will fall, and therefore the nature of its motion, are indeterminate" (Prigogine & Stengers, 1984, p. 73). Physicist James Clerk Maxwell reflects on the significance of these events, which he terms singular points:

> In all such cases there is one common circumstance—the system has a quantity of potential energy, which is capable of being transformed into motion, but which cannot be so transformed till the system has reached a certain configuration, to attain which requires an expenditure of work, which in certain cases may be infinitesimally small, and in general bears no definite proportion to the energy developed in consequence thereof. For example, the rock loosed by frost and balanced on a singular point of the mountain-side, the little spark which kindles the great forest, the little word which sets the world a fighting, the little scruple which prevents a man from doing his will, the little spore which blights all the potatoes, the little gemmule which makes us philosophers or idiots. Every existence above a certain rank has its singular points, the higher the rank, the more of them. At these points, influences whose physical magnitude is too small to be taken account of by a finite being, may produce results of greatest importance. All great results produced by human endeavor depend on taking advantage of these singular states when they occur. (Maxwell, 1882, p. 443; Prigogine & Stengers, 1984, p. 73)

Herbert Simon's concept of the limits of rationality, as set forth in his classic, *Administrative Behavior*, also illuminates the contemplative view of determinism and freedom, as well as the previously discussed concept of the incompleteness of knowledge. "[K]nowledge of consequences is always fragmentary" (Simon, 1976, p. 81). Not only is there incomplete knowledge about consequences, but there is uncertainty regarding values that will be attached, in the future, to the various consequences that might be chosen in the present (p. 81). Simon identifies some of the problems as using the information available about relevant factors and consequences and observes that not all that one does know about causality can be used in making decisions about the future.

> Only those factors that are most closely connected with the decision in cause and time can be taken into consideration. The problem of discover-

ing what factors are, and what are not, important in any given situation is quite as essential to correct choice as a knowledge of the empirical laws governing those factors that are finally selected as relevant.

Rational choice will be feasible to the extent that the limited set of factors upon which decision is based corresponds, in nature, to a closed system of variables—that is, to the extent that significant indirect effects are absent. Only in the cases of extremely important decisions is it possible to bring to bear sufficient resources to unravel a very involved chain of events. (pp. 82–83)

Simon's view of the limits of rationality leaves room for a certain openness about the future and allows the possibility of surprise, break-through, and transformation, as opposed to a view of the future that is closed, predictable, and static.

Business consultant Peter Schwartz also offers insights on the openness of the future. He views uncertainty and ambiguity as presenting the possibility of freedom. In assisting businesses and other organizations facing an uncertain future, Schwartz (1991) presents the concept of scenario building and its relation to freedom.

This book is about freedom. In western societies, people are ostensibly free, but they feel constrained by the unpredictability of events. . . . How can people, businesses, and institutions plan for the future when they do not know what tomorrow will bring? . . . In this unpredictable context, freedom is the ability to act both with confidence and a full knowledge of uncertainty. (p. 3)

For Schwartz, uncertainty is what allows freedom. Again, for Schwartz, life is not so completely chaotic and unexplorable as to preclude planning and strategizing. In responding to the uncertainty of the future, he proposes the creation of various scenarios that allow one to anticipate and prepare for, but not control, the future.

For the contemplative, life has the excitement, possibility, and challenge—as well as the frustration and uncertainty—that confront a big-league batter. He can never be sure of what kind of pitch will be thrown or where the ball will go after it leaves the bat, but there are intelligent choices to be made regarding data to be observed and evaluated, preparatory moves to be made, and responses to be executed that give the batter some choice, some freedom, some influence in the situation so that he is neither an automaton nor the ball that is thrown and batted about.

Reverence and Wonder

Every human being experiences wonder, whether it be while viewing a beautiful sunset or hearing a Beethoven symphony or witnessing the birth of a child, but reverence and wonder are often ignored in public life. These experiences, although potentially very powerful, are pushed to the fringes of discourse and given little attention in organizational life. The contemplative, however, brings the experience of reverence and wonder closer to the center of attention and is mindful of this phenomenon. In the contemplative approach to life, the numinous is found not only in the rare occurrences, such as childbirth, but in the midst of the ordinary. Each mundane moment has the potential for breaking through to the truly awesome, to meaning overflowing, to the extraordinary in the midst of the ordinary. For the contemplative, it is as if people were living in a rice-paper prison set in the midst of a beautiful, sunny meadow. It is possible to see the light shining through the thin walls, something that beckons us to what is beyond the mundane and routine. At times we dare to test the walls and find that they are made only of paper. We push through to the bright light and open space—at least for a moment. These can be the breakthrough moments that happen in the midst of a meeting, in a chance comment, a sudden insight.

The metaphor breaks down at this point in that it is possible to remain in the brightness of wonder for only brief periods. Life necessarily returns to the ordinary. The fall of the Berlin wall may be an example of this brief glimpse, on a global scale, of awe and wonder. For a brief moment in history, there was a breakthrough, both literally and figuratively, that was unexpected, wondrous, and awesome. The breakthrough was not entirely unambiguous and did not last forever. The barriers that the wall symbolized and that were breached in the midst of the crumbling of the concrete and metal were soon replaced by new complexes of problems and obstructions, but for that moment in history there was a breakthrough that was not previously deemed possible. These breakthroughs into the numinous take place on a more limited or less public scale also, but are recognized and remembered and valued by the contemplative leader. One of the functions of the contemplative executive is to recognize and point to these breakthroughs on behalf of the whole group, whether in regular reporting, in creating the stories that form part of any organizational culture or in a particular form such as the Wall of Wonder, described earlier, in which the significant events of the past year are collectively and symbolically portrayed and celebrated by the group.

Organizational consultant Harrison Owen (1987) relates a story, for the purpose of illustrating how the vision of an organization comes alive. The story is repeated here because it seems to illustrate also how an ordinary encounter in the coffee room became a signal moment for Jean and also for the organization.

For Jean, access to the Vision occurred in an apparently happenstantial way. One day, sitting alone on the 21st floor, feeling estranged, disconnected and down in the dumps, he wandered out to the executive coffee suite for a little caffeine and a change of scene. While he felt just about as low as he could go, he also found a strange new sense of clarity. The 21st floor wasn't where it was at, and while he still had Understanding of how things worked, he knew there had to be more. In short, Jean was ready, and as he sipped his second cup, feeling worse with every swallow, a little old man walked in to pour himself a cup. As he turned around and faced Jean, the old man smiled in a wistful way and remarked how things had changed, and yet how very much it all followed the original dream. . . . In fact it was old JP, the founder. . . . With some embarrassment, Jean started to go, but the old man touched him on the arm and asked if they could talk. Said the Old man, "It's been a long time since I was around, and I am sort of curious as to what's been happening."

The unlikely pair sat down in the corner, and Jean began to tell the story as best he could. But scarcely had he opened his mouth to begin, and the old man interrupted. "You know," he said, "back in the old days we knew the world would be our oyster. There were no limits to our expectations. The customers were out there with real needs, and if we could meet those needs with a quality product in a timely fashion at a fair price, well, anything could happen. . . . Our first store was a small one. We never seemed to have enough stock or hands to move it with. . . . I invented some new positions to move things faster. I think we called them expediters, and special forms to keep track of what was going on, the old 1040-Bs. That's all gone, I suppose, and well it should be. . . . It's a funny thing, good dreams just get better and richer. They sort of reach out to the world around, to find new ways of doing business." . . .

The old man left and Jean was left alone with his thoughts. . . . But what different thoughts they were. It wasn't so much that Jean was thinking differently, or reasoning differently, it was almost as if he were seeing differently. Suddenly everything was connected in a fluid pattern. The parts no longer retained the same iron fixation on the past, but rather, like a kaleidoscope, the same colors kept evolving into new and different forms, all different, yet all connected. . . .

In the days that followed, Jean discovered some quite remarkable changes in his work. It wasn't so much that he was doing different things as that the results were different. He couldn't quite put his finger on it, but somehow it related to seeing things in connectedness as opposed to difference. (pp. 65–66)

Whatever transpired in this chance encounter, something changed for Jean. He saw things in a new way; he had an *aha!* experience. Although Owen does not use these terms, it appears that that was a momentary breakthrough to the awe, a breakthrough that resulted in some long-lasting changes. Often these occasions are trivialized and discounted as *gee-whiz* experiences. Individuals steeped in the contemplative paradigm are practiced in identifying, acknowledging, and appreciating these awesome moments, both individually and collectively.

For the contemplative, there is also is a sense of reverence toward and appreciation of all of life and being. The material world is a gift to be celebrated in the contemplative paradigm. It makes a difference for the contemplative manager whether the offices are attractive, inviting places to work, whether the space in which a team spends its time is beautiful and inspiring, whether one would expect awesome and wondrous events to occur there. Beauty need not be expensive. Whether one is meeting in a walnut-paneled boardroom around a mahogany table or in a boiler room around a piece of plywood supported by concrete blocks, the manager can prepare the space to say, "What happens here is important, and we have taken the time to prepare a space that will support your efforts," rather than, "This is just another meeting, and as long as everyone has a place to sit, we don't care."

Intuition and Rationality

In the contemplative paradigm intuition, along with sensing and rationality, is an important way of knowing. Intuition is a way of knowing something without being able to explain how one knows it. For the contemplative, intuition operates in tandem with rational, logical thinking. Experientially, intuition is often associated with gestalt shifts, breakthroughs, insights, the sudden emergence of order out of chaos, the immediate apprehension of a situation, and other transformative events, although intuition may also manifest itself as a slowly growing awareness and sense of assuredness (see de Bono, 1985, p. 62).

In some of the contemplative methods illustrated later, there is an emphasis on trusting the group's or the individual's intuitions. However, in these circumstances it is usually understood that this means trusting an informed intuition. For example, in developing strategies for a rural village, the participants, whether the village residents themselves or the outside consultants, would be assumed to have steeped themselves in the situation either by everyday living or by experience in similar circumstances aided by systematic study of the current location. Edward de Bono (1985) notes that there is nothing infallible about intuition, and includes experience in his description of one aspect of intuition:

> The other use of the word *intuition* is the immediate apprehension or understanding of a situation. It is the result of a complex judgment based on experience—a judgment that probably cannot be itemized or even expressed in words. (de Bono, 1985, p. 62)

Intuition is a knowing that involves listening to one's internal senses. It is related to the concept of bodiliness (to be discussed in more detail later), or the importance of the entire human body, rather than just the brain or the mind, in thinking, in the broadest sense of that term. De Bono, in categorizing ways of thinking, links intuition with feelings and emotions.

Psychiatrist Gerald May (1983), in a discussion on contemplative spirituality, begins to define intuition and its place in the contemplative paradigm:

> What is known in spiritual traditions as contemplation is very similar if not identical to the philosophical term intuition. It should be immediately understood that the meaning here is not at all the popular interpretation of intuition as a sort of "hunch." Instead, intuition refers to a very specific and long-acknowledged way of knowing. In epistemology—the study of ways of knowing—intuition is often considered to be the highest, purest form, surpassing even reason and inferential thought. It is the state of apprehending or appreciation that occurs *before* any thinking takes place. If, for example, one closes one's eyes for awhile and then suddenly opens them to look at an object, there is a fraction of an instant in which the object is perceived purely, before any thought or response occurs. If this instant were protracted, we would have the *intuitus* that Descartes described as "pure," "ready," and "so distinct that we are wholly freed from doubt." Spinoza also emphasized the purity of that which he called *scient[i]a intuitiva*, noting its rarity in daily life. "But those things which I have hitherto been able to know by such knowledge," he said, "are very few."
>
> Will Durant suggested, "Let us for a while stop thinking, and just gaze upon that inner reality. . . . We see life in its subtle and penetrating flow. . . . This direct perception, this simple and steady looking-upon (*intueor*) a thing, is intuition; not any mystic process, but the most direct examination possible to the human mind." Durant goes on to affirm that this high praise of intuition is not meant to disparage other ways of knowing. Most philosophers, except perhaps for Rousseau, would maintain that all ways of knowing are important and necessary for a balanced approach. It is just that intuition has a slightly special place because of its purity, directness, and apparent rarity.
>
> Thus religion and philosophy have a well-established conceptual meeting ground in this arena. Intuition and contemplation are so closely related that, at least for the purpose of our discussion, we can assume that they refer to the same state. The difference is simply that one is a philosophical term and the other, religious. In further defining contemplation, Hugh of St. Victor, called it "the piercing and spontaneous intuition of the soul." (pp. 25–26)

The value of intuition in a manager's decision-making has been recognized by a variety of contemporary authors. Herbert Simon observes that "some direct evidence also suggests that the intuitive skills of managers depend on the same kinds of mechanisms as the intuitive skills of chessmasters or physicians" (Simon, in Agor, ed., 1989, p. 33). Simon also emphasizes the relationship between intuitive and analytic styles of management.

> It is a fallacy to contrast "analytic" and "intuitive" styles of management. . . . Every manager needs to be able to analyze problems systematically (and with the aid of the modern arsenal of analytical tools provided by management science and operations research). Every manager needs also to be able to respond to situations rapidly, a skill that requires the cultivation of intuition and judgment over many years of experience and training. (in Agor, ed., 1989, p. 38)

Weston Agor (1989), in the introduction to *Intuition in Organizations*, identifies five settings in which intuition is particularly useful for leaders:

- Where there is a high level of uncertainty
- Where there is little previous precedent
- Where reliable "facts" are limited or totally unavailable
- Where time is limited and there is pressure to be right
- Where there are several plausible options to choose from, all of which can be plausibly supported by "factual" arguments (p.11)

Business administration professor Daniel J. Isenberg identifies five distinct ways senior managers use intuition:

> First, they intuitively sense when a problem exists. . . .
> Second, managers rely on intuition to perform well-learned behavior patterns rapidly. . . .
> A third function of intuition is to synthesize isolated bits of data and experience into an integrated picture, often in an "aha!" experience. . . .
> Fourth, some managers use intuition as a check (a belt-and-suspenders approach) on the results of more rational analysis. . . .
> Fifth, managers can use intuition to bypass in-depth analysis and move rapidly to come up with a plausible solution. (in Agor, ed. 1989, pp. 97–98)

The contemplative's reliance on both rational and intuitive methods is in accord with recent literature stressing the value of a variety of modes of thinking (see, for example, Agor).

There is also a way of thinking that includes techniques of visualization or visioning that could be included under the category of intuition and rationality in the contemplative paradigm. Kenneth Boulding (1956) has said that our actions are affected by our images or mental pictures of reality (p. 6). (See also Garfield, 1984; Bry, 1972; Gawain, 1978.) This is true for groups as well as individuals. This may have been an element of the source of the determination that St. Teresa of Avila exhibited in confronting her opponents in the founding of St. Joseph after an image or vision had formed in her consciousness of beginning a new religious community in that location. Management consultant Harrison Owen (1987) describes vision and its role in organizations:

> **VISION** Literally, a picture or image of what all this might mean. In color, shape and form, the idea is embodied in some descriptive way. A story is told, images are called forth.... Powerful Visions are inclusive, they gather all to themselves, and see everything from their point of view.... Vision thus has the potential to arm, protect and possibly blind—but in any event, make comfortable, those who come to share in it. (p. 43)

Visualization or visioning, as alternative ways of thinking that include both rational and intuitive aspects, have offered powerful ways for organizations to discern new directions and motivate action.

OPENNESS AND DETACHMENT

The contemplative leader adopts a stance of openness and detachment. This openness and detachment are manifest in a variety of forms. This includes an attitude of receptivity or innocent ignorance in which one initially encounters situations with as much openness and as little judgment as possible. The second aspect of openness and detachment is the letting go that is characterized as maintaining a loose grip, or an attitude of being responsible in a situation without having to control all aspects of it. The third area of discussion included in openness and detachment involves the manner in which the contemplative paradigm regards pain and death, failure and disillusionment. Finally, the contemplative paradigm is based on a fundamental assumption that existence is trustworthy.

Innocent Ignorance

In the contemplative paradigm life is approached with an openness and receptivity that can be termed innocent ignorance. It is as if one arrived as a newborn with no preconceived idea of what was to be encountered or what was to take place. The situation is allowed to reveal itself. This attitude is grounded in the characterization of the contemplative experience as open awareness (G. May, 1987, p. 29). One cannot control what happens in the deep state of attentive listening that is part of the contemplative experience.

An aspect of learning termed by David A. Kolb (1984) as concrete experience, one of four parts of his cycle of experiential learning, requires this open awareness, a lack of immediate judgment or analysis. Kolb identifies a cycle of concrete experience, reflective observation, abstract conceptualization, and active experimentation (p. 42). Kolb terms this mode of knowing *apprehension*:

> Pause in your reading for a moment and become aware of your surroundings. What you see, hear and feel around you are those sensations, colors, textures, and sounds that are so basic and reliable that we call them reality. The continuous feel of your chair as it firmly supports your body, the smooth texture of your book and its pages, the muted mixture of sounds surrounding you—all these things and many others you know instantaneously without need for rational inquiry and analytical confirmation. They are simply there, grasped through a mode of knowing here called apprehension. (p. 43)

Kolb contrasts apprehension with comprehension:

> Yet to describe these perceptions faithfully in words, as I have attempted here, is somewhat difficult. It is almost as though the words are vessels dipped in the sea of sensations we experience as reality, vessels that hold and give form to those sensations contained, while sensations left behind fade from awareness. The concept "chair," for example, probably describes where you are sitting. . . . It is a convenient way to summarize a whole series of sensations you are having right now, although it tends to discourage attention to parts of that experience other than those associated with "chairness." The concept ignores particular aspects of your chair that may be important to you, such as hardness or squeakiness.
> . . . Through comprehension we introduce order into what would otherwise be a seamless, unpredictable flow of apprehended sensations, but at the price of shaping (distorting) and forever changing that flow. (p. 43)

The contemplative does not ignore the other modes of knowing, but perhaps can be said to give concrete experience or apprehension its due. By judging, naming, or labeling immediately, one loses the freedom of allowing a situation to unfold and reveal itself. In order to interact with the world, it is necessary to judge, name, and label, but to the extent this is done with finality, the chance to see something more or something else is lost. In many of the contemplative methods described here, the opportunity is given for the apprehension of a situation before the next step to analysis, abstraction, and judgment is taken.

Loose Grip

The concept of letting go or letting be, of not having to be in control, is at the heart of the contemplative paradigm and contrasts sharply with the dominant paradigm. The image of the surfer riding the wave, presented earlier, is one of many metaphors for communicating this attitude, as is the image of loosely held reins. Goals, strategies, roles, ideas, and impressions are all held with a loose grip. To grasp too tightly or become attached to any goal or role or impression is to surrender a measure of freedom. Conversely, with a loosened grip, new possibilities appear. People need egos, personae, roles, plans, and the like, in order to function in life and interact with the world, but the contemplative knows that these are tentative models and forms that can be held loosely instead of tightly grasped. A contemplative has the freedom to find meaning in any role, situation, or circumstance. A person can prefer a particular role or idea or course of action because it gives her something that she desires or to which she is attached. But if she cannot release it, her freedom is limited. A loose grip allows the future to unfold and reveal itself. One cannot, of course, control what happens in the contemplative state of attentive, hands-off listening, the primary metaphor for the contemplative paradigm.

In the contemplative paradigm people and situations cannot and do not need to be controlled. The contemplative executive can interact with life but is not in control of it. From a surfer's perspective a wave is not subject to his control. A surfer can read a wave to a certain extent but can never be sure of what the wave is going to do. A surfer can make moves that help him stay on top of the wave or travel in particular directions. Perhaps only a mad surfer will make a claim that he can control the wave. It is enough to let the wave reveal itself and respond in a meaningful way.

Participatory methods, almost by definition, involve a relinquishment of control, a loosening of the reins, by the manager. Fear of losing power or control has been identified as one of the major barriers to a participative approach to management (Spencer, 1989, p. 18).

> Many managers resist participation because they fear it will erode their power. "The failure or refusal at many organizations to make the necessary conversion [to a participative approach]," writes Bill Saporito in *Fortune*, "is hung up on old issues of authority." Such authority remains a clear badge of rank to many managers, for whom the idea of participation still doesn't sit right. William P. Anthony agrees that many managers think participation is "a management style that has little power or influence over subordinates. They feel that they will lose control and that subordinates will run roughshod over them" (Anthony, p. 4).
>
> Such fear of losing power often results from a conscious or unconscious distrust of subordinates. (Spencer, 1989, p. 18)

Frederick Thayer (1981), in his attack on hierarchy and competition, is also proposing a new way of dealing with the issue of control: "The formal, or officially acknowledged, interactions within any hierarchical structure are those of *ruling* and *being ruled, issuing commands* and *obeying them, repressing* and *being repressed*" (p. 52). The underlying values of the contemplative paradigm suggest an organizing mode other than hierarchy and competition.

The addiction and codependency literature, including the various twelve-step programs, identifies the need for control as an important element of the addictive system and explores alternatives. Schaef and Fassel (1988) analyze the addictive organization:

> A major preoccupation of the addictive system is *control*, or more accurately, *the illusion of control*. The addict and the addict's family are constantly preoccupied with controlling one another. . . .
>
> We call this the *illusion* of control because none of us can truly control anything. However, the addictive system harbors a belief that it is possible to control everything. (pp. 65–66)

Schaef and Fassel find the individual addict's need for control reflected in organizations and society as a whole and identify these addictive behavioral patterns as a systemic and organizational problem (p. 53).

Although in the contemplative paradigm there is no assumption that one can control a situation or make things happen, it is possible to set a context that will unblock a course of action and enable it to develop and move forward. Just as a gardener can water and fertilize a plant but cannot force it to grow, so a contemplative administrator can foster and create a situation in which a particular outcome is encouraged, without the assumption that he can control the situation.

Embracing Loss

The contemplative is neither a Pollyanna nor an idealist—nor a cynic. Life, including organizational life, includes pain and death, failure and loss. Pain and death are fundamentally mysterious and paradoxical. The contemplative assumption is that these negative elements can be faced without denial, stoicism, or sugarcoating. Failure and disappointment can be acknowledged and celebrated as significant events. There is no illusion of control, particularly control of the entire universe.

There is an inherent permission in the contemplative paradigm, in the midst of loss and failure, to continue the journey into life. Certainly accountability is real, but so is absolution, the permission to move on. The adventure does not end with mistakes or failures. Human beings have a freedom to move into the future. This freedom is related to the core value of detachment. No project or role or relationship or goal holds the key to the meaning of someone's existence. What is seen as a loss is not fatal because one has not put one's trust in it. It is possible to let go of failure and make a 180 degree turn. There is no situation that is beyond the bounds of meaningfulness. The most hopeless situation can be faced directly. There is no denying the pain, but there is light in the darkness. There is possibility in every situation.

Death and pain and loss are not things to be avoided at all costs, but neither are they to be sought after. Injustice and oppression are to be resisted. The contemplative manager is neither a victim nor a passive observer.

There has been a theme in recent management literature regarding the need for mistakes and failure in the corporate endeavor. Some companies, such as Westinghouse, recognize and publicize failures as a means of saying, "We do not have to do it this way any longer." Peters and Austin (1985) cite the need for toleration of failure in an innovative organization:

A crucial corollary is that the organization that would nourish champions must also tolerate, even celebrate, failures. General George Doriot . . . said . . . "If failure can be explained, and it's not based on a lack of morality, then to me failure is acceptable." The best of the companies we've looked at explicitly support failures in the sense that they admit that failure along the way is normal. Their philosophies say so, and tolerance for it is fostered through war stories. Setbacks—not sloppy foul-ups, but thoughtful missteps along the way—are considered normal. The winners are seen as people who persist. People who fail, sometimes in rather big ways, may get demotions or lateral transfers—but the ranks of corporate vice presidents are densely peppered with those who have returned from "Siberia" to bring a critical product to the market or contribute in some other important way. Even egregious failure is thus seen as a natural way-stop on the path to eventual success. (p. 136)

Organizational analysts Kiefer and Senge (1982) also point to the history of the invention of flight and discuss the role of failure:

For example, the viewpoint that flight is impossible was rendered untenable by man's first flight. . . . Previously every failure had been one more debilitating "proof" that it was. Failures then suddenly became useful as learning experiences. They revealed the flaws in design that needed correction. Metanoic organizations develop a remarkable tolerance for error and adopt an experimental posture vis-à-vis internal policies and external activities. They recognize that outstanding achievement is an inherently uncertain process that requires continual course correction to reach the final destination. Planning is valued but is subordinated to concerted, flexible effort to produce results. (p. 16)

Although there is recognition of the need for failure in these quotations, and even the celebration of it, there is the need for ultimate success, even if it is deferred success.

Trustworthy Existence

A necessary corollary to the contemplative stance of being open to whatever life has to offer, including pain and suffering, is that existence is trustworthy. This does not imply that nothing bad ever happens, but that it is possible not only to live through adversity but to find meaning within it. The awe and wonder can appear in the midst of difficult as well as glorious moments. This aspect of the contemplative paradigm is in contrast to unwarranted optimism, stoicism, or uncontrolled cynicism. It allows one to risk.

There is security in insecurity and detachment. If one is always riding the unpredictable wave, an unexpected turn of events is not unexpected. For the contemplative, life is an adventure.

ENGAGEMENT AND RESPONSIVENESS

The contemplative embodies a stance of engagement and willingness. Although the contemplative is both open and detached, he is neither a victim nor a floater who does not get involved. On the contrary, the one who lives out of the contemplative paradigm assumes that authentic living includes passionate engagement in life and responsiveness to the depths of the situation.

Willingness

A contemplative embodies an attitude of willingness instead of willfulness (see G. May, 1983, especially pp. 1–21). Bluntly stated, this means not having to have one's own way. Willingness presumes an openness of mind, an attitude of listening. It presupposes a willingness to lose everything. It does not imply passivity. When a contemplative manager decides on a course of action, he gives it all he has while being ready to drop it and move in another direction at a moment's notice if that is what is indicated. It is both a radical detachment and a radical engagement. The contemplative is available to the situation and to his colleagues. There is a stance of mutual service that makes authentic teamwork possible.

The willingness to take on any role or persona or course of action that is necessary gives freedom and new possibility. If one is willing, when necessary, to drop what appeared to be the required course of action, and is also willing to engage in a new way of thinking or acting, one has the freedom to do—or not to do. To the extent there are things a manager must have or do, her freedom is compromised. By giving up what she clings to, she is given new opportunities for thinking, relating, acting. This contemplative stance yields flexibility in assignments, roles, and plans.

Kiefer and Senge, in their reflections on metanoic organizations, refer not only to the balancing of intuition and rationality or the alignment of individual goals within the organization, but to the ability of the organization to make radical shifts in direction. (*Metanoic* is derived from the Greek word *metanoia* meaning, among other things, a 180 degree turn or a radical change of heart) (Kiefer & Senge, 1982, p.2; Newman, 1988, p.115).

Creativity

A basic assumption of the contemplative paradigm is that human beings have an unlimited source of interior energy that can be tapped. In the contemplative state there is a deepened awareness and openness. The contemplative executive assumes that breakthrough events, in which new insight and creativity blossom as he allows himself to let go of what is familiar and secure, will occur. When images and ideas are held loosely and then let go, something new can break forth. It is in allowing old images of life to die that the contemplative manager can be open and receptive to an utterly new conception. There is the possibility of an "aha"!

Creativity is a gift to which one can be open, but it cannot be manufactured. Contemplative managers and leaders assume that they can gain access to new insight and creativity by ceasing to do the things that block this insight and creativity. They can be silent. They can listen. They can play, be silly, be wild and crazy. Dancing, painting, singing, joking, and writing poems can all be vehicles for the creative spirit to come into organizational lives. For the contemplative, these activities can spring loose deeper insights than words can convey. Meetings need not be dull, controlled, overformalized situations that never touch on what is truly important for the participants. There is a time for telling stories and jokes, sharing visions, and celebrating organizational life together. In the contemplative paradigm, all are artists and all have something to contribute. For the contemplative, play and artistic creativity need not be utilitarian. Simply being alive is a celebration of one's inherent creativity.

Creativity is on behalf of all who share the organizational universe. The gifts that are given birth in the midst of wild creativity are to be shared with others, to enable them to participate in the mystery of life and to participate in their own depths and creativity.

Organizational consultant David Nicoll (1984) identifies play as an idea-producing, creative activity: "*Play* is behavior that is not serious but is nonetheless intensely and utterly absorbing. As such, it is important in creating new ideas and in generating loose and relaxed thinking and associations" (p. 159).

Freedom

Although the contemplative paradigm includes the assumption that people are inherently creative, this creativity may be used for good or ill. People are seen as capable of both tremendous good and tremendous evil. Ultimately, human beings cannot be controlled. Participants in an organization have the capacity to be involved and responsive or to refrain from involvement.

A second assumption with regard to freedom is that to become attached to any role, relationship, goal, or thing, that is, for it to become something one must have or to become addicted to somebody or something—is to compromise one's freedom. As stated earlier, human beings need roles, egos, relationships, and things in order to function, but these are not what define our humanity. No one can take away the freedom of another, only the individual can surrender her own freedom.

Discernment

In the contemplative paradigm, attention is paid to the sense or style of being in sync. In the 16th-century Ignatian spiritual tradition, would-be contemplatives are taught to pay attention to their daily experience of consolation, which is defined in various ways as a sense of being at peace, of being in sync, as well as their experience of desolation or being bored, restless, disturbed, and the like. This sense of peace or *in-syncness* seems to be common to various contemplative traditions. A contemplative manager with a developed interior awareness might ask, either himself or his team members, regarding a proposed course of action, "Does this feel right?"

Kiefer and Senge, in *Metanoic Organizations*, allude to a contemporary sense of discerning a rightness of action or of being in sync. Basketball star Bill Russell describes an intuitive sense of being in alignment with the other players of the team and uses the phrases "magical" and "playing in slow motion" (Kiefer & Senge, 1984, p. 72).

> Every so often we hear of a group of people who unite under extreme pressure to achieve seemingly miraculous results. In these moments human beings transcend their personal limitations and realize a collective synergy with results that far surpass expectations based on past perfor-

mance. Anyone hearing a fine symphonic or jazz group hopes for one of those "special" concerts that uplift both audience and performers. Perhaps less frequent . . . are examples in sports, such as the 1980 U.S. Olympic Hockey Team. . . . These occurrences, although unusual, are much more frequent in American business than is commonly expected.

People recall these experiences vividly. There is a sense of sustained exhilaration, a moment of peacefulness in the midst of frantic activity, when time seems to flow in slow motion. Maximum effort is extended, and things come together effortlessly and in astonishingly effective ways that could never have been planned, yet at the same time with a sense of predestination. There is a feeling of unity with everything and everyone, from which deep personal relationships grow. Most yearn to relive the experience, and some find it so transforming that life becomes a search for duplicating it. (Kiefer & Senge, 1982, p. 1)

On the same topic futurist Willis Harman speaks of alignment as listening to an inner voice and acting in accord with a life plan that is revealed by that inner voice (Kiefer & Senge, 1984, p. 72). The Hebrew sacred scriptures use the term *sedaq* to point to this rightness of action. In one descriptive anecdote a tourist in Israel has car trouble. When the car is finally running smoothly, the mechanic closes the hood and, with confidence and satisfaction, announces "*sedaq.*"[3]

This sense of rightness is beyond ordinary questions of ethics and morality. There is a more subtle issue of whether a direction is indicated, under all the circumstances, even when an action is ethical or moral. The concept of discernment is related also to issues of interdependence, intuition, and synchronicity or having things fall into place.

HUMAN SIGNIFICANCE

Human beings, indeed, have significance first by being part of the universe. We are made of the same material as everything else in the universe and thereby have a kinship with it. Humans are, after all, made of stardust.[4] We cannot separate ourselves from the physical medium in which we live. But, from the contemplative perspective, as well as from many others, human beings occupy a unique place in the universe, and the relationship with other human beings and with the rest of the universe requires special attention.

Bodiliness

For the contemplative, the body, as well as the mind or spirit, is important. It is more than a home for the mind. Human beings perceive through their bodies, think through their bodies and act through their bodies. A contemplative is not a disembodied spirit. On the contrary, the contemplative understands himself as an embodiment of awe, creativity, and compassion.

The creative arts, almost by definition, involve the body, whether music, dancing, painting, or sculpture. Participation in the arts awakens the human body and mind and is a source of empowerment and creativity. The arts often offer a voice when ordinary words fail and can be a means through which awe and wonder are experienced. Contemplative methods include such nontraditional activities as singing, movement, poetry, and drawing.

Educator Howard Gardner has recognized that intelligence resides not only in the mind but in the body and has articulated the concept of multiple intelligences. A person will possess a degree of musical intelligence, kinesthetic intelligence, intrapersonal intelligence, and so forth, as well as the traditional verbal, spatial, and mathematical intelligences (Gardner, 1984, passim; see also Masters and Houston, 1978; Houston, 1982).

In the contemplative paradigm, the physical surroundings or context, as well as the agenda for a meeting, merit attention and are part of the contemplative method.

Love

A fundamental assumption in the contemplative paradigm is that human beings are significant and unique. They are valued and loved in themselves and not for what they can produce or do. People are not fungible or expendable. They embody the mystery that is the core quality of the universe. Self-awareness is uniquely human. Only human beings can have a contemplative experience. The contribution of each individual is important.

In his development of the concept of servant leadership in the book with the same title, retired AT&T executive Robert K. Greenleaf (1977) reflects on love in the context of community:

> Love is an undefinable term, and its manifestations are both subtle and infinite. But it begins, I believe, with one absolute condition: unlimited liability! As soon as one's liability for another is qualified to any degree, love is diminished by that much.
>
> Institutions, as we know them, are designed to limit liability for those who serve through them. . . . But any human service where the one who is served should be loved in the process requires community, a face-to-face group in which the liability of each for the other and all for one is unlimited or as close to it as is possible to get. Trust and respect are highest in this circumstance and an accepted ethic that gives strength to all is reinforced. . . . Living in community as one's basic involvement will generate an exportable surplus of love which the individual may carry into his many

involvements with institutions which are usually not communities: businesses, churches, governments, schools. (pp. 38–39)

Love can also be understood as a primary value undergirding the concept of the team, an essential element for effective participatory methods. Greenleaf defines love as a manner of structuring relationships among human beings rather than as a feeling or emotion. In an organizational context, the contemplative paradigm does not assume that members of an organization will necessarily like each other or have warm feelings for each other—although that may happen. Love, in this sense, does mean that people will live for each other and, if necessary, die for each other. This love is akin to the foxhole ethic portrayed in the popular culture in which soldiers give themselves for each other because they belong to the same unit. In the contemplative understanding of life, human beings are in the same unit by virtue of their shared humanity.

Meaningfulness

Human beings appropriate meaning. Every situation has the potential for disclosure of the awe and mystery at the core of life and is, therefore, meaningful. No situation is beyond the bounds of meaningfulness. In the contemplative worldview, a situation will unfold or reveal itself, if allowed to do so. Just as meanings are not contrived or manipulated to serve a predetermined purpose, there is also no single, exclusive meaning for any event or situation. Human beings are limited creatures: Knowledge is always incomplete. The significance of data or of a situation may not be immediately or entirely apparent. Meaning or significance is slowly revealed. A meaning or significance may be revealed in the midst of an *aha!* experience.

The contemplative assumption is that there is meaning in every situation. Articulation of meaning through story and myth is an everyday management function. Storytelling and myth creation play a major role in allowing human beings to appropriate meaning in mundane situations. Organizational consultant Harrison Owen (1987) develops the concept of leadership as collective storytelling. In doing so, he sketches a picture of groups beginning to forge a collective set of meanings for their situation.

> So the name of the game is Collective Storytelling. This process may begin with the leader's tale, his personal understanding of how things might go, but in telling this tale, the leader, if wise, will say infinitely less than more. . . . Artfully done, the leader will actually create a vacuum which not only invites participation, but demands it. . . .

Effectively practicing the art of Collective Storytelling is rigorous and demanding business. It is also, potentially, painful. For the leader must have sufficient investment in the tale that he tells in order to tell it with conviction and feeling, but the leader must be prepared to let it go. This is no straw man, and if the story is ever perceived as such, it will lack the essential power. (p. 113)

Owen also uses the concept of *mythos* to articulate how a group begins to appropriate the meanings of its activities and existence. Meaning unfolds from the mundane and ordinary.

Mythos begins in the everyday events and activities of an organization. Early on, and even in maturity, it appears as "little stories" about the way things are around here. In form, these stories are short, pointed and graphic, for in their early uses, they are called upon to illustrate the life of the group to new members, and to occasional outsiders who may have the need to know. For example, when a new individual joins the group and raises the question—What's going on around here?—a usual response will go something like, "Well, back in '81 when all this got started, we all worked out in the garage."

It is critically important to note that these "stories" are about some action, event or activity in the life of the group. (p. 17)

Owen continues this discussion to examine how this meaning creation is most powerfully expressed in action, that is, as ritual.

And although [the stories] may eventually assume verbal form, initially, it was *act* that counted. This point may seem so obvious as to be inconsequential, but the issue is that myth and ritual are together from the start. In later times, the tale may be told in words alone, but it becomes infinitely more powerful when represented in physical terms—ritual. To *really* tell a tale, it should be produced in such a way that you can see it, touch it, taste it, and smell it—and best of all, move with it. (p. 17)

Deal and Kennedy (1982) also emphasize the power of storytelling as a conveyor of meaning in their book *Corporate Cultures: The Rites and Rituals of Corporate Life*:

For the corporation, storytellers maintain cohesion and provide guidelines for everyone to follow. It's the most powerful way to convey information and shape behavior. The beauty of a story is that just by remembering the punch line you can recreate the entire occasion. (p. 87)

The appropriation of meaning is an important element in planning in the contemplative paradigm. One looks back on the past and discerns the meaning of events rather than evaluating whether one has done what one had planned to do. Planning is, in part, a matter of articulating and embracing the meaning of the past, present, and future.

Justice

In the contemplative paradigm it is assumed that human beings are equal and interdependent, with other human beings and with the universe. Human beings are inherently worthy of love and concern as part of the human family. Love is the highest value, even at the cost of losing one's life. To be human is to care about other human beings and their freedom. The wounds of others are also our wounds. When interdependency and love are linked together, it results in compassion and a quest for justice for all. The contemplative paradigm recognizes the reality of evil and injustice, both of which are to be resisted and opposed.

Meaning is found in justice making. The contemplative methods are not designed to be used in an ethically neutral situation. They are designed to be used for justice, not just to get what one wants. There is an underlying assumption that the participants will *give up* whatever it is they think they want if the situation reveals to them that something else is needed.

We now turn to the style of contemplative leadership.

NOTES

1. Note such common terms as *quantum leap* and the popularization of certain aspects of modern physics by authors such as Capra, Swimme, Prigogine, Bohm, and so on. See also Beam and Simpson, 1984, pp. 194 ff. for a discussion of how modern physics offers altered assumptions about reality and how these altered assumptions can lead to a new understanding of politics.

2. *Planck's constant* refers to the h in $\Delta q \Delta p \geq h$, the *Heisenberg inequality* discussed here (Heisenberg, 1930, p. 104).

3. Anecdote contributed by Professor Gerald Christiansen, the Lutheran Theological Seminary at Gettysburg, Gettysburg, Pennsylvania.

4. Metaphor attributed to Matthew Fox.

PART V

The Contemplative Paradigm and Organizational Life

The first task for this exploration was to explicate the role of paradigms in human interactions and, in particular, in organizational life. Paradigms are the foundation for the theories, metaphors, and images that form the architecture of intellectual constructs that are regularly employed in almost any field. A particular manner of approaching life or understanding a situation, that is, a particular paradigm, opens up certain possibilities for perceiving, thinking, valuing, inquiring, and acting.

Leaders are called upon to tame a variety of wicked problems that have bedeviled organizational life. How one thinks about these problems, frames the issues for further investigation, and finally acts upon them is dependent upon his or her fundamental paradigm or worldview. A new paradigm or worldview arguably would open and make available additional modes of thinking, inquiring, perceiving, valuing, and acting that could be brought to bear on these wicked problems.

The second task was to delineate an alternative paradigm—the contemplative paradigm. Our 20th-century Western culture has inherited the rational-logical paradigm from the Enlightenment. The contemplative paradigm offers alternative assumptions about life, assumptions that would offer ways of thinking, perceiving, valuing, inquiring, and acting that differ from those of the dominant paradigm.

Having outlined the assumptions of the contemplative paradigm, the challenge now is to begin to explore the implications of that alternative paradigm for organizational life, that is, how these alternative ways of thinking, perceiving, inquiring, valuing, and acting would affect organizations.

There are several options for a consideration of the implications of the contemplative paradigm for organizational life. For example, one could examine a contemplative view of power, a contemplative approach to research, a contemplative way of evaluation, a comprehensive toolkit of contemplative group methods—or one of many other specific aspects of organizational life.

However, in order to maintain judicious boundaries for this project, we focus only on contemplative leadership, that is, the style of a leader grounded in the contemplative assumptions. Even with a narrow focus, the reader is offered only a brief glimpse, a tentative outline, a narrow slice of a contemplative style of leadership. The final chapter reflects on the journey that has been charted thus far and begins to raise additional issues for further exploration in the arena of the contemplative paradigm and organizational life.

16

The Contemplative Leadership Style

A description of the style of contemplative leadership is reminiscent of Frederick Hart's stone carving, *Creation Tympanum*, above the main entrance to the Washington Cathedral. The background is a dynamic swirling sea from which human figures are emerging. None is yet complete. Some are more detailed than others. The viewer is not offered a completed work, a finished picture, but the human form is still easily recognized. One experiences a sense of mystery rather than confusion. Much is left to the imagination. The work makes an impression, but it does not supply all the answers. The following outline of contemplative leadership attempts to communicate in a similar manner. This portrait of the contemplative leadership style is an unfinished jigsaw puzzle, but the intent is to present sufficient detail and example to warrant a nod of recognition and to lay a foundation for further exploration of the contemplative way.

Before beginning to outline the style of contemplative leadership, a few points of clarification are necessary. No claim is being made that the contemplative leadership style is better than any other leadership style (although some of the authors chosen to illustrate the contemplative way clearly advocate the contemplative approach to life). Ways of thinking, perceiving, valuing, inquiring, and acting can authentically be judged and evaluated only within their own paradigm. It is not possible to determine the validity or contribution of different leadership strategies grounded in different paradigms unless one would find an independent point of reference against which the nature and claims of the various leadership strategies can be assessed (Morgan, 1983, p. 370). The following is only an outline of a contemplative leadership style, not a recipe or prescription for better leadership in the currently dominant paradigm. The description of a contemplative leadership style illustrates and suggests the kind of leadership that might follow from the contemplative approach to life, that is, a leadership style that would be grounded in the contemplative assumptions and understandings.

A second clarification is prompted by the difficulty of straddling two paradigms. Just as it would be difficult for Galileo to imagine physics research in the relativistic, Einsteinian paradigm of the 20th century, so it may be challenging for contemporary organizational leaders to consider a contemplative leadership style when we are situated squarely in the dominant, logical-rational paradigm. The contemplative leadership style may not work in the office or department—as currently constituted. This alternative leadership style may not help a manager achieve his or her established objectives, for example. It may not give more control over the situation. In fact, it is not clear what would happen if one did embody the contemplative leadership style. But contemplative leadership may generate additional, alternative ways of thinking and acting, perceiving and inquiring that could be brought to bear on the wicked problems we now face.

A related observation is that a leader does not exist in a vacuum. A contemplative leader functioning in the dominant paradigm may be like a fish out of water. Styles of leadership are intimately related to the surrounding culture. There are, of course, the prophets, the outcasts, the pioneers who break new ground for a society. But a leader arises out of and is supported by a particular community or subculture. Leadership is an interactive process, and being a contemplative leader without a contemplative community in which to relate is almost unthinkable.

A third observation is that contemplative leadership does not easily surrender itself to the print medium. The contemplative leadership style cannot be reduced to a set of principles, a list of activities to be undertaken, or even a description of characteristics. There may be other strategies for communicating the nature of contemplative leadership—for example, a biography of someone who could be identified as a contemplative leader. Such biographies would paint a more detailed and compelling portrait, assuming that the essential historical details would be available. Perhaps an artistic presentation of dance, music, and drama might provide a better medium.

A fourth and final preliminary observation is that the contemplative leadership style is not an ideal to be achieved. Embodying the contemplative leadership style is more a matter of unlearning, of letting go of what one already knows, of loosening one's grip on the current grasp of reality. Gerald May's description of the range of responses when confronted with the possibility of a contemplative lifestyle emphasizes the absence of specialness. May (1988) explains that one of many options is to be present in the midst of life

> in a gentle, open-handed, and cooperative way. This is the *contemplative* option—not any system of complicated exercises, but the simple and courageous attempt to bear as much as one can of reality just as it is. To be contemplative, then, is not to be a special kind of person. Contemplation is simply trying to face life in a truly undefended and open-eyed way. (p. 107)

Finally, there is no single style or view of leadership in the dominant paradigm, although one might define a range of leadership styles acceptable within the rational-logical paradigm. Similarly, there is no single approach to leadership within the contemplative paradigm. The following is an outline within which the various styles of contemplative leadership could be defined.

Leadership that is grounded in the assumptions of the contemplative paradigm, that is, contemplative leadership, is defined here in terms of a style rather than as a set of principles or list of functions. Broadly conceived, leadership is a matter of how one engages in life and interacts with the world and particularly with one's fellow human beings. It is concerned with an individual's particular manner of thinking, inquiring, perceiving, valuing, and acting in a collective rather than an individual context.

The style of contemplative leadership is framed in terms of four qualities or characteristics: lucid, attentive, vulnerable, and disciplined (see Figure 16.1). The following narrative description, enhanced by imagery, poetry, legend, story, and the personal reflection of others, begins to articulate the nature of those fundamental qualities. The contemplative leadership style is described here in somewhat idealized

Figure 16.1
The Style of Contemplative Leadership

Lucid	Attentive	Vulnerable	Disciplined
About Suffering	To the Comprehensive	Acts Decisively	Without Habits
About Colleagues	Without Judgment	In Ambiguity	Without Rewards
About Self	To the Depths	With Detachment	With Passionate Joy
About Gratitude	In Multiple Dimensions	With Accountability	Toward Freedom

terms, without much subtlety or nuance in order to highlight and accent the key characteristics of the contemplative paradigm.

THE CONTEMPLATIVE LEADER IS LUCID

Lucidity means gazing upon raw existence without turning away. It is seeing clearly and directly to the depths. There is no need for rose-colored glasses or protective illusions or an idealized fantasy of how one would like the world to be. The contemplative leader is free to move into any situation with not only open eyes but also a joyous heart: He is lucid about the irrepressible possibilities as well as the tragic, broken realities of life.

Lucid About Suffering

The contemplative leader need not excise, dismiss, or deny the irrational, unjust, chaotic, and uncontrollable aspects of life. The raw human suffering that one encounters in organizational life, and one's participation or complicity within it, are within the range of the contemplative leader's awareness. He is lucid about the suffering and tragedy of life and sensitive to the deep anguish that lurks just below the surface. The unexplained data, the unanswered questions, the issues that one is currently unable to address, the wicked problems, are not pushed outside the scope of acknowledgment or responsibility. Life is not reduced to manageable proportions. The contemplative leader lives uncomfortably with eyelids propped open in order to view a situation fully and unreservedly with all its contradiction, pain, and complexity.

The contemplative leader has the lucidity of Sisyphus who, in full consciousness, is condemned forever to roll a rock to the top of a mountain only to have it fall back again—and again and again. He stands present to the stark tragedy of life. Contemplative leadership acknowledges the waste, fraud, and abuse and does not hide behind a facade of efficiency, rationality, and fairness. She is aware of the absurdity and evil that is present.

The contemplative leader is lucid about the demands and limitations of the situation. They too are part of the full reality: goals, principles, values, job descriptions, budgets, legislative history, rules, and regulations. These demands and limitations are acknowledged, considered, and even used, but not clung to as if they were the final reality that completely defines the organizational universe. The leader is sensitive to death and loss in the midst of life, the passing-away of all things—control, roles, plans, agencies, and the like.

Contemplative leadership also involves a paradoxical stance of love in the midst of lucidity about contingency and death, that is, a willingness to engage in less than ideal circumstances. It may be easy to give oneself to an excellent operation, a success-oriented, fast-track organization. It is wonderfully motivating to be a case study in the latest best-seller in the business section of the local bookstore, but not all organizations are grist for the management guru's mill. They are frayed, limping, disorganized, confused, and/or inefficient organizations. Nevertheless, the contemplative leader presents his or her gifts—abilities, energies, vision— unreservedly to that same imperfect, but significant, situation.

> Is it possible for the rose to say, "I will give my fragrance to the good people who smell me, but will withhold it from the bad?" Or is it possible for a lamp to say, "I will give my light to the good people in this room, but I will withhold it from the evil people?" Or can a tree say, "I will give my shade to the good people who rest under me, but I will withhold it from the bad?" These are images of what love is about. (de Mello, 1990, pp. 60–61)

The legend of St. Francis kissing the leper, that is, giving oneself fully to that which is personally considered the most repulsive, is illustrative. The contemplative leader kisses not only the excellent organizations but also the diseased and disfigured ones.

J. D. Salinger (1961) captures this stance of love in the midst of lucidity in the last pages of his novel *Franny and Zooey*, with the image of the anonymous Fat Lady, for whom one of the characters shined his shoes before each radio broadcast:

> Anyway, I started bitching one night before the broadcast. Seymour'd told me to shine my shoes just as I was going out the door with Walker. I was furious. The studio audience were all morons, the announcer was a moron, the sponsors were morons, and I just damn well wasn't going to shine my shoes for them, I told Seymour. I said they couldn't see them *any*way, where we sat. He said to shine them anyway. He said to shine them for the Fat Lady. I didn't know who the hell he was talking about, but he had a very Seymour look on his face, and so I did it. He never did tell me who the Fat Lady was, but I shined my shoes for the Fat Lady every time I ever went on the air again—all the years you and I were on the program together, if you remember. I don't think I missed more than a couple times. This terribly clear, clear picture of the Fat Lady formed in my mind. I had her sitting on this porch all day, swatting flies, with her radio going full-blast from morning till night. I figured the heat was terrible, and she probably had cancer, and—I don't know. Anyway, it seemed goddamn clear why Seymour wanted me to shine my shoes when I went on the air. It made *sense*. (pp. 198–199)

With full and wide-eyed consciousness the contemplative leader shines his shoes for the Fat Organization. It makes sense as love in the midst of lucidity.

Lucid About People

Love, for the contemplative leader, has nothing to do, in the first instance, with one's affection for another. There will always be coworkers, for example, who irritate and annoy, with whom, for whatever good or bad reason, one does not prefer to work. The contemplative leader is lucid about the frailties of others. He is painfully aware of the full range of man's inhumanity from genocide to petty office gossiping. There is no need for romantic illusions about humanity. But there is also the freedom to acknowledge and recognize humankind's unexpected and unexplainable random acts of kindness and senseless beauty.

The recognition of the inherent value of human beings, without regard to what they can do or produce, is a fundamental assumption of the contemplative paradigm. It is again an acknowledgment of the paradoxical juxtaposition of the wonder of being human and the human capacity for dreadful atrocities. The contemplative leader understands that human beings do not get what they deserve. There is an acknowledgment of the disordered, even unfair nature of reality. There is no universal scorekeeping. The equally paradoxical concept of forgiveness is one mode of dealing with lucidity about the imperfections of others.

> To forgive is not to excuse an unjust behavior. There are evil and destructive behaviors which are inherently inexcusable: fraud, theft, emotional abuse, physical violence, economic exploitation, or any denial of human rights. Who could possibly claim that these are excusable? To excuse such behaviors—at least in the sense of winking and pretending not to notice, or of saying, "Oh, that's all right," or even "I'll overlook it this time, just don't do it again"—is to tolerate and condone them. . . .
>
> If we now have greater clarity concerning what forgiveness is not, then what is it? Let me characterize it this way: to forgive is to make a conscious choice to release the person who has wounded us from the sentence of our judgment, however justified that judgment may be. It represents a choice to leave behind our resentment and desire for retribution, however fair such punishment might seem. . . .
>
> Moreover, without in any way mitigating the seriousness of the offense, forgiveness involves excusing persons from the punitive consequences they deserve to suffer for their behavior. The behavior remains condemned, but the offender is released from its effects as far as the forgiver is concerned. (Thompson, 1992, pp. 18–19)

In forgiveness the contemplative leader surrenders control and rejects the temptation to maintain a record of offenses. In embodying both lucidity and forgiveness, one has the freedom to engage enthusiastically in imperfect situations.

Lucid About Himself or Herself

The contemplative leader is lucid about the neuroses, frailties, hidden agendas, and warpings of her neighbors and coworkers—because she knows her own. The contemplative is lucid about her own gifts and limitations—her weaknesses, strengths, failures, and possibilities. Self-awareness is an essential aspect of contemplative leadership. Indian contemplative Anthony de Mello (1990) suggests:

> Come home to yourself. Observe yourself. . . . After a while you don't have to make any effort, because, as illusions begin to crumble, you begin to know things that cannot be described. It's called happiness. Everything changes and you become addicted to awareness. . . .
> That's what it is to watch yourself. No one can show you how to do it, because he would be giving you a technique, he would be programming you. But watch yourself. When you talk to someone, are you aware of it or are you simply identifying with it? When you got angry with somebody, were you aware that you were angry or were you simply identifying with your anger? Later, when you had the time, did you study your experience and attempt to understand it? Where did it come from? What brought it on? I don't know of any other way to awareness. You only change what you understand. What you do not understand and are not aware of, you repress. You don't change. But when you understand it, it changes. . . .
> . . . There are some lucky people who see this in a flash. They just become aware. There are others who keep growing slowly into it, slowly, gradually, increasingly. They begin to see things. Illusions drop away, fantasies are peeled away, and they start to get in touch with facts. There is no general rule. (pp. 56–57)

Lucidity born out of self-awareness and observation supports lucidity about one's fellow human beings.

Although growth in self-awareness is often associated in contemporary culture with psychological issues and explorations, it is not so limited. The contemplative leader is particularly lucid about his or her own attachments, areas where freedom is compromised. Self-awareness and self-exploration are not, however, a matter of searching for defects in order to fix them. Psychiatrist Gerald May and others have used the term *addictions* in a broad sense to encompass attachments. The issue is to become aware of these areas of unfreedom and their effect on decisions and action. The more one is unaware of addictions, attachments, or other important aspects of the inner life, the greater the danger in their having an unwanted or unwarranted effect on one's leadership decisions.

This advocacy for self-awareness almost necessarily presumes a knowledge that one belongs in the universe, that is, that at some deep level, he or she is good and acceptable. Self-awareness could otherwise become far too painful to bear. The contemplative style of leadership is grounded in the contemplative assumption that—just as any other human being—the leader has innate significance and value. One can stand before the raw truth of self–awareness because of that underlying affirmation.

There is also a seemingly necessary presumption that life is good as it is, that nothing needs to be fixed or changed before peace or happiness or satisfaction is possible. There is glory in the given moment—just as it is. The contemplative leader is not driven, but drawn to action. She takes action because it is what is indicated by the comprehensive situation, not to prove herself, not to establish her worth, not to compensate for some past deficiency or failing.

Lucid, With Gratitude

Contemplative leadership does not necessarily presume or aspire to perfection or excellence (although there may be times when the situation demands such). The contemplative leader is lucid about life as it is, but is at the same time grateful within the broken, warped, contradictory situation. He may not be grateful for all things, but is grateful in the midst of all things as they are. Life is possible in all its fullness and wonder now, in the present moment. One is invited to embrace that moment and wring the meaning from it. There is no need to wait for something different, something better. The contemplative leader engages in life with open eyes and a joyous heart.

There is a two-sided contemplative lucidity about both the absurdity and wonder of life—as well as the fundamental awareness of the necessity of living fully and completely in that absurdity and wonder. This meta-awareness is dramatized in an old *Peanuts* cartoon. Charlie Brown is consulting Lucy in her role as psychiatrist. Charlie Brown laments, "What do you do when the world is passing you by? What do you do when you don't fit in?" Lucy takes Charlie to a hilltop. Sweeping the horizon with a broad gesture, Lucy asks a series of questions. "Do you know of any other world out there? . . . Is there any other place you can go?" Charlie answers, "No," to each question; whereupon Lucy advises, at the top of her lungs, "Well, live in it then!"

The contemplative leader is lucid to the possibilities in the midst of a situation as it unfolds. Neither cynicism nor idealism is helpful. Both often expose ingratitude, that is, the insistence on having one's own way rather than receiving the current situation with open hands, as a gift. A contemplative leader is lucid not only about tragedy but also about hope in the midst of despair. The contemplative leader is grounded in the assurance that nothing else is needed to make life complete. Anthony de Mello (1990) sets forth one contemplative perspective on the completeness, wholeness that he terms *happiness*:

> Happiness is our natural state. Happiness is the natural state of little children . . . until they have been polluted by the stupidity of society and culture. To acquire happiness you don't have to do anything, because happiness cannot be acquired. Does anybody know why? Because we have it already. How can you acquire what you already have? Then why don't you experience it? Because you've got to drop something. You've got to drop illusions. You don't have to add anything in order to be happy; you've got to drop something. Life is easy, life is delightful. It's only hard on your illusions, your ambitions, your greed, your cravings. (pp. 77–78)

> [W]e have a subtle way of making our happiness depend on other things, both within us and outside us. We say, "We refuse to be happy until my neurosis goes." I have good news for you: You can be happy right now, *with* the neurosis. You want even better news? . . . There's only one reason why you're not experiencing bliss at this present moment, and it's because you're thinking or focusing on what you don't have. Otherwise you would be experiencing bliss. You're focusing on what you don't have. But, right now you have everything you need to be in bliss. (p. 61)

THE CONTEMPLATIVE LEADER IS ATTENTIVE

Not only is the contemplative leader lucid, facing life without illusion, but she is also attentive. A contemplative is radically aware, sensitive, mindful. He listens deeply—but first without judging. This attentiveness is like a huge satellite dish that sweeps the sky and picks up the faintest of signals from every possible part of the spectrum. The contemplative leader is the Superman/Clark Kent with x-ray vision who can see through the surface concerns to the depth issues. The attentive leader has the sanded-down fingertips of a safecracker who can slowly turn the dial, detecting the delicate tripping of tumblers. The contemplative leader is tuned-in to the situation. Such sensitivity is essential for effective, carefully-discerned action.

Attentive to the Comprehensive

The attention of the contemplative leader is not narrowly focused or limited, but spacious, expansive, and comprehensive. The contemplative leader stands before life as it unfolds and reveals itself. A metaphor for this attentiveness is the mundane encounter of a mother listening to her child after school. As the mother is busy preparing dinner, she asks the child, "How was your day, dear?" Although the mother may continue her tasks while listening to her child with half an ear, the mother may, at times—for example, if the child announces that she has been expelled from school—stop her other activities, stoop down, look directly into her daughter's eyes, and listen carefully to every word that is said—or unsaid. A manager may often set his or her attention at a surface level, being jarred to another level of awareness only by the catastrophic or unusual. Ordinary consciousness and awareness are somewhat dulled and muted—and perhaps with good reason: Sometimes the massive amount of data leaves one in a state of overload. A contemplative leader is deeply attentive, not only during times of crisis, but also during the daily routine.

One might question this capacity for attentiveness and argue that there is only so much that one can take in and absorb. However, attentiveness, in the contemplative paradigm, is expandable, elastic. There is an illustrative phenomenon in some traditional contemplative practices in which a focus of attention—for example, a mantra—is used to broaden attentiveness. The contemplative practitioner may begin the exercise with his mind racing, his consciousness crammed with restless thoughts, like a cage full of overactive hamsters. He gently directs his attention to the mantra, a word constantly repeated in his mind. It is not necessary to force out the other thoughts: The repetition of the mantra often has the effect of gradually calming the mind, putting the restless hamsters to sleep. The mind becomes clear, and new data are easily received and assimilated. In a similar manner, the contemplative leader can be fully present and attentive to a particular situation without blocking out other aspects of the environment, in fact, being present and attentive to what appear to be peripheral matters.

There is a necessary component of leadership of tuning in, picking up the context, expanding one's awareness. There is, for example, the common experience in which one is introduced to a roomful of people and then immediately asked to address them. There is only enough time to walk to the podium before beginning to speak. There is no opportunity to get one's bearings or even to notice who is sitting in the front row. It can be disorienting and unnerving. Under those circumstances, one is not tuned in or in sync with the audience. Such an occasion serves as a metaphor for the mundane experience of finding oneself in a new situation—arriving at work in the morning, being assigned a new project, or being promoted to a new position—in which one must become tuned in to the new situation and calm the hamsters so that one can be fully attentive to the new environment. It is possible, however, to go through the entire day—or career—without becoming fully attentive to the situation, without ever becoming aware of what is happening. The contemplative leader takes the time to allow attentiveness to overcome him.

A recent forum in a medical ethics journal provides some insight into this aspect of contemplative leadership. John Carmody, an assistant professor in the occupational therapy department at the University of Chicago, describes his experience as a patient himself, the recipient of treatment from two different physical therapists. William F. May, an ethics professor, comments on Carmody's case study. Although the patient-therapist relationship may not initially seem analogous to the leadership relationship, the discussion of attentiveness or sensitive and caring presence (often explicitly distinguished from problem-solving activities), in the context of contemporary helping professions, touches certain issues regarding the nature of contemplative leadership.

Briefly summarized, Carmody contrasts the treatment given by two physical therapists: the big, overbearing, 6-foot, 200-pound Queen Mary; and Ruby, the good caregiver who substitutes for the first. William May (1994) comments on the interactions:

> Cases in medical ethics usually concentrate on the question of *what* one should say and do. This case reminds us that at least as much turns on the question of *how* one says and does something. In content, for example, the two women say very much the same thing. The Queen Mary says, "It's mainly a question of your will." Ruby, the sister of mercy, says, "You can do this." Yet how they say it makes a world of difference: one commands, overbears, intimidates; the other invites and encourages.
>
> Such matters of decorum and manner count for much more, ethically, than the words *style, tact* or *tactics* can convey. The *how* of right action depends ultimately upon the character and the virtue of the actor. Carmody pleads, in effect, for what the ancients called prudence, the eye of the soul. Decorum requires a kind of metaphysical tact, what the Stoics called a sense of the fitting. The healer must first "take in" what's out there in order to know both what to do and how to do it. . . .
>
> A plea for the virtue of prudence in caregivers underlies several "home truths" that emerge from Carmody's experience. He criticizes the over-bearing professional, who is too busy influencing her environment to take it in, too driven by her own agenda to know who her patient is, and too controlling to permit the patient a share in the "joint venture" of healing. The imprudent practitioner is trapped in the first-person singular; she or he does not know how to move from the "I" to a "we."
>
> Prudence makes a difference in the apparently similar content of what each caregiver summons from the patient. Each asks the patient to will something. But the exercise of the will for the first therapist means pushing through pain, battling the body and the cosmos, whereas the exercise of the will for the second therapist requires making friends with one's body and the cosmos. . . . Command at that level turns into encouraging invitation; effort passes over into effortless grace. (pp. 47–48)

William May makes several points here relevant to the contemplative style of leadership. First, an individual's manner of being or quality of presence is as important as what one says or does. Knowing what is fitting requires an attentiveness to the situation, a "taking in of what is out there." The full context is critical. In this case study the context included Carmody's personal history; his current, physically and emotionally painful experience in the unfamiliar role of patient; and his unstated concerns about maintaining his human dignity while facing diminishment and death. Every human being comes complete with a personal history, a collection of current (often unstated) concerns and hopes for the future. Although a leader cannot know everything about another individual or situation, the leader can be sensitive and attentive to the broader context. This attentiveness to internal as well as external issues is facilitated by one's own self-awareness.

Another aspect of attentiveness highlighted by this story is the effect of one's own agenda in an encounter with another individual, particularly if one is not aware of that agenda. The Queen Mary therapist was described as being "too busy influencing her environment to take it in, too driven by her own agenda to know who her patient is, and too controlling" to allow true collaboration with the patient. In the contemplative paradigm there is a fundamental assumption of collaboration, a collaboration not only with another individual but with life. Whatever agenda or desire or intent one may bring to a situation, the contemplative leader does not cling to that agenda, but holds it loosely and surrenders it (or does not surrender it) when it is fitting. This kind of collaboration is a dance with life, requiring a sensitivity and responsiveness to the movements of one's partner.

Carmody's experience as a patient contrasts two ways of exercising one's will or, perhaps, two styles of engaging in life, of leading. For the first therapist this meant "pushing through pain, battling the body and the cosmos," whereas for the second, the exercise of the will involved "making friends with one's body and the cosmos." Life is less a battle and more a cooperative endeavor.

Attentive, but First Without Judgment

The attentiveness of the contemplative leader is first an open, receptive attentiveness. The situation is assimilated on its own terms without judgment. This requires a stance of initially listening and watching, without getting entangled in an attempt to fix anything. It is an attentiveness without the assumption that one knows what something should be. This approach does not preclude action. Carefully discerned action comes after one has allowed a situation to present itself without interference. Listening is one aspect of being attentive. Two authors reflect on their experience with listening:

> Critical listeners dry you up. But creative listeners are those who want you to be recklessly yourself, even at your very worst, even vituperative,

bad–tempered. They are laughing and just delighted with any manifestation of yourself, bad or good. . . .

In order to learn to listen, here are some suggestions: Try to learn
tranquillity, to live in the present a part of the time every day. Sometimes
say to yourself: "Now. What is happening now? This friend is talking. I
am quiet. There is endless time. I hear it, every word." Then suddenly you
begin to hear not only what people are saying but what they are trying to
say, and you sense the whole truth about them. And you sense existence,
not piecemeal, not this object and that, but as a translucent whole. (Ueland,
1992, p. 109)

Attention. Deep listening. . . . In academic culture . . . most listening is
critical listening. We pay attention only long enough to develop a counter–
argument; we critique the student or the colleague's ideas; we mentally
grade and pigeon-hole each other. In society at large, people often listen
with an agenda, to sell, or petition, or seduce. Seldom is there deep,
open-hearted, unjudging reception of the other. (O'Reilley, 1994, p. 22)

With an attentive contemplative presence, it is unnecessary to pigeon-
hole ideas or persons, no need to judge now—although later there will
be time for careful discernment.

No judgment, no commentary, no attitude: one simply observes, one
studies, one watches without the desire to change what is. Because if you
desire to change what is into what you think *should* be, you no longer
understand. A dog trainer attempts to understand a dog so that he can
train the dog to perform certain tricks. A scientist observes the behavior of
ants, to learn as much as possible about them. He has no other aim. He's
not attempting to train them or get anything out of them. He's interested
in ants, he wants to learn as much as possible about them. That's his
attitude. (de Mello, 1990, pp. 37–38)

This is an attentiveness that initially sets aside predetermined categories. It crushes the boxes into which we place people, ideas, actions.
The boxes will, of course, be remade again and again. The categories
are like clay that is never baked into permanent forms.

The concept always misses or omits something extremely important,
something precious that is only found in reality, which is concrete uniqueness. The great Krishnamurti put it so well when he said, "The day you
teach the child the name of the bird, the child will never see that bird
again." How true! The first time the child sees that fluffy, alive, moving
object, and you say to him, "Sparrow," then tomorrow when the child sees
another fluffy, moving object similar to it he says, "Oh, sparrows. I've seen
sparrows. I'm *bored* by sparrows."

If you don't look at things through your concepts, you'll never be bored. Every single thing is unique. Every sparrow is unlike every other sparrow despite similarities. It's a great help to have similarities, so we can abstract, so we can have a concept. It's a great help, from the point of view of communication, education, science. But it's also very misleading and a great hindrance to seeing *this* concrete individual. If all you experience is your concept, you're not experiencing reality, because reality is concrete. The concept is a help, to *lead* you to reality, but when you get there, you've got to intuit or experience it directly.

A second quality of a concept is that it is static whereas reality is in flux. We use the same name for Niagara Falls, but that body of water is constantly changing. . . .

Ideas actually fragment the vision, intuition or experience of reality as a whole. This is what the mystics are perpetually telling us. Words cannot give you reality. They only point, they only indicate. You use them as pointers to get to reality. But once you get there, your concepts are useless. A Hindu priest once had a dispute with a philosopher who claimed that the final barrier to God was the word "God," the concept of God. . . . "The ass that you mount and that you use to travel to a house is not the means by which you enter the house. You use the concept to get there; then you dismount, you go beyond it." (de Mello, 1990, pp. 121–123)

This nonjudgmental reception of life allows a joyous celebration of the ordinary—that is, an innocent delight in the fluffiness of the sparrow, the unexpected comment at a staff meeting.

Attentive to the Depths

The contemplative leader is not the one who knows everything or has all the answers, but the one who is more likely to point to the white-hot center of meaning in the most mundane of circumstances, the one who is sensitive to the wonder of the moment. He knows there is no other situation that is more worthy, no other task that is more significant than the current one. In the words of poet D. H. Lawrence, it means kindling the life quality. Whatever the task that engages us—scrubbing the kitchen floor, preparing for a board meeting, writing a letter—if life goes into that task, we transmit life in an ongoing flow. Lawrence also makes it clear that transmitting life, kindling life does not mean letting any mean fool suck us dry, to allow a zombie to eat us alive (Lawrence, 1959, pp. 105–106). The contemplative leader blows on the sparks of possibility and brings the mundane situation blazing to life.

The contemplative leader is attuned to what is really going on. She is not fooled by outward appearances. She listens to the unsaid words and sorts out the meanings behind the meanings. It also means trusting those insights, being willing to deal with ambiguity and contradiction while allowing the situation to unfold and reveal itself. Patricia Clark, a director of operations for a small nonprofit organization, in reflecting on her experience with attentiveness or practicing the presence in the workplace, identifies some of the factors involved in being present in the midst of mundane circumstances: to be open to not having the answers, to be willing to not answer questions at all, to contradict oneself, to live with the contradictions, and to laugh about it, to be confused, to let things remain unspoken, to be willing not to be logical and rational, but to follow the heart, to "feel freedom to go for my heart's desire," and to not be overly sensitive to another's problems. Clark also lists *"things they didn't teach me in business school"*:

> ... (3) That it's not rational, careful, sensible thinking but crazy, irrational things that create the beauty of the day.
>
> (4) That it's not worrying about my role, my job, my identity that gets me anywhere. It's sitting back to see the gifts blossoming in others, letting go and finding more help and good ideas than could be asked for.
>
> (5) That it's not getting more organized or using my time better that keeps me sane. It's taking things as they come, not panicking but being aware of what's important; giving a job its time and then letting go. (P. Clark, 1991, p. 4)

This is the stuff of storytelling, myth making, and symbol creation. A contemplative leader points to the depths and allows others to see the richness and significance of the mundane moment.

Attentive in Multiple Dimensions

Every leader is attentive to something. Managers pay attention to the bottom line. Some watch selected input and output measures. Public administrators pay attention to the mood of Congress. Team leaders watch for signs of flagging morale.

A contemplative leader is attentive in multiple dimensions. An earlier chapter introduced the concept of multiple intelligences (see Gardner, 1984), the view that human beings have a variety of fundamental abilities or that intelligence includes multiple dimensions—most of which are not usually measured or considered. For example, standardized academic testing focuses on a person's mathematical and verbal abilities, but not much attention is paid to an individual's kinesthetic or musical talents. One might well argue that such a focus is appropriate for the dominant paradigm. It is possible to have a successful career in business or government with two left feet and without being able to carry a tune, but one probably has limited opportunities if he or she is unable to read or perform basic computations.

The multiple dimensions in which the contemplative leader is attentive are analogous (but not necessarily identical) to the multiple dimensions of intelligence that others have discerned. A contemplative leader is free, of course, to use any of the traditional tools or roles or strategies that are available—depending on her particular circumstances. There is no reason a contemplative leader would not acquire the skills to read balance sheets, edit technical writing, or interpret statistics, or any of the other basic skills required in our society. A contemplative leader will, if the situation requires it, be sensitive to the bottom line, the mood of Congress, or team morale. There are however, other dimensions to which a contemplative leader is attentive—dimensions that are not as well recognized in the dominant culture.

It is almost as if the contemplative leader has the eyes to see and ears to hear—and perhaps the third eye or the third ear—what is often not perceived. In John Carmody's experience with the two physical therapists, the Queen Mary did not perceive what Ruby had seen or heard. A scientist may be particularly sensitive and responsive to patterns and rationality. An artist may be especially attentive to beauty. A politician may be keenly aware of power relationships.

It should be remembered that perception requires more than a sense organ to register the data. Kuhn's example of the research subjects who did not perceive the red six of spades or the black four of hearts illustrates this fact (Kuhn, 1970, pp. 63, 113). Sometimes one does not see what is there. Without some kind of training and experience, for example, it is difficult to gaze into a starry night and see anything more than a thousand randomly scattered points of light. But after spending some time with a star chart, one can perceive Orion, Ursa Major, Betelgeuse, and Polaris.

Allusion has already been made to some of these multiple dimensions to which a contemplative is attentive. Many have been explored by other authors, within or without the field of administration and management. For example, the contemplative leader is attentive to the intuitive as well as the rational, to the depth issues of meaning and significance as well as the objective surface data. The multiple dimensions of attentiveness may offer multiple ways of answering the question, "What is going on here?" Such a question might be considered by a contemplative leader from an artistic, ethical, mythological, psychological, or some such similar perspective.

Considering the contemplative assumptions that have been articulated, several dimensions are deserving of special mention, that is, they are arenas of particular importance in the contemplative paradigm. The contemplative leader is particularly attentive to the intuitive (or interior), the artistic, the physical, and to justice.

The intuitive here includes not only the common understanding of intuition as the complementary partner of rationality, about which a great deal has been written.[1] A contemplative leader certainly acknowledges and pays attention to the hunches and the sense of knowing that one sometimes has without ever being able to articulate how one knows it. This is one aspect of intuition or interiority. Another important dimension of interiority for the contemplative leader concerns the interior movements of the heart. The concept of heart here is something like an interior sensing organ or internal compass that registers something beyond fleeting emotions or feelings. In traditional Ignatian spirituality the terms *consolation* and *desolation* are used to describe the two aspects of these interior movements of the heart. *Desolation* is associated with interior experiences such as discontent, agitation, anxiety, fear, disruption, inertia, boredom, apathy, restlessness, dejection, self-pity, discouragement, sadness, and the like. Consolation, on the other hand, is associated with peace of mind, tranquillity, courage, harmony, joy, hopefulness, self-acceptance, simplicity, and clarity of thought.[2] Though everyone has experienced these sensations, they are often dismissed as having no significance or perhaps even ignored or shoved aside. The contemplative leader, however, takes note of the patterns of consolation and desolation and learns to use this interior compass of the heart. With practice, one begins to sense when a course of action seems fitting or right or in sync.

One need not be a professional artist to become aware of and attentive to the artistic dimension of reality. Each human being is an artist, although in our culture, it may be a hidden or stifled artist.

> "Not every artist is a special kind of person but every person is a special kind of artist." And Erich Fromm . . . observes how telling it is that our language does not even have a word for "folk art." This lack of a word is symptomatic of something worse: the lack of art and creativity as an ideal for all. . . .
> . . . "What do we mean by *artist*? The idea of 'professional artist' should be tossed away. Everyone should feel as an artist does. Everyone should be free to let his inner mind speak to him. And everyone is an artist when he does this. . . . Here, then, are many truly free artists. Unique billions of geniuses live together in our world." (Unpublished address by Buddhist philosopher and poet, Kenji Miyazawa; quoted in Fox, 1990, pp. 107–108)

The contemplative leader is sensitive to creativity in the midst of everyday life and is an artist in the midst of the ordinary. He is attentive to beauty (or lack of beauty) and responds to it, recognizing its significance.

The psychological dimension of life, and particularly as it relates to self-awareness, is certainly one of the multiple dimensions to which a contemplative leader is attentive. But one aspect of self–awareness that has not been as thoroughly explored or popularized in contemporary management literature as psychological awareness—and which is of importance in the contemplative paradigm—is awareness of the physical aspects of life and their affect on one's openness and presence. The contemplative leader certainly pays attention not only to the life of the mind but also to the life of the body (although the distinction between these two dimensions is becoming increasingly blurred). For example, many contemporary managers have had their psychological type determined with the Myers-Briggs Type Indicator (see, for example, Kroeger and Thuesen, 1988, passim) and are aware of the significance of being an introvert or extrovert or any of the other various type categories for one's approach to leadership strategies. But one wonders how many managers have a similar grasp of the significance—or even identity—of analogous physical types (however one might name them). Identifying oneself as a morning person, noticing a heightened alertness after physical exertion, or being aware of drowsiness after lunch all point to simple physical factors that influence one's quality of presence and open awareness.

Most people probably have articulated rules for their lives that have grown out of psychophysical awareness—for example, "I never talk to anybody before my first cup of coffee." Physical awareness could encompass the effect of music, color, art, temperature, and other aspects of the physical environment. A self-aware contemplative leader would know the significance of surroundings and physical cues such as smell, taste, or touch. Compare, for example, the effect of walking into a hushed cathedral, smelling the incense, and listening to chant with the experience of a midnight visit to a crowded dance hall filled with flashing lights, cigarette smoke, and loud music. Each of these experiences carries a different significance for individuals.

The broader contemplative tradition throughout the centuries has developed a rich heritage of experience with physical factors, such as sleep deprivation on a watch or vigil, food deprivation on a fast, or repetitive movement in an activity such as a walking meditation. Serious athletes may also have special insight into the nature of physical awareness that is of importance for contemplative leadership (see also, Tulku, 1978; Houston, 1982; and Masters and Houston, 1978). One area of interest for contemplative leaders in the future might be methods to identify physical factors that influence behavior in the workplace, just as the Myers-Briggs psychological inventory has helped many today to become more aware of individual psychological differences and their effect on individual and group performance.

Finally, attentiveness to justice is not limited, of course, to the contemplative paradigm. Compassion or concern for justice, for the contemplative leader, is born out of the interdependence of all creatures. "Compassion, one might say, works from a strength born of awareness of shared weakness, and not from someone else's weakness. And from the awareness of the mutuality of us all" (Fox, 1990, p. 2). As with the other particular dimensions of awareness, the contemplative leader pays attention to and gives significance to her perceptions of justice or injustice, the sense of rightness in a particular situation, whether or not the circumstances pass the test of rationality or due process. Rationality and due process, of course, are to be taken into account, but for the contemplative leader the range of awareness is broader.

THE CONTEMPLATIVE LEADER IS VULNERABLE

The third dimension of the contemplative leadership style is vulnerability. Professor Michael Downey (1993) offers a fresh perspective on vulnerability, viewing it as an openness to life rather than as a weakness:

Vulnerability is often thought to refer to a weakness that places us in a position of being forced to give in indiscriminately to any and all powers and forces. It is often thought that vulnerability causes us to be adversely affected by persons, events, and circumstances beyond our control. Human vulnerability is often overlooked or flatly denied by individuals and by whole societies wherein cults of the young and of youth flourish, where the advertising industry exalts human perfection and longevity, and where pain, impairment, and limitations are to be avoided at any and all costs. Properly understood, however, the term describes the fundamental openness of the human being to be affected by life, persons, and events. To be human is to be vulnerable, indeed defenseless, in the face of so many events and persons that touch us, for good or ill. At the most fundamental level, human vulnerability is part and parcel of being a person, having a body, being embodied.

. . . It is vulnerability that enables us to enter into relationships of interpersonal communication and communion with others who recognize their own weakness and need. Vulnerability requires the integrity and strength, indeed the power, to risk enormous pain, to bear the burdens of the darkest hour without avoidance, denial, or deception. It demands the stamina to open ourselves in order to be touched in our fragility. Being vulnerable means a willingness to lose ourselves in the hope of finding our true self. (pp. 19–20)

The contemplative leader lives an unprotected life. She acts decisively when action is necessary. Although the contemplative acts after taking into account a wide variety of input—data, principles, rules, values, insights, and hunches—and after careful discernment, there is no one, nothing to which she can shift responsibility for her decisions.

Decisions are born out of one's own personal freedom with no guarantee of rightness or final exoneration. Actions are taken in the midst of ambiguity and uncertainty, but also in the face of accountability. There is no promise of reward. The risks are high. Nevertheless, the contemplative engages fully and unreservedly in life as a vulnerable human being.

The Contemplative Leader Acts Decisively

The contemplative leader is patient and discerning, waiting for the situation to reveal itself. But he is not inert. Timing is a critical aspect of discernment. The contemplative waits for the *kairotic*[3] moment and then strikes, like a powerful slapshot delivered at the precise moment the goalie has left an opening to the net.

There is the legend[4] of the famous World War II general, George S. Patton, trying to move his troops quickly into position. An Italian farmer's mules are blocking a narrow bridge the men must cross. The soldiers try a variety of ways to coax the mules, but to no avail. No one seems to know what to do. Patton strides up to the mules, quickly assesses the situation, and then pulls out his sidearm and shoots the mules, ordering the soldiers to shove the carcasses off the bridge. The contemplative discerns and then acts—decisively and quickly. Discernment may be a lengthy, deliberative process, but not always. The point is that when it is the right time, the contemplative leader moves.

The Contemplative Leader Acts in Ambiguity and Uncertainty

The contemplative leader engages in this decisive action in the midst of uncertainty and ambiguity. She does not usually have the luxury of waiting until the situation has been clarified and her position is unassailable. German theologian Dietrich Bonhoeffer (1955), who was executed by the Nazis for his involvement in a plot to assassinate Hitler, reflects on free action in ambiguity and uncertainty:

> The responsible man acts in the freedom of his own self, without the support of men, circumstances or principles, but with a due consideration for the given human and general conditions and for the relevant questions of principle. The proof of his freedom is the fact that nothing can answer for him, except his own deed and his own self. It is he himself who must observe, judge, weigh up, decide and act. It is man himself who must examine the motives, the prospects, the value and purpose of his action. But neither the purity of the motivation, nor the opportune circumstances, nor the value, nor the significant purpose of an intended undertaking can

become the governing law of his action, a law to which he can withdraw, to which he can appeal as an authority, and by which he can be exculpated and acquitted. For in that case he would indeed no longer be truly free. . . . At the same time it is performed wholly within the domain of relativity, wholly in the twilight which the historical situation spreads over good and evil; it is performed in the midst of the innumerable perspectives in which every phenomenon appears. It has not to decide simply between right and wrong and between good and evil, but between right and right and wrong and wrong. . . . Precisely in this respect responsible action is a free venture; it is not justified by any law; it is performed without any claim to a valid self-justification, and therefore also without any claim to an ultimate knowledge of good and evil. Good, as what is responsible, is performed in ignorance of good and in the surrender to God of the deed. (pp. 248–249)

The contemplative leader certainly uses every appropriate analytical tool in making a decision. He will "observe, judge, weigh up, decide and act" in the tradition of logic and rationality. He will examine his own purposes, motives, values, and prospects. The relevant principles and laws will be taken into account. But finally, the contemplative leader is left with the raw decision for which he takes personal responsibility. There are no guarantees. There are no proper procedures that will exculpate him (although an organization or society may excuse him). The contemplative leader acts without knowing everything, without certainty, and without assurance that he is doing the right thing— but he does act.

The Contemplative Leader is Detached

For the contemplative leader *detached* or *indifferent* does not have the same meaning as *uncaring* or *unconcerned*. Theologian Karl Rahner (1965) defines these terms in the tradition of St. Ignatius Loyola and comments on the role of detachment or indifference in decision making:

Indifference is a kind of removal or distance away from things that makes true vision possible and is required for a proper decision. . . .

The very possibility of the influence of previously held views (for example, "That would be stupid!" or, "That cannot possibly be for me!") points up the fact that by our very nature we are not indifferent when it comes to making a free decision. Indifferent is what we must become. But this does not come through good will alone, or by saying that I am indifferent; for indifference is something that must enter into the nerves and the very marrow of the bones. Nor is indifference the mere resolution not to let oneself be carried along by the crowd; it demands, rather, the existential distance from things that is self-appropriated in such a way that it even frees the will to accept its own previous prejudices. Even the attitude of accepting everything that happens in silence—which itself is very difficult—is less than what is demanded here. [What is proposed is] an *active indifference* in virtue of which we are to act in such a way that both the using and leaving of things can and must be our own responsibility. . . .

This distance from things is a goal that must always be re-won again and again. . . . We love things, . . . we have tasted them in sweetness and in sorrow, we have absorbed them in love or in fear. Therefore, we need the courage to undertake ever new beginnings, and we need the power to break loose from that which holds us. . . .

If we consider all this, then it seems that we can never attain this kind of indifference by ourselves and permanently. (pp. 23–25)

Detachment or indifference can also mean making oneself radically and completely available and embracing loss. It is inapposite to being in control or to possessing something. Philosophy professor Jerome Miller (1994) reflects on attachment and control, using Willa Cather's heroine in *Song of the Lark*. Thea attends a concert as a young woman studying music. The Dvorak symphony evokes memories of her childhood, and Thea is suddenly filled with the amazement of seeing her life anew. As she ventures out of the concert hall and into the noise and crowding of city life, she resolves that the world will not rob her of the experience she just had. Miller (1994) comments on Thea's attachment to that experience:

Every event that happens *in* our world can turn into a crisis happening *to* our world, if we do not find a way to control it. The very fact that things happen—that they occur without regard for whether we will enjoy or be upset by them—makes us vulnerable. The bond of trust between ourselves and life has been irreparably severed. Life is not a simple radiance. It is a torrent of vicissitudes, filled with unsuspected vortices of anguish. The amount of enjoyment in our lives seems, therefore, to be directly proportional to how much control we have over life, how effective we are in making it conform to our plans. We respond to the threat of losing what is most precious to us by *holding onto it* so that it will not be taken away from us.

But the question is . . . whether our very effort to hold onto joy transforms it into something else entirely. [Willa] Cather's heroine [in *Song of the Lark*] does not think so. Thea vows that she will "have" the music that has just transported her and never let those who do not appreciate it deprive her of it. But there is a painful irony at work here of which she is, I am afraid, entirely unaware. In the concert hall, Thea allows herself to be transported by the music. She surrendered to it without reservation and let it carry her beyond herself. Nothing existed for her, when she was caught up in this riveting and draining experience, except the music itself. *Afterward* she is determined to seize hold of this fragile and elusive experience, to make sure that life does not take it from her. But seizing something is an exercise in control—the exact opposite of abandoning oneself to something. One cannot be possessive toward something and at the same time lose oneself in it. One cannot let oneself go if one is steeling one's will and straining every nerve to hold on. But, without realizing it, she is subverting the very relationship with the music that she wants to preserve. . . . At the very moment that she resolves not to let the music be taken away from her, the music itself ceases to be what matters most to her. It is subordinated to a more pressing concern—her desire to *have* it.

Now this seems to me to illustrate, with uncommon clarity, the inescapable conundrum of our middle years. . . . Once we realize that it can happen, we resolve to avert the heartbreaking loss of what is most precious to us. But holding onto it makes it impossible for us to spend ourselves on it. Determined to have it, we become incapable of losing ourselves in it. In the childlike moments of our childhood, we experienced joy by entering into life without holding anything back from it. But now we work to secure our grip on life—to "cope with," "deal with," "handle," and "manage" every situation that arises—so as [to] ensure that we eventually get some enjoyment from it. We think of joy as something we have to *get* from the world, not as something *given* to us when we surrender ourselves to it, because, surrendering to it, we would risk losing it entirely and being crushed under the leaden weight of loss. (pp. 62–63)

An essential aspect of the style of contemplative leadership is detachment, a letting-go of what seems to give security, a willingness to not be in control of life. Once again, a contemplative is free to use or enjoy any role, tool, object, relationship, or other aspect of life. But it is as if each of these—roles, tools, objects, relationships—were on loan, rather than being a permanent possession or acquisition.

Jan LaWall, a woman who had made the transition at age 35 from a career woman to a homemaker reflects on the contemplative, detached approach to roles and status. Although her focus is the family, her comments could easily be transferred into the workplace or other area of organizational life. LaWall (1988) first comments on the gender roles and the *shoulds* that are inherent in these roles and that threaten to define and affirm these roles for themselves. She suggests that instead of creating a new set of rules defining family roles, the roles could be negotiated, based on gifts, talents, energy, personal nature, needs, and other factors—but without the assignment of superiority or inferiority.

[P]erhaps, contemplative awareness offers another way. Perhaps one can *sit* in a role, noticing that expectations, performance and status shift from moment to moment. As this shifting is observed, perhaps attachment and importance can lessen and freedom increase. Perhaps this view could not represent a reconciliation for decades to come, but some of the time, in our personal lives if not in our rhetoric, a social role can be performed with lightness, humor, good will, and with no particular attention to status. (p. 7)

La Wall's comments illustrate the interplay of the concepts of freedom, detachment, and awareness, as well as the importance of humor and lightness for the contemplative leader. Humor and play often are the key to letting go, to loosening one's grip and transforming the seriousness of a situation. A contemplative leader will foster this humor and lightness in a manner appropriate to a particular situation.

Finally, detachment means allowing room for the new and being open to the future. Anthony de Mello (1985) offers a poetic reflection on detachment from one's treasures:

> In the measure that my heart is in past treasures
> I am fossilized and dead,
> for life is only in the present.
> So to each of those past treasures,
> those golden yesterdays, I say goodbye.
> To each I speak, explaining that,
> grateful though I am that it came into my life,
> it must move out
> —or my heart will never learn to love the present.
>
> My heart is in the future too.
> Its anxious fears of what will be tomorrow
> leave little energy to fully live what is today. . . .
>
> My heart is in my dreams, ideals, hopes
> which make me live in future fiction. . . .
>
> Having reclaimed the portion of my heart
> that was captured by the future and the past,
> I now survey my present treasures.
> To each beloved person
> I say with tenderness, "You are so precious to me,
> but you are not my life. . . ."
>
> I say to places . . . things . . . I am attached to, . . .
>
> I say to the things
> that seem to constitute my very being:
> my health,
> my ideologies,
> my good name, reputation,
> and I must say it even to my life,
> which must succumb some day to death,
> "You are desirable and precious,
> but you are not my life.
> My life and destiny are separate from you." (pp. 38–40)

The Contemplative Leader Is Accountable

A contemplative leader is not an independent, isolated individual, but fully recognizes the fundamental interdependence of human beings. Her context for decision making is broad enough to encompass this interdependence. There is nothing outside of her sphere of concern—although she does not presume to exercise universal control. This fundamental interdependence accounts, in part, for the ambiguity and uncertainty in decision making. It is easier to make the right decisions when there are circumscribed responsibilities and clearly articulated rules and principles that govern a situation.

In one form or another, the contemplative leader stands before the piercing gaze of the rest of humanity—the great cloud of witnesses—past, present, and future to whom each human being is intimately related. There must be someplace in a leader's life where he knows he cannot hide, someone who confronts him with the truth about his life, who can expose the fabrications and dissembling. But this encounter involves neither judgment nor advice. Through this one human being the leader answers to the rest of humanity. He stands before all those who have brought him to this moment, the giants upon whose shoulder he now stands, as well as the future generations that will be affected by his decisions.

Again, this radical accountability is grounded in the individual's unmistakable acceptance and significance as a human being. Otherwise such accountability would crush a person.

There is yet another legend of St. Francis that gives insight into the nature of contemplative leadership, and particularly accountability, in this case the ability to gaze upon others with eyes of love. A ravenous wolf was terrorizing a small hill town of Gubbio near Assisi. It devoured not only animals, but also human beings. Francis approached the wolf, in effect, for the purpose of accountability.

> Francis approached the snarling wolf and, making the sign of the cross, spoke gently to the animal, who we are told lay down at the saint's feet with the docility of a lamb. Francis addressed the wolf as his brother and pointed out to him the seriousness of his crimes. But then he offered his forgiveness and proposed that he, Francis, act as a peacemaker between the beast and the people of the town. If the wolf would promise to cease harassing the inhabitants, Francis pledged that he would see that the people not only would not harm the wolf but would tend to his hunger by feeding him. (Wright, 1988, pp. 13–14)

The wolf offered Francis his paw in promise, and the people of Gubbio agreed to treat the creature with respect and not harm him. For two years, the people fed the wolf until he died a natural death.

Professor Wendy Wright (1988) reflects on this legend as an example of seeing with the eyes of love. Although the focus of her discussion is not accountability per se, seeing with the eyes of love is one aspect of accountability for the contemplative leader.

> What moves me deeply about this quaint tale . . . is that Francis' seeing, his perception of the situation, was so different from anyone else's. He did not see from the wolf's perspective (if a wolf can be said to "see" in this sense). He was not dominated by sheer need, driven out of biological necessity to kill in order to stay alive. Neither did he see the situation from the perspective of the good people of Gubbio. He did not have eyes clouded by fear that saw only their own survival and the threat to it. Neither did Francis attempt to solve the "conflict" by dealing with the situation in the terms which had been set up: adversaries battling to the death for survival. Instead Francis saw through the dilemma of the wolf and people of Gubbio with eyes of love. He looked into the hearts of the people and awakened them to their mutual needs. He showed them how their shared life on this earth could be lived for their mutual enhancement.
>
> There is an art . . . in learning to see with the eyes of love. I do not mean seeing with the rose-colored glasses of sentimentality but seeing with a heart and mind awakened to the other as "self." There is a Buddhist practice which can be translated into something like "benevolent glancing" which involves training the eye to see with compassion. For example, if there has been some disagreement between monks in a Buddhist monastery and they are brought together to achieve some resolution of their conflict, they are expected first to sit silently face to face and gaze benevolently on one another. They are asked to look into the heart of the other as if it were their own heart. This is a giant step beyond simply learning to listen to another's position and reach a compromise. In the experience of seeing differently, the very way the issue has been constellated—as a conflict between two separate wills—is transformed by the vision of the common humanity of the persons involved. . . .
>
> It is very hard to see each other with eyes of love. For the most part even the most sensitive of us tend to see each other with eyes informed by our own agendas, our own beliefs, and our own needs. (pp. 14–15)

Accountability involves opening oneself to another's perspective; it is being vulnerable to the viewpoint of another, it is the willingness to be detached from one's own deeds and decisions and even frameworks. It is allowing one's perspective to be called into question. There is a certain mutuality in accountability in seeing each other with the eyes of love.

The Contemplative Leader Is Disciplined

The fourth and final dimension of the style of the contemplative leader style is discipline. Being disciplined does not mean being rigid or inflexible. Rather, a contemplative leader is disciplined in situating himself in a context that fosters the contemplative life. Contemplative discipline requires that one be unhabituated. Furthermore, the contemplative leader does not allow herself to be trapped by rewards. Just as an athlete trains for endurance, speed, strength, and the like, a contemplative leader trains for passionate joy. The contemplative leader's way of life is directed toward freedom. He embraces those colleagues, communities, customs, and routines that abet and encourage a lifestyle of awareness and freedom and avoids those that do not.

The Contemplative Leader Is Not Habituated

A contemplative leader does not program himself or herself to have any particular number of beneficial habits. Being disciplined means living before the reality of one's freedom. Spacious, open awareness is inapposite to operating on automatic pilot. Psychiatrist Gerald May has discussed at length the concept of attachments or addictions and here considers whether there might be positive addictions. Responding to the question whether some kinds of attachments could be positive and beneficial—for example, a mother's attachment to her children, a husband's attachment to his wife—May states unequivocally that there are no addictions, no attachments that are beneficial; although some attachments and addictions, for example, chocolate and golf, are less destructive than others such as alcoholism or bigotry. However, all addictions and attachments interfere with human freedom. The issue is the free choice rather than compulsion that initiates participation in positive activities such as mothering or eating. Are we participating in freedom or slavery? May then considers the hypothetical example of "being attached to feeding starving people" and observes that if a person were truly unhabituated, truly free from addiction and attachment, he would have no reason not to respond to the one in need. The love that is at the core of our being would spontaneously evoke such a response. "The only reason we could have for 'choosing' against true compassion and charity is that we are addicted to something else" (G. May, 1988, pp. 39–40).

A contemplative leader then, is concerned with freedom from attachments of any kind (or inordinate attachments) inasmuch as these attachments interfere with one's ability to make a free decision. Any human being has desires and needs but is not necessarily a prisoner to them.

The Contemplative Leader Acts Without Rewards

Related to the freedom from habits and attachments is the detachment from rewards. Anthony de Mello (1990) reflects on the energy that is released when one no longer is trapped by rewards.

There's a lovely saying by Tranxu, a great Chinese sage. . . . "When the archer shoots for no particular prize, he has all his skills; when he shoots to win a brass buckle, he is already nervous; when he shoots for a gold prize, he goes blind, sees two targets, and is out of his mind. His skill has not changed, but the prize divides him. He cares! He thinks more of winning than of shooting, and the need to win drains him of power." Isn't that an image of what most people are? When you're living for nothing, you've got all your skills, you've got all your energy, you're relaxed, you don't care, it doesn't matter whether you win or lose. (pp. 58–59)

The contemplative leader is one who knows there is nothing to be lost because nothing is possessed. In the contemplative paradigm there is no bait to be taken, other than the possibility of living consciously and gratefully before the awesome mystery of life—and that possibility is a gift, not something to be earned or acquired.

Detachment does not imply that one is not attracted or moved, that is, that one is an inert, passive, unengaged automaton. On the contrary, the contemplative leader uses the deepest desires of the human heart as a guide, desires that are not extinguished by adversity or failure but the desires that remain and draw one deeper into life. The contemplative leader acts on those desires and does not dismiss or ignore them. Gerald May (1990) discusses the relationship of desire, intention, and control, defining desire as wanting to do something, intention as acknowledging the desire and consciously choosing to follow it, and control as what we can do to gratify the desire:

A child wants to fly like a bird; that is desire. She decides to try; that is intent. She tries and fails; that is control—or rather the absence of it. The failure will not take away her desire, and if she is spunky she will keep her intent. But there are forces beyond her control that will, probably, prevent her from succeeding.

We desire much, and can intend anything we choose, but our control is limited. (p. 5)

May continues and explains that our desire is not concerned with practicality. For example, if the child wants to fly, the actual possibility of flying does not affect her desire. However, if she actually attempts to fly, the practical aspects of control come to the fore. "In between, gently intervening in the space between desire and control, is intention" (p. 5). In an authentic, contemplative life, according to May, intention—the reaching out of the will, the stretching forward of one's self—moves toward love. This intention gives love a greater significance than control.

The world will say that the road to hell is paved with good intentions; that only accomplishment counts. Against this worship of success, the intention toward love must stand undefended, without rationale or justification. . . .

Intention is everything because it is the only way we can truly say "yes" to love. Desire can only be a wanting of love, wistfully arising amidst the confusion of countless other impulses and addictions. Control cannot even begin to address love, for love cannot be controlled. . . . Only in between, in intention, is there freedom for human authenticity. [We may fail or make poor choices.] Still, we have done our best in the choosing and in the doing, and that is where our authenticity is found. A conscious, freely chosen "no" to love is truer and more human than a thousand reflexive, conditioned, addicted yeses. (p. 5)

The Contemplative Leader Is Passionately Joyful

Philosophy professor Jerome Miller (1994) begins a reflection on the relationship between joy and letting go of control with an observation on the similarity between recollection of childhood joy and the joy that is sometimes experienced by the dying. It is "as if some uncanny bond connects the unadulterated love of life with the unadulterated loss of it" (p. 57).

> I have noticed that, for some dying people, life again becomes something infinitely precious, similar to but not the same way it was in their childhood. . . . But the uncanny thing is that this happens after the dying person has finally given up all hope of *holding onto* life. It seems that the very willingness to relinquish life allows its radiance to be enjoyed in a way that is not otherwise possible. (p. 64, emphasis added)

Miller does not seem to be saying that one gives up hope, but that one gives up hope of hanging onto life. There is a certain freedom when one acknowledges—either on a deathbed or much earlier in life—that we are all mortal. Like a couple swirling with wild abandon around the dance floor—touching, but not clinging—such an acknowledgment and embrace of mortality can allow human beings to dance with life, whether for four minutes or 40 years.

Miller (1994) then explores the spontaneity, energy, and joy that characterize childhood and relates the exuberance and energy to the child's response to the sheer glory of life that beckons her:

> It is a mistake to think that this elation is simply the result of discharging excess biological energy. . . . Running into the world would not be possible if energy were not available, but the child does not run simply to discharge it. The child runs into the world *because the sheer glory of it beckons and animates her.* . . . The glory of the world itself is what provokes the child to throw open the door to her affections. Wonder is

the hinge. Running is the headlong "yes"! But the radiance of the world calls forth the fervor.

But if this is the case, then we must say that the child who is "full of life" *receives* this fullness of life *from* the world, and her running into the world is, as it were, only her way of giving it back. Here we are starting to appreciate the fecundity of the phrase "full of life." The child we use it to describe seems to have tapped into some inexhaustible spring within herself that fills her again to overflowing every time she empties it. But all her enthusiasm, all her passion, is evoked in her by life—by the world to which she devotes it. We might say that between the child and the world there is a kind of absurd circulation of gifts in which each gives back to the giver what each receives. The world, as the child experiences it, does not hoard its glory; the child, offered this glory, does not try to possess it.

. . . Wonder is drawn by unlimited expanses; fervor is awakened by the extremities. Childlike passion thinks only of spending itself without reserve in response to what is beckoning it. Such self-expenditure, made without any thought of reward, is quite literally absurd from any practical point of view. But for the child, caught up in the throes of what beckons here, it is, quite literally, what it means to be alive. The world, inexhaustible and without limit, evokes a passion that throws caution to the wind and holds nothing back. Racing down the hill on her sled, the child feels as if she is stepping out of her own body into the world itself.

To say "yes" unreservedly to what beckons, without holding anything back or thinking to get anything in return: this means to give praise. . . . Joy is the state of being of the praise-giver—not a result of praise-giving but an attribute of it: we enjoyed life fully when we spent ourselves on it without remainder. The uninhibited passion with which we played in our childhood was, it seems to me, our first and most profound response to the sanctity of life. (pp. 59–60)

The contemplative leader, like the child, runs into the world because of the sheer glory that beckons and animates. The radiance of the world calls forth the fervor of the contemplative leader. It is an exuberance and energy that spends itself without reserve in response to the wonder of life that is beckoning. For the contemplative leader, of course, this presumes that one is attentive to wonder in the midst of everyday life, that one is not playing it safe and clinging to the complex reward system implicit in organizational life. An outwardly wonderful organization is not required for the release of exuberance and joy. The contemplative leader recognizes the mystery and wonder in the most ordinary situations and embraces the leprous organizations as well as the excellent organizations. There is action, risky action, that is born from this exuberance and wild abandon. But it is discerned action, taken after due consideration for the given human and general conditions and for the relevant questions of principle, as Bonhoeffer explained.

The contemplative leader is passionately joyful. A clarification is probably needed to distinguish the contemplative approach to leadership from hedonism:

> Some word must then be found for the many counterfeits that we substitute and mistake for joy. Let us call them pleasures. They are too diverse to enumerate, but for each of us a few that we most "enjoy" undoubtedly come to mind. They may not be pleasures of the body in any obvious sense, but our pursuit and enjoyment of them always have the flavor of erotic possessiveness. We see something that attracts us and decide we must have it. Desire concentrates on what arouses it just as intently as childlike enthusiasm concentrates on the radiance that awakens it. But desire has *acquisition* in mind. Like passion, it will run out into the world—but only for the purpose of bringing something back to its private chambers for the purpose of hoarding or consuming it. Desire throws open the door to our hearts—but only to take something in and bolt them shut.
>
> Desire, then, is not, as we like to think, a synonym for passion. Obsessively wanting something is not the same as passionately loving it. Even when we spare no expense and throw caution to the wind in the pursuit of a desired object, the experience is entirely different from the extravagance of headlong running. Both desire and passion tend to override our reservations and tolerate no half-measures; both concentrate our energies into a single flame. But desire's aim is to quench this flame. Passion, on the other hand, is a conflagration. Desire wants to get and keep, possess or consume. Passion throws itself into the fire of praise and wants only to spend itself utterly. Desire might "go to any length"—but only in the hope of capitalizing on its expenditures. Passion simply empties all its coffers. Desire is calculative, passion exorbitant. Desire leads us to seize hold; passion leads us to abandon ourselves.
>
> And so the pleasure in which desire culminates cannot but be profoundly different from the joy with which passion expends itself. . . . [P]leasure makes us oblivious of everything except our sensation of it—indeed, oblivious even of the object that is providing it. Joy, on the other hand, transports us into the world and out of ourselves. Pleasure provides us a respite from the world; joy comes unbidden when we awaken to it. . . .
>
> But joy is contingent on the exorbitance of passion, and passion is not ready-made. It is awakened only by the radiance of the world and is extinguished when this radiance is no longer appreciated. (Miller, 1994, pp. 63–64)

What would it mean to train for passionate joy? What does being disciplined toward exuberance involve? The contemplative leader places himself in a context, a community that aids and abets passionate joy. There is much more to explore here, but it is clear that play and creativity and even some aspect of craziness are essential. The contemplative leader also aids and abets lucidity, attentiveness, and vulnerability among those who surround him.

The Contemplative Leader Is Disciplined Toward Freedom

Finally, a contemplative leader is disciplined toward freedom. She is free in terms of being able to engage fully and passionately in whatever situation she finds herself, to act in accord with her most fundamental sense of what is right and fitting, and to persist for as long as is necessary. But the contemplative leader is also able to walk away at a moment's notice and never look back. There is nothing—no task, no role, no project or legacy that she cannot give up. Her significance is grounded in her existence. There is nothing she must accomplish. She lives in consciousness of her humble, yet glorious kinship with the universe. In the contemplative paradigm, all human beings are made of stardust. The molecules of oxygen, hydrogen, carbon, and nitrogen that comprise our physical beings, that make up the air we breathe and the food we eat, are interchangeable. They are on loan. We do not possess them—at least not for very long. The air we breathe is the air that Aristotle, Moses, and Cleopatra breathed. The atoms that form human bodies and sustain conscious life originated in the stars. And it is to dust that all return. Meister Eckhart often points out that the word *humility* has the same linguistic origins as *humus*, good black dirt made from living matter now in decay (Fox, 1983, p. 59). The contemplative leader lives in the awareness that we are people of dust. To live in the consciousness of this glory and mundanity is to have freedom. There is nothing to lose. There is nothing more that is worth having.

One of the main characters in *The Ronin*, a novel based on a Zen myth, is engaged, for the major part of the story, in a quest to dig a tunnel through a mountain after having encountered an impassable cliff on one side. The story comes to a close after years spent chipping through solid rock.

[T]here was a spike of hard, pale light thrust in at him and a whirring of cold air that raped the warm and musky dark.

They stood and looked at it, and felt the cold.

Then in a sudden frenzy, they attacked the dot of sky and ripped it wide and stretched it big enough to make a window on the world. They pressed forward and leaned out as if there were some special scene to see that had not been seen before. They saw, of course, no view but Destination.

Both looked down. The Tunnel ended in the face of a cliff higher, steeper, wider and more deadly than its mild brother at the other end. They stared.

The big man pulled back and pressed against the wall. He murmured as if stunned: *"But I was so sure of my direction!"*

The other whispered, "It will take again as long to make a path down there."

The big man said, "Oh, no."

The young man looked at him: "But we must, we can't stop here." . . .

The big figure was striding naked toward the other light: "Not mine! No more! Not me!"

The young man screamed after him: "But you can't leave a thing like this undone! It's wrong not to finish what you start!"

And the big voice echoed from a vast distance in the dark, "*The hell with it!*"

—THE END—

(Jennings, 1968, pp. 157–159)

CONCLUDING OBSERVATIONS

The preceding description of the style of contemplative leadership is an unfinished tapestry of ragged edges and missing threads. Much of what it means to lead as one firmly rooted in the assumptions of the contemplative paradigm, that is, to be a contemplative leader, remains to be discovered and invented. The portrait of the contemplative leader was articulated in terms of four fundamental qualities or, perhaps, attitudes toward life: lucid, attentive, vulnerable, and disciplined. At this point one may ask, "But what does the contemplative leader *do*?"

The first response is that the contemplative leader does not necessarily do anything different than any other leader in any other paradigm. The actions of a contemplative leader may look just the same. He may use the same tools, data, words, structures, procedures, and so forth, as anyone else. He may look like Patton or Ghandi. Being a contemplative leader is a matter of how one goes about the tasks of leadership. Much of it takes place below the surface of observable actions. A contemplative leader embodies the style of lucidity, attentiveness, vulnerability, and discipline.

A second response to this question is that the contemplative leader creates an environment in which those she leads can be lucid, attentive, vulnerable, and disciplined. She allows others the opportunity to be contemplative leaders. She invites them to this approach to life. (It is not impossible, in the contemplative paradigm, for there to be any number of leaders in a situation. One can lead from the back of the room.[5]) Leading means assisting the contemplative presence of others, allowing them the freedom to live out of the contemplative style. Rather than telling or teaching others how to be lucid, sensitive, vulnerable, and disciplined, the contemplative leader enables others to remain in the ambiguity, the vulnerability, the tension, the discomfort, that is involved in contemplative presence. He disarms the attempts to resolve the ambiguity, to paper over the mystery, to revert to favored roles and status and knowledge and procedures that give security. The contemplative leader gives support for the wide-open presence for reality as it is, for careful but courageous discernment, for risk taking and vulnerability. The contemplative leader also has a discerning eye for the many diversions and false reductions of the contemplative style, for example, the grasping after any method or technique that will be the answer for the organization, the dissolution of the contemplative style into yet another achievement or status symbol.

There is also the issue of how one can communicate or teach the contemplative style. A contemplative apprenticeship comes close, but there is no master of contemplative leadership who can teach techniques or impart wisdom. There are no lessons to be mastered.

> There's the story of a disciple who told his guru that he was going to a far place to meditate and hopefully attain enlightenment. So he sent the guru a note every six months to report the progress he was making. The first report said, "Now I understand what it means to lose the self." The guru tore up the note and threw it in the wastepaper basket. After six months he got another note, which said, "Now I have attained sensitivity to all beings." He tore it up. The third report said, "Now I understand the secret of the one and the many." It too was torn up. And so it went on for years, until finally no reports came in. After a time the guru became curious and one day there was a traveler going to that far place. The guru said, "Why don't you find out what happened to that fellow." Finally, he got a note from his disciple. It said, "What does it matter?" And when the guru read that, he said, "He made it! He made it! He finally got it! He got it!" (de Mello, 1990, pp. 94–95)

One existing model that suggests what contemplative leadership might look like—or even what a contemplative apprenticeship could be—is the system used in initial and continuing professional training for psychotherapists, hospital chaplains, and others in related professions. It is a process termed *supervision*, although the term is used for a process that is not within the common understanding of supervision. The supervision can take place with another individual or with a peer group. The supervisee will present a verbatim, a report similar to a brief case study in which he relates an encounter with a client. The supervisor or peer group will reflect on the report with the supervisee.

For a hospital chaplain trainee, for example, the verbatim interview will include a brief description of the circumstances—the patient's diagnosis and age, the chaplain's initial plans for the visit with the patient, observations regarding cards or flowers in the room, the patient's physical appearance, the presence or absence of others in the room, and the like. A verbatim account of the conversation with the patient follows. The supervisee then evaluates the visit in terms of what is happening with the patient, including the more subtle or hidden issues, and also in terms of the supervisee's own responses to the visit.

For example, the chaplain trainee may report that he noticed his own anger when the patient described how her family refused to talk about her impending death.

The role of the supervisor or peer group is not to critique the comments made or actions taken by the chaplain trainee, for example, not to suggest that it would have been more helpful to tell the patient x,y,z, or that the proper way to deal with that situation was to do such and such. Instead the peer group or supervisor will help the trainee to be more aware of his own internal state, how his past history affects his relationships with patients, where the trainee is hindered by his own fears, and other similar issues. One of the ways the peer group or supervisor facilitates this reflection is by sharing his or her own internal observations or hunches with the trainee. The quality of presence or attentiveness of the supervisor or peer group with the trainee is significant for the success of the supervision experience. If the peer group is not listening deeply and attentively, they will have nothing significant to offer. If the group members or supervisor are unable to gaze lovingly on the trainee, with lucidity about their own areas of unfreedom, the session will be useless or even destructive. The supervisory sessions foster the lucidity, attentiveness, vulnerability, and even discipline of both the trainee and the supervisor or peer group.

An analogous peer group to encourage contemplative leadership might not have quite the same focus. In fact, it may not even be a formal process, but an ongoing process in a contemplative leadership situation. A similar reflection process could enable the contemplative leader to grow in lucidity, attentiveness, vulnerability, and discipline in the context of organizational life. For example, after relating a mundane management encounter, a peer group might help the contemplative leader reflect on where his lucidity is blocked, what illusions he is harboring, where his attentiveness is disturbed, what his current attachments are, and so on. What the contemplative leader trainee actually did is not the focus of the reflection. A second level of reflection is how, with the new awareness, lucidity, and so on, the leader might think, perceive, inquire, value, or act differently in the future.

Once again, the contemplative leadership style is not an accomplishment but a gift, an ever deepening awareness of oneself and the situation.

NOTES

1. See, for example, Agor, 1989.
2. From unpublished notes provided by the Jesuit Center for Spiritual Growth, Wernersville, PA, 1979.

3. *Kairotic* is derived from the Greek word *kairos*, meaning time (viewed as an occasion rather than an extent) or appointed or proper time or at the right time.

4. This scene is portrayed in the movie *Patton*.

5. See, for example, the servant leader Leo in Hesse's (1956) *The Journey to the East* described in Greenleaf's (1977) *Servant Leadership*.

17

Alternative Paradigms for Wicked Problems

We began with an exploration of how paradigms, images, maps, metaphors, theories, and other intellectual constructs shape our thinking, perception, inquiry, valuing, and action—both opening and closing off possibilities. Alternative intellectual constructs would then yield additional approaches, additional ways of thinking, perceiving, inquiring, valuing, and acting that could be brought to bear on the complex, intractable, wicked problems that we face. In the second segment of the journey, we ventured into an alternative paradigm, that is, the contemplative paradigm, first to articulate and delineate that paradigm and then to investigate the style of leadership that would emanate from the contemplative assumptions about life.

REFLECTIONS AND QUESTIONS

It is appropriate at the end of the journey to reflect and raise questions about future directions.

My first question is whether the choice of alternative paradigms was unimportant. I suggested that one might choose any other alternative paradigm—perhaps the basic assumptions of 19th-century Australian aboriginals or even the contemporary Yanomamo culture—to explore whether an alternative set of assumptions about life would yield alternative ways of thinking and acting. I am wondering now whether the approach taken here—stepping into another paradigm—is deeply rooted in the contemplative paradigm itself. The freedom, the detachment, the willingness to deal with uncertainty and ambiguity, the understanding that one can never get a firm grasp on the facts—all of which are required to leave one's own paradigm behind and step into another—are, of course, central elements of the contemplative paradigm. Would the Yanomamo paradigm allow or even consider such a possibility? I wonder.

A related question is whether one can choose another paradigm and simply enter into it. Inventing one's own, individual paradigm is probably close to any definition of insanity. A paradigm is almost certainly a communal project. Basic assumptions about life seem to develop in the midst of ordinary human interaction over a long period of time, rather than simply being chosen or invented. Perhaps one needs to be presented with or confronted by an alternative paradigm in order to enter into it. In my own case, I found myself with my experiential toe in the contemplative waters before I started reflecting on the nature of the contemplative paradigm. Sometimes one finds oneself thrown in another world—usually somewhat bewildered and out of place—and struggling to make sense of the situation. When one comes to terms with that alternative reality, there is a return to (or at least a new relation to) the dominant or home reality with new gifts (see also Dunne, 1978.)

An example that is at least analogous to an alternate paradigm involves the alternative perceptual reality in which some autistic individuals find themselves. Dr. Temple Grandin (1995), an animal scientist and high-functioning autistic, describes her alternative ways of perceiving, thinking, inquiring, and acting in *Thinking in Pictures*. Grandin is able to participate in the dominant culture although her perceptual abilities are distinctly different from the norm. She is able to bring exceptional gifts to her field of animal science by taking the perspective of the animals when she is designing livestock-handling facilities. Grandin has extraordinary abilities in visualizing a space or a process— as well as severe limitations in other areas. Because of her creative abilities and unique insights, she has designed the facilities that handle about a third of all animals processed in the United States. In a sense, Grandin lives in, or at least has access to, an alternative paradigm as well as the dominant paradigm. She is able to take advantage of the alternative ways of perceiving and acting that that alternative paradigm offers. This example involving autism causes one to wonder whether the ability to visit another paradigm is affected by the brain's hard wiring—and how the participation in a particular paradigm alters brain physiology and chemistry, making casual trips to another paradigm difficult.

It may be that an attempt to place oneself in an alternative paradigm presents problems analogous to the tourist returning home from another country with great recipes and art objects that simply are out of context in the home environment and do not accurately reflect the culture that was visited. The American cook can follow a recipe for an East African dish, for example, and even try to re-create the setting in which it would be eaten by an East African, but it is never quite the same. It may appear on the surface to be an East African meal, but an East African might not even recognize it. In some sense—especially with regard to contemplative leadership—the contemplative paradigm is a total experience that cannot be replicated by simply following a recipe book.

However, if one can truly and fully enter into another paradigm, with innocent seeing and unselfconscious participation, the alternative paradigms represented in our diverse and multiethnic society may be a gold mine of alternative approaches to today's wicked problems. Although there is always a temptation to translate one worldview into another, to squeeze another culture into the logical-rational box, it may be possible to experience another paradigm on its own terms. This approach would be akin to the immersion language training that is used to teach English as a second language. The student never uses her first language in the learning process. An English speaker with no knowledge of Swahili can teach English to a Swahili speaker by modeling the English language. For example, the teacher stands up and says, "I am standing up." She motions the student to arise and repeat the phrase. No one translates. This process is experienced to its fullest when the Swahili speaker takes up residence in an English-speaking area and simply learns English as he participates in life. Perhaps a better way to communicate the contemplative paradigm would have been to immerse the reader in a contemplative culture in order to experience this alternative worldview. (Unfortunately, such an environment may not exist.)

A final question is whether one needs a home paradigm. Burrell and Morgan (1979) emphasized that alternative paradigms cannot be seen as mere satellites of the dominant paradigm if they are to offer alternative ways of thinking, inquiring, and acting. Is it possible to be a citizen of the universe with the ability to move from one paradigm to another with no place to call home, nothing on which to stand firmly? Physicist Wolfgang Pauli shared his distress when caught without a firm paradigm beneath him. Flanigan (1992) describes at length the difficulty of having your paradigm ripped away. Perhaps only an authentic contemplative could live in the ambiguity and detachment of not having a home paradigm!

FURTHER EXPLORATIONS

There are several paths for further exploration that present themselves. First, how does the contemplative paradigm manifest itself in everyday life? The best we may hope for is to catch a glimpse of authentic contemplative living here and there. The exploration may be analogous to seeing the reflections in the polished marble floor of the National Cathedral. At first you just notice the luster of reflected overhead lights. But as you begin to follow that first insight, you also notice the reflection of the stained glass windows in the floor—and then of the stone carvings on the wall, the people in the pews. Soon you are looking into a dimmed but vibrant universe. Things become clearer, more visible, more identifiable. What was once obscure begins to reveal its outlines. Once I know there is a contemplative understanding of life, I can start to look for it and perhaps point it out to a colleague.

Second, what are other forms of contemplative leadership? What does contemplative leadership look like in other contexts? Who is an exemplar of contemplative leadership? How does one look beneath the surface of action and discover underlying assumptions? Not every agency director who gives up his large office with a window and bookshelves is necessarily a contemplative leader. How do we begin to sniff out the contemplative style? But finally, contemplative leadership is not a phenomenon to be reported but a process to be invented and lived.

A first focus of exploration of alternative paradigms might be one's own underlying assumptions. What do we dismiss as foolishness—or worse? What are we unwilling to consider? Where is our creativity blocked? What are the well-used images and metaphors? Where are we stuck in our ways? What are favorite operating modes? This may be analogous to psychological therapy or growth experiences in which the client, with the assistance of a mental health professional discovers underlying assumptions, patterns, and understandings that hinder full psychological functioning. It is as if the therapist helps the client bring to consciousness his psychological paradigm. Perhaps with the help of another, a manager could probe broader areas of her underlying assumptions and understandings, that is, her common sense to bring it to awareness and perhaps to recognize the limitations as well as the possibilities.

References

Agor, Weston H. (Ed.). (1989). *Intuition in organizations*. Newbury Park, CA: Sage.

Anthony, William P. (1978). *Participative management*. Reading, MA: Addison-Wesley.

Beam, George, & Simpson, Dick. (1984). *Political action: The key to understanding politics*. Chicago: Swallow Press.

Benson, Herbert. (1975). *The relaxation response*. New York: Morrow.

Benz, E., & Koch, J. (Eds.) (1938–1975). *Meister Eckhart: Die lateinischen Werke* (Vols. 1–5). Stuttgart: W. Kohlhammer.

Beyth-Marom, Ruth, & Shlomith Dekel (1985). *An elementary approach to thinking under uncertainty*. Hillsdale, NJ: Lawrence Erlbaum Associates.

Blakney, Raymond. (1941). *Meister Eckhart: A modern translation*. New York: Harper & Row.

Bohm, David. (1980). *Wholeness and the implicate order*. London: Ark.

Bonhoeffer, Dietrich. (1955). *Ethics*. New York: Macmillan.

Boulding, Kenneth E. (1956). *The image*. Ann Arbor: University of Michigan Press.

Bry, Adelaide. (1972). *Visualization*. New York: Harper.

Burrell, Gibson, & Morgan, Gareth. (1979). *Sociological paradigms and organisational analysis*. Portsmouth, NH: Heinemann.

Butterfield, Herbert (1949). The Origins of Modern Science, 1300–1800. London: G. Bell & Sons Ltd.

Capra, Fritjof. (1984). *The Tao of physics* (Rev. ed.). New York: Bantam.

Capra, Fritjof. (1982). *The turning point: Science, society and the rising culture.* New York: Bantam.

Chagnon, Napoleon A. (1968). *Yanomamo.* New York: Holt.

Clark, James M. (1957). *Meister Eckhart: An introduction to the study of his works with an anthology of his sermons.* London: Thomas Nelson & Sons, Ltd.

Clark, James M., & Skinner, John V. (1958). *Meister Eckhart: Selected treatises and sermons translated from Latin and German with an introduction and notes.* London: Faber & Faber.

Clark, Patricia. (1991, February). Putting God first at work. *Shalem News, 15*(1), 4.

Clissold, Stephen. (1979). *St. Teresa of Avila.* London: Sheldon Press.

Colledge, Edmund, O.S.A., & McGinn, Bernard. (1981). *Meister Eckhart: The essential sermons, commentaries, treatises and defense.* New York: Paulist.

De Bono, Edward. (1985). *Six thinking hats.* Boston: Little Brown.

de Mello, Anthony, S. J. (1990). *Awareness.* New York: Doubleday.

de Mello, Anthony, S. J. (1985). *Wellsprings: A book of spiritual exercises.* New York: Doubleday.

Deal, Terrence E., & Kennedy, Allan A. (1982). *Corporate cultures: The rites and rituals of corporate life.* Reading, MA: Addison-Wesley.

Del Mastro, M. L. (1977). *Juliana of Norwich: Revelations of divine love.* New York: Doubleday.

Downey, Michael. (1993, July/August). Brief gold. *Weavings, 8*(4), 17.

Dunne, John S. (1978). *The way of all the earth.* Notre Dame: University of Notre Dame.

Edwards, Tilden. (1990, February). God in our laughter. *Shalem News, 14*(1), 1.

Edwards, Tilden. (1987). *Living in the presence: Disciplines for the spiritual heart.* San Francisco: Harper & Row.

Edwards, Tilden. (1977). *Living simply through the day: Spiritual survival in a complex age.* New York: Paulist.

Egan, Harvey D., S. J. (1978, Fall). Christian apophatic and kataphatic mysticisms. *Theological Studies,* pp. 399–426.

Eggert, Nancy. (1990). Contemplation and administration: An alternative paradigm. In Christopher Bellavita (Ed.), *How public organizations work.* New York: Praeger.

Eisler, Riane. (1987). *The chalice and the blade: Our history, our future.* San Francisco: Harper & Row.

Elgin, Duane. (1981). *Voluntary simplicity: Toward a way of life that is outwardly simple, inwardly rich.* New York: William Morrow & Co.

Fayol, Henri. (1978). General principles of management. In Jay M. Shafritz & J. Steven Ott (Eds.), *Classics of organization theory.* Chicago: Dorsey Press.

Ferguson, Marilyn. (1980). *The aquarian conspiracy: Personal and social transformation in the 1980s.* Los Angeles: Tarcher.

Flanigan, Beverly. (1992). *Forgiving the unforgivable: Overcoming the bitter legacy of intimate wounds.* New York: Macmillan.

Fox, Matthew. (1990). *A spirituality named compassion.* San Francisco: Harper & Row.

Fox, Matthew. (1983). *Original blessing.* Santa Fe, NM: Bear.

Fox, Matthew. (1982). *Meditations with Meister Eckhart.* Santa Fe, NM: Bear.

Fox, Matthew. (1980). *Breakthrough: Meister Eckhart's creation spirituality in new translation.* Garden City, NY: Doubleday.

Fox, Matthew (Ed.). (1981). *Western spirituality.* Sante Fe, NM: Bear.

Gardner, Howard. (1984). *Frames of mind.* New York: Basic Books.

Garfield, Charles A., & Bennett, Hal Zina. (1984). *Peak performance: Mental training techniques of the world's greatest athletes.* New York: Warner Books.

Gawain, Shakti. (1978). *Creative visualization.* New York: Bantam.

Grandin, Temple. (1995). *Thinking in pictures.* New York: Random House.

Green, Thomas H., S. J. (1979). *When the well runs dry.* Notre Dame: Ave Maria.

Green, Thomas, S. J. (1984). *Weeds among the wheat.* Notre Dame: Ave Maria.

Greenleaf, Robert K. (1977). *Servant leadership.* New York: Paulist.

Hammarskjöld, Dag. (1964). *Markings.* New York: Knopf.

Harman, Willis. (1988). *Global mind change: The promise of the last years of the twentieth century.* Indianapolis, IN: Knowledge Systems.

Harman, Willis, & Rheingold, Howard. (1984). *Higher creativity: Liberating the unconscious for breakthrough insights.* Los Angeles: Tarcher.

Harmon, Michael M., & Mayer, Richard T. (1986). *Organization theory for public administration.* Boston: Little, Brown.

Hauerwas, Stanley, & Jones, L. Gregory (Eds.). (1989). *Why narrative?* Grand Rapids, MI: Eerdmans.

Heisenberg, Werner. (1930). In Carl Eckhert & F. C. Hoyt (Trans.), *The physical principles of the quantum theory.* Chicago: University of Chicago.

Hesse, Hermann. (1956). *The journey to the east.* New York: Farrar.

Hodgson, Bryan. (1994, April). Kamchatka. *National Geographic, 185*(4), 36–67.

Hoffman, Bengt. (1976). *Luther and the mystics.* Minneapolis: Augsburg.

Houston, Jean. (1982). *The possible human: A course in enhancing your physical, mental, and creative abilities.* Los Angeles: Tarcher.

Hummel, Ralph P. (1991, January/February). Stories managers tell: Why they are as valid as science. *Public Administration Review, 51*(1), 31–41.

Jennings, William Dale. (1968). *The ronin.* Rutland, VT: Charles E. Tuttle.

Johnston, William (Ed.). (1973). *The cloud of unknowing and the book of privy counseling.* New York: Image.

Jung, Carl. (1962). In Richard Wilhelm (Trans.). *The secret of the golden flower.* New York: Doubleday.

Kavanaugh, Kieran, & Rodriguez, Otilio (Trans.). (1987). *The collected works of St. Teresa of Avila* (2nd ed., Vols. 1–3). Washington: Institute of Carmelite Studies.

Kavanaugh, Kieran, & Rodriguez, Otilio. (1979). *The collected works of St. John of the Cross.* Washington: Institute of Carmelite Studies.

Kavanaugh, Kieran, & Rodriguez, Otilio. (1973). *The collected works of St. John of the Cross.* Washington: Institute of Carmelite Studies.

Keating, Thomas. (1986). *Open mind, open heart: The contemplative dimension of the gospel.* Amity, NY: Amity House.

Kiefer, Charles F., & Senge, Peter M. (1984). *Metanoic organizations.* In John Adams (Ed.). *Transforming work.* Alexandria, VA: Miles River.

Kiefer, Charles F., & Senge, Peter M. (1982). *Metanoic organizations.* Framingham, MA: Innovation Associates.

Kolb, David. (1984). *Experiential learning: Experience as the source of learning and development.* Englewood Cliffs, NJ: Prentice Hall.

Kroeger, Otto, & Thuesen, Janet M. (1988). *Type talk.* New York: Bantam, Doubleday, Dell.

Kuhn, Thomas S. (1970). *The structure of scientific revolutions* (2nd ed.). Chicago: University of Chicago.

Kuhn, Thomas S. (1957). *The Copernican revolution.* Cambridge: Harvard.

Lakoff, George, & Johnson, Mark. (1980). *Metaphors we live by.* Chicago: University of Chicago.

LaWall, Jan. (1988, June). Homemaking as context for spirituality & spiritual direction. *Shalem News, 12*(2), 7.

Lawrence, D. H. (1959). *Selected poems.* New York: Viking.

Lenz, Barbara, & Myerhoff, Barbara. (1985). *The feminization of America: How women's values are changing our public & private lives.* Los Angeles: Tarcher.

Masters, Robert, & Houston, Jean. (1978). *Listening to the body.* New York: Delta.

Maxwell, J. C. (1882). Science and free will. In L. Campbell & W. Garnett, *The life of James Clerk Maxwell.* London: Macmillan.

May, Gerald G. (1991, February). If our lives depended upon it. *Shalem News, 15*(1), 5.

May, Gerald. (1990, October). The best of intentions. *Shalem News, 14*(3), 5.

May, Gerald. (Introducer). (1989). Contemplative prayer forms (Introduction). [Audio cassette recording]. Washington: Shalem Institute.

May, Gerald. (1988). *Addiction and grace.* San Francisco: Harper & Row.

May, Gerald G. (1987, Summer). To bear the beams of love: Contemplation and personal growth. *The Way* (Supp. 59), 24–34.

May, Gerald G. (1983). *Will and spirit: A contemplative psychology.* San Francisco: Harper & Row.

May, William F. (1994, July). Commentary: Listening carefully. *Second Opinion, 20*(1), 47–49.

Merton, Thomas. (1961). *New seeds of contemplation.* New York: New Directions.

Miller, Jerome. (1994, July). Joy and gravity: A meditation on the will to live. *Second Opinion, 20*(1), 57–69.

Morgan, Gareth. (1986). *Images of organization.* Beverly Hills, CA: Sage.

Morgan, Gareth. (1980). Paradigms, metaphors, and puzzle solving in organization theory. *Administrative Science Quarterly, 25,* 605–622.

Morgan, Gareth (Ed.). (1983). *Beyond method: Strategies for social research.* Beverly Hills: Sage.

Newman, Barclay M. (1988). *A concise Greek-English dictionary of the New Testament.* Stuttgart, Germany: United Bible Societies.

Nicoll, David. (1984). Consulting to organizational transformations. In John D. Adams (Ed.), *Transforming work.* Alexandria, VA: Miles River.

O'Reilley, Mary Rose. (1994, May/June). Deep listening: An experimental friendship. *Weavings, 9*(3), 17.

Owen, Harrison. (1987). *Spirit: Transformation and development in organizations.* Potomac, MD: Abbott Publishing.

Pasquier, Jacques. (1977). Experience and conversion. *The Way, 17*(2), 114–122.

Peers, E. Allison (Trans. & Ed.). (1959). *Dark night of the soul by St. John of the Cross* (3rd ed.). Garden City: Image.

Peters, Thomas J., & Austin, Nancy. (1985). *A passion for excellence.* New York: Random House.

Peters, Thomas J., & Waterman, Robert H., Jr. (1982). *In search of excellence.* New York: Harper & Row.

Pieper, Josef. (1993, March/April). Leisure as a spiritual attitude. *Weavings, 8*(2), 6–12.

Prigogine, Ilya, & Stengers, Isabelle. (1984). *Order out of chaos: Man's new dialogue with nature.* New York: Bantam.

Puhl, Louis J., S. J. (1951). *The spiritual exercises of St. Ignatius.* Chicago: Loyola.

Quint, Josef (Ed. & Trans.). (1963). *Meister Eckhart: Deutsche Predigten and Traktate.* Munich.

Quint, Josef (Ed.). (1958–1976). *Meister Eckhart: Die deutschen Werke* (Vols. 1–3 and 5). Stuttgart: W. Kohlhammer.

Rahner, Karl, S. J., & Baker, Kenneth (Trans.). (1965). *Spiritual exercises.* New York: Herder.

Reynolds, Paul Davidson. (1971). *A primer in theory construction.* New York: Macmillan.

Rittel, Horst W. J., & Webber, Melvin. (1973). Dilemmas in a general theory of planning. *Policy Sciences, 4*(2), 155–169.

Salinger, J. D. (1961). *Franny and Zooey.* Boston: Little, Brown.

Schaef, Anne Wilson. (1985). *Women's reality.* San Francisco: Harper.

Schaef, Ann Wilson, & Fassel, Diane. (1988). *The addictive organization.* San Francisco: Harper & Row.

Schwartz, Peter. (1991). *The art of the long view.* New York: Doubleday.

Simon, Herbert A. (1976). *Administrative behavior: A study of decision-making processes in administrative organizations* (3rd ed.). New York: Macmillan.

Sölle, Dorothy. (1976, June). *Christianity and Crisis, 36*(10).

Spencer, Laura J. (1989). *Winning through participation.* Dubuque, IA: Kendall/Hunt.

Swimme, Brian. (1984). *The universe is a green dragon.* Sante Fe, NM: Bear.

Taylor, Frederick Winslow. (1978). The principles of scientific management. In Jay M. Shafritz & J. Steven Ott (Eds.), *Classics of organization theory.* Chicago: Dorsey Press.

Thayer, Frederick C. (1981). *An end to hierarchy and competition.* (2nd ed.). New York: Franklin Watts.

Theobald, Robert. (1987). *The rapids of change: Social entrepreneurship in turbulent times.* Indianapolis, IN: Knowledge Systems, Inc.

Thompson, Marjorie J. (1992, March/April). Moving toward forgiveness. *Weavings, 7*(2), 16.

Toner, Jules J., S. J. (1982). *A commentary on St. Ignatius' rules for the discernment of spirits.* St. Louis: The Institute of Jesuit Sources.

Tulku, Tarthang. (1978). *Kum Nye relaxation.* Berkeley: Dharma.

Ueland, Brenda. (1992, November/December). Tell me more. *Utne Reader* (544), 104.

van Kaam, Adrian C.S.Sp. (1994). *Spirituality and the gentle life.* Pittsburgh: Epiphany Books.

Weber, Max. (1978). Bureaucracy. In Jay M. Shafritz & J. Steven Ott (Eds.), *Classics of organization theory.* Chicago: Dorsey Press.

Welch, John. (1990). *When Gods Die: An Introduction to John of the Cross.* New York: Paulist.

Wright, Wendy M. (1988, September/October). For all the saints. *Weavings, 3*(5), 6.

Yockey, James Francis. (1987). *Meditations with Nicholas of Cusa.* Santa Fe: Bear.

Selected Bibliography

Adams, John D. (Ed.). (1984). *Transforming work: A collection of organizational transformation readings*. Alexandria, VA: Miles River.

Adler, Mortimer J. (1986). *A guidebook to learning for the lifelong pursuit of learning*. New York: Macmillan.

Alvarez, Karin B., & Stupak, Ronald J. (1993, December). An analytical essay and annotated compendium on organizational theory: Paradigms lost and needed in public administration. *International Review of Modern Sociology, 23*(2).

Bell, Daniel. (1976). *The cultural contradictions of capitalism*. New York: Basic Books.

Bellah, Robert N., Madsen, R., Sullivan, M., Swidler, A., & Tipton, S. M. (1985). *Habits of the heart: Individualism and commitment in American life*. Berkeley: University of California.

Bellavita, Christopher. (Ed.) (1990). *How public organizations work*. New York: Praeger.

Brandon, Joel, & Morris, Daniel. (1997). *Just don't do it! Challenging assumptions in business*. New York: McGraw-Hill.

Buzan, Tony. (1983). *Using both sides of your brain* (Rev. ed.) New York: Dutton.

Campbell, Camille. (1985). *Meditations with Teresa of Avila*. Santa Fe, NM: Bear.

Cather, Willa. (1965). *Song of the lark*. Boston: Houghton Mifflin.

Eckhart, Meister. In Josef Quint (1963) (Ed. & Trans. into modern German), *Meister Eckhart: Deutsche Predigten and Traktate*. Munich.

Eckhart, Meister. In Josef Quint (1938 ff) (Ed., Vols. 1–3 & 5), *Meister Eckhart: Die deutschen Werke*. Stuttgart: W. Kohlhammer.

Fromm, Erich. (1955). *Sane society.* NY: Holt, Rinehart & Winston.

Gelb, Michael. (1995). *Thinking for a change.* New York: Harmony Books.

Hackney, Peggy. (1988, Winter). Moving wisdom. *In Context* (18), 26–29.

Handy, Charles. (1996). *Beyond certainty.* Boston: Harvard Business School.

Handy, Charles. (1994). *The age of paradox.* Boston: Harvard Business School.

Handy, Charles. (1989). *The age of unreason.* Boston: Harvard Business School.

Herbert, Nick. (1987). *Quantum reality—Beyond the new physics.* Garden City, NY: Anchor Books.

Huse, Edgar F., & Cummings, Thomas G. (1980). *Organizational development and change* (3rd ed.). St. Paul: West.

Isenberg, Daniel J. (1989). How senior managers think. In Weston H. Agor (Ed.), *Intuition in organizations.* Newbury Park, CA: Sage.

Janis, Irving L. (1982). *Groupthink.* Boston: Houghton Mifflin.

Jockey, James Francis. (1987). *Meditations with Nicholas of Cusa.* Sante Fe, NM: Bear.

Joranson, Philip N., & Butigan, Ken (Eds.). (1984). *Cry of the environment.* Santa Fe, NM: Bear.

Kanter, Donald L., & Mirvis, Philip H. (1980). *The cynical Americans: Living and working in an age of discontent and disillusion.* San Francisco: Jossey-Bass.

Kiersey, David, & Bates, Marilyn. (1984). *Please understand me.* Del Mar, CA: Prometheus.

Kilmann, Ralph H., Saxton, Mary J., & Serpa, Roy. (1985). *Gaining control of the corporate culture.* San Francisco: Jossey-Bass.

Manchester, William. (1992). *A world lit only by fire.* Boston: Little, Brown.

Nims, John Frederick (Trans.). (1979). *The Poems of St. John of the Cross* (3rd ed.). Chicago: University of Chicago.

Ornstein, Robert E. (1977). *The psychology of consciousness* (2nd ed.). New York: Harcourt.

Palmer, Parker J. (1988, July/August). The clearness committee. *Weavings, 3*(4), 37–40.

Pearson, Carol S. (1991). *Awakening the hero within.* San Francisco: Harper Collins.

Schon, Donald A. (1983). *The reflective practitioner.* New York: Basic Books.

Senge, Peter M. (1990). *The fifth discipline.* New York: Doubleday.

Simon, Herbert A. (1989). Making management decisions: The role of intuition and emotion. In Weston H. Agor (Ed.), *Intuition in organizations.* Newbury Park, CA: Sage.

Spretnak, Charlene, & Capra, Fritjof. (1986). *Green politics.* Santa Fe, NM: Bear.

Strauch, Ralph. (1985). *Reality illusion.* Wheaton, IL: Theosophical Press.

Tart, Charles T. (1986). *Waking up: Overcoming the obstacles to human potential.* Boston: Shambala.

Toffler, Alvin (1980). *The third wave.* New York: William Morrow.

Troxel, James P. (Ed.). (1993). *Participation works.* Alexandria, VA: Miles River Press.

Tulku, Tarthang. (1977). *Gesture of balance: A guide to awareness, self-healing, and meditation.* Berkeley: Dharma.

Valle, Ronald S., & von Eckartsberg, Rolf (Eds.). (1989). *Metaphors of consciousness.* New York: Plenum.

Welch, John. (1982). *Spiritual Pilgrims: Carl Jung and Teresa of Avila*. New York: Paulist.

Wheatley, Margaret J. (1994). *Leadership and the new science*. San Francisco: Berrett-Koehler.

Wilber, Ken. (1984). *A sociable God: Toward a new understanding of religion*. Boulder, CO: Shambala.

Wilber, Ken. (1983). *Eye to eye: The quest for the new paradigm*. Garden City, NY: Doubleday.

Wilber, Ken. (1977). *The spectrum of consciousness*. Wheaton, IL: Theosophical Publishing.

Yankelovich, Daniel. (1981). *New rules: Searching for self-fulfillment in a world turned upside down*. New York: Random House.

Zohar, Danah. (1990). *The quantum self-human nature and consciousness defined by the new physics*. New York: William Morrow.

Index

ABOUT THE AUTHOR

NANCY J. EGGERT has been an attorney and manager for the National Labor Relations Board for 25 years. She holds a doctorate in public administration, a J.D., and master's degrees in urban education and divinity. An ordained minister and current pastor of a Lutheran church in Alexandria, Virginia, Eggert has been active in international development and literacy organizations, and has been an adjunct faculty member of the Washington Theological Union, a Roman Catholic seminary in Washington, D.C.